The BEST Book of
FOOTBALL
FACTS
& STATS

A FIREFLY BOOK

Published by Firefly Books Ltd. 2004

First printing

Publisher Cataloging-in-Publication Data   (U.S.)

Mehno, John.
   The best book of football facts and stats / John Mehno.
Rev. ed.
[304] p. :   cm.
Summary: A reference guide to all NFL teams, important players,
coaches, games, and statistics.
ISBN 1-55407-016-3 (pbk.)
1. Football -- Records. 2. Football players. 3. National Football League. I. Title.
796.332/ 64/ 0973021 dc22   GV955.M446 2004

National Library of Canada Cataloguing in Publication

Mehno, John
   The best book of football facts & stats / John Mehno.
ISBN 1-55407-016-3
   1. National Football League--Miscellanea. 2. Football--United States--Miscellanea.
3. Football players--United States. I. Title.
GV950.5.M44 2004   796.332'64'0973   C2004-902058-7

Published in the United States in 2004 by
Firefly Books (U.S.) Inc.
P.O. Box 1338, Ellicott Station
Buffalo, New York 14205

Published in Canada in 2004 by
Firefly Books Ltd.
66 Leek Crescent
Richmond Hill, Ontario L4B 1H1

Commissioning Editor: Martin Corteel
Project Editor: Luke Friend
Production: Lisa French
Cover Image: Elsa/Getty Images

Printed and bound in Great Britain

The BEST Book of
FOOTBALL
FACTS
& STATS
REVISED

John Mehno

STATS INC.

FIREFLY BOOKS

CONTENTS

CONTENTS

CONTENTS

CONTENTS

L et baseball cling to the sleepy title of "national pastime." Football is the national passion. It's purely American—offering fast, spirited, violent action that fits perfectly on a television screen.

No wonder Super Bowl Sunday has become an unofficial holiday.

From modest beginnings as a dust-churning game played mostly on the ground and between the tackles, football has become an aerial show. There's still a need to run the ball but a strategy that restrictively simple doesn't work. Not when coaches spend hours poring over films and analyzing tendencies. Better be able to loosen up that defense with the occasional pass downfield.

Pro football was born shortly after the turn of the century and got its first spark in the 1920s when Red Grange signed on after a spectacular career at the University of Illinois. The game was a distant second to baseball until the 1960s.

Then the emergence of television helped establish pro football as a Sunday afternoon tradition in the fall and winter months. The NFL had a TV-savvy commissioner in Pete Rozelle and his vision helped the game grow and surpass baseball in the 1960s. ABC, a network that had nothing to lose, bought Rozelle's idea of a weekly Monday night game and America's viewing habits—and lifestyle—changed.

Rozelle may not have been able to diagram a power sweep because his background was in public relations. He knew how to sell, though, and officially-licensed NFL merchandise was soon on every kid's Christmas wish list. The league expanded prudently and continually adjusted its rules to give fans the action they wanted.

There was an alphabet soup of competitors—the AAFC, AFL, WFL, USFL and the laughable XFL. The All America Football Conference brought the Cleveland Browns, Baltimore Colts and San Francisco 49ers to the NFL in 1950. The wholesale merger with the American Football League in 1970 diluted the original attraction of the Super Bowl but made the NFL stronger. The other upstarts fell by the wayside, arriving far too late to chip away at the NFL's dominance.

Stars ranged from Johnny Unitas, who came to work in business-like

INTRODUCTION

black high tops, to Broadway Joe Namath, whose shoes seemed to stay white on the muddiest fields. Vince Lombardi's Packers put tiny Green Bay, Wisconsin on the map. The Miami Dolphins were perfect one year. President Richard Nixon suggested plays for the Washington Redskins while the Dallas Cowboys built a national fan base.

Jim Brown's rushing records fell but no one ever suggested he wasn't the game's best running back. There was a Fearsome Foursome, a Steel Curtain and Purple People Eaters. San Francisco had Bill Walsh's West Coast Offense and a western Pennsylvania quarterback, Joe Montana, who made it hum. Old-guard 1960s powers like the Packers, Bears and Giants all came back to prominence. Too many teams moved. O.J. Simpson went from famous to notorious.

Through it all, though, the NFL flourished, helped by an economic system that makes worst-to-first scenarios possible and ignites hope in many cities.

AMERICAN FOOTBALL CONFERENCE

NORTH

Cincinnati Bengals
Cleveland Browns
Pittsburgh Steelers

BALTIMORE RAVENS

The Ravens were an old team in a new city. Or maybe they were a new team in an old city.

The NFL returned to Baltimore in 1996 after an 12-year absence that was created when the beloved Colts loaded trucks and moved out of town in the middle of the night. Baltimore got pro football back under reverse circumstances—this time, fans got a franchise that had abandoned an established city.

Owner Art Modell, frustrated by his inability to get a new stadium in Cleveland, began shopping the Browns. He closed a deal to move the team to Baltimore. It was determined that the Browns' name and history would remain in Cleveland so a new identity was sought for the relocated team.

"Ravens", a nod to former Baltimore resident Edgar Allen Poe, was chosen after it was the favorite of more than two thirds of the respondents in a fan poll. The other finalists were Americans and Marauders. The list started with more than 100 possibilities, then was narrowed to 17 by team management.

The familiar Halloween-tinged orange, brown and white was left in Cleveland and the Ravens sported uniforms that were primarily purple and black.

The first Ravens coach was Ted Marchibroda, which was also an indirect acknowledgment of Baltimore's NFL past. Marchibroda had enjoyed great popularity as the Colts coach from 1975-79, especially when he transformed a 2-12 team into a 10-4 playoff qualifier in his first season.

Although Modell was anxious to cut ties with Cleveland, much of the front office staff moved to Baltimore, including former Browns tight end Ozzie Newsome, the franchise's director of player personnel.

After Marchibroda left, the Ravens hired highly-regarded assistant Brian Billick as their head coach. The high-profile Billick constructed one of the NFL's most effective defenses and led the team to a Super Bowl victory in its fifth year.

FRANCHISE RECORD			
	W	**L**	**T**
Regular Season	63	64	1
Playoffs	5	2	0
AFC Championships	**1** *(2000)*		
Super Bowls	**1** *(2000)*		

BALTIMORE RAVENS

1996 — The Cleveland Browns moved to Baltimore on February 9 and were renamed the Ravens.

1996 — Offensive lineman Jonathan Ogden of UCLA became the Ravens' first draft choice.

1996 — Quarterback Vinny Testaverde ran nine yards for the Ravens' first touchdown on September 1.

1996 — The Ravens won their first game, beating Oakland 19-14 on September 1.

1998 — Ravens Stadium opened with a preseason game against the Chicago Bears on August 8.

1998 — Priest Holmes ran for a franchise-record 227 yards on November 22 against Cincinnati.

1999 — Minnesota Vikings offensive coordinator Brian Billick was named head coach on January 19.

1999 — Qadry Ismael collected a team-record 268 receiving yards on December 12.

2000 — Baltimore's defense set a 16-game record for fewest points allowed in a season (165).

2001 — The Ravens defeated the New York Giants 34-7 in the Super Bowl.

2002 — Billick tied Tom Flores' record for most consecutive playoff wins at the start of a career (five).

2003 — Jamal Lewis set an NFL record by rushing for 295 yards in a 33-13 victory over Cleveland on September 14.

CINCINNATI BENGALS

Paul Brown helped found the Cleveland Browns, only to be pushed out of the franchise he'd created.

He was eager to get back into football and determined not to make the mistake of losing control of his franchise again.

Three years after he was forced out in Cleveland, Brown began studying ways to land an expansion team. He and Ohio Governor James Rhodes worked on the project in 1965 and targeted Cincinnati. Local government approved funds for a new stadium that was to open in 1970 and Brown was granted an American Football League franchise that was to start play in 1968.

Brown returned to coaching for the first time since 1962 and the Bengals became Ohio's second pro football team. Brown coached the team until 1975, when he turned the job over to assistant Bill Johnson. Brown moved into the front office as the Bengals' General Manager, a position he held at the time of his death in 1991.

Former Green Bay Packers Hall of Famer Forrest Gregg coached the team from 1980-83 and finished seven games over .500, making him the most successful coach in Bengals' history. Gregg's 1981 team went to the Super Bowl but lost to San Francisco.

The Bengals were a contender again later in the 1980s under Sam Wyche. They reached the Super Bowl in 1988 but again lost to San Francisco, this time when the 49ers scored a pair of touchdowns in the fourth quarter. Wyche left after the 1991 season and a succession of coaches—David Shula, Bruce Coslet and Dick LeBeau—have failed to restore the team to contender status.

Brown's two sons have run the franchise without much success. However, hiring Marvin Lewis as head coach resulted in an immediate improvement in 2003. The Bengals finished 8-8 and went into the last week of the season with a chance to win the AFC North.

FRANCHISE RECORD			
	W	**L**	**T**
Regular Season	234	313	1
Playoffs	5	7	0
AFC Championships	**2** *(1981, 1988)*		

CINCINNATI BENGALS

1965 — Paul Brown began exploring the possibility of a second pro football franchise in Ohio.

1966 — Cincinnati leaders approved construction of a new multi-purpose stadium to open in 1970.

1967 — Brown was granted an American Football League franchise on May 24, to begin play in the 1968 season.

1968 — The Bengals lost 29-13 to San Diego in the franchise's first game on September 6.

1968 — Cincinnati got its first win, defeating Denver 24-10 on September 15.

1970 — The Bengals moved into Riverfront Stadium and posted their first winning season (8-6).

1970 — Cincinnati qualified for the playoffs for the first time but lost 17-0 to the Baltimore Colts on December 26.

1981 — The Bengals unveiled new uniforms with tiger stripes on the helmets and pants.

1982 — San Francisco defeated the Bengals 26-21 in the Super Bowl on January 24.

1991 — Franchise founder Paul Brown died on August 5.

2000 — The Bengals moved into Paul Brown Stadium.

2003 — Marvin Lewis was hired as head coach in January.

2003 — With the top pick in the draft, the Bengals selected quarterback and Heisman Trophy winner Carson Palmer of Southern California.

CLEVELAND BROWNS

The Cleveland Browns are one franchise with two separate histories.

The "original" Browns were launched by Paul Brown and were a powerhouse in the old All-American Football Conference. When that league folded, the Browns joined the NFL in 1950 and continued their tradition of excellence.

After winning four AAFC titles, the Browns quickly won three in the NFL. All seven of the titles came with Brown running the organization. The legendary coach was pushed out after the 1962 season when he and new owner Art Modell clashed over control issues. Blanton Collier took over as head coach and the Browns won the NFL title in 1964, defeating the Baltimore Colts in the championship game.

Running back Jim Brown, who keyed the Browns' offense, abruptly retired after the 1965 season to become an actor. The Browns continued to have winning seasons but they were no longer a championship caliber team. The Browns couldn't overtake the powerful Pittsburgh Steelers in the 1970s but they won five AFC Central titles in the '80s without reaching the Super Bowl.

The franchise again fell on hard times in the 1990s and the unthinkable happened when Modell moved the team to Baltimore and renamed it the Ravens. In a deal between the city and the NFL, it was determined that the Browns' name, colors and records would remain in Cleveland while the Ravens would start from scratch. Thus, when the Browns returned in 1999, they were an expansion team that had a legacy of eight league championships and five retired uniform numbers.

The new stadium is not far from old Municipal Stadium site on the shores of Lake Erie. The Browns are again sporting their traditional orange, white and brown with a completely new cast—making them a franchise that is both old and new.

Although the Browns took a step back with a 5-11 record in 2003, head coach Butch Davis was given a two-year contract extension.

FRANCHISE RECORD			
	W	**L**	**T**
Regular Season	400	320	10
Playoffs	11	20	0
NFL Championships	**4** *(1950, 1954, 1955, 1964)*		

CLEVELAND BROWNS

1944 — The Browns were a charter member of the All-American Football Conference.

1950 — One year after they won the defunct AAFC's last title, the Browns won the NFL title by beating Los Angeles.

1958 — Jim Brown followed a Rookie of the Year season by becoming Cleveland's first 1,000-yard rusher, gaining 1,527 yards.

1961 — Art Modell purchased the Browns for the record sum of $4 million.

1963 — Paul Brown was released as coach and General Manager with six years remaining on his contract.

1964 — The Browns won the Eastern Conference title game 52-20 over the New York Giants and beat Baltimore 27-0 for the NFL championship.

1970 — The Browns moved to the American Football Conference as part of the NFL-AFL merger.

1980 — The Browns lost the AFC Championship game to Oakland in the final minutes, missing their best chance to get to the Super Bowl.

1986 — Cleveland had another heartbreaking outcome in the AFC Championship game, losing to Denver in overtime.

1995 — Weeks after a 5-11 season ended, Modell announced he was moving the team to Baltimore.

1996 — The NFL agreed to assign Cleveland an expansion franchise in 1999 that would inherit the history of the Browns.

1999 — The Browns returned to the NFL by losing 43-0 to the Steelers in the first regular season game at their new stadium.

PITTSBURGH STEELERS

When Arthur J. Rooney founded the Pittsburgh Steelers in 1933, he had no idea 40 years would pass before his team could claim a championship.

The Steelers didn't have lean years, they had lean decades. But when their fortunes finally changed, the Steelers had one of the greatest runs in NFL history, winning four Super Bowls in six years and firmly establishing Pittsburgh as the team of the 1970s.

Rooney was an all-around athlete who boxed, played minor league baseball and semi-pro football. When he started the Steelers, the franchise was known as the Pirates to capitalize on the fame of the city's professional baseball team.

The Steelers stumbled from the start in the 10-team NFL. They had only 22 wins in their first seven seasons and went through five head coaches. The franchise's first winning season came in 1942 but personnel shortages brought on by World War II forced the Steelers to combine with the Philadelphia Eagles and Chicago Cardinals for two seasons.

Pittsburgh reached the postseason for the first time in 1947 but wouldn't return until 1972. Good players came through Pittsburgh but the Steelers could never seem to come up with a formula for success. Low attendance corresponded with the team's futility but Rooney rejected offers to move his team to another city.

The turning point came in 1969 when Art Rooney handed over day-to-day responsibility for the franchise to his son Dan. After being spurned by Penn State's Joe Paterno, Dan Rooney hired Baltimore Colts assistant Chuck Noll as head coach, the first move in assembling the team that would dominate.

The Steelers had phenomenally successful drafts in the early 1970s and their championship rosters were home-grown.

Noll stayed on the job for 23 seasons. His successor, Bill Cowher, has kept the Steelers in the playoffs but they lost to Dallas in their only other Super Bowl appearance.

The Steelers were expected to contend in 2003 but had a disappointing 6-10 record.

FRANCHISE RECORD			
	W	**L**	**T**
Regular Season	464	464	20
Playoffs	23	17	0
AFC Championships	**5** *(1974, 1975, 1978, 1979, 1995)*		
Super Bowls	**4** *(1974, 1975, 1978, 1979)*		

PITTSBURGH STEELERS

1933 — Arthur J. Rooney was granted an NFL franchise for Pittsburgh on July 8.

1940 — The franchise changed its name from Pirates to Steelers.

1942 — After 10 years, the Steelers posted their first winning record, 7-4 under head coach Walt Kiesling.

1948 — Coach Jock Sutherland died suddenly during a scouting trip. Sutherland had led the Steelers to an 8-4 record and a share of the Eastern Division title in 1947.

1955 — The Steelers drafted Louisville quarterback Johnny Unitas on the ninth round. They cut Unitas without letting him appear in a preseason game.

1969 — Chuck Noll, an assistant to Don Shula in Baltimore, was hired as head coach on January 27.

1970 — The Steelers won a coin flip with the Chicago Bears and the right to choose quarterback Terry Bradshaw with the first overall pick in the draft.

1972 — The franchise's first postseason victory was a 13-7 win over Oakland, decided on Franco Harris' "Immaculate Reception."

1974 — The Steelers had one of the greatest drafts in NFL history, selecting four future Hall of Famers in the first five rounds—receivers Lynn Swann and John Stallworth, linebacker Jack Lambert and center Mike Webster.

1975 — Pittsburgh beat the Minnesota Vikings 16-6 in Super Bowl IX on January 12 for the Steelers' first championship.

1980 — The Steelers won their fourth championship in six years, defeating the Los Angeles Rams 31-19 in Super Bowl XIV on January 20.

1991 — Noll retired on December 26, after compiling a 209-156-1 record in 23 seasons.

AMERICAN FOOTBALL CONFERENCE
SOUTH

Houston Texans
Indianapolis Colts
Jacksonville Jaguars
Tennessee Titans

HOUSTON TEXANS

It's hard to imagine a team leaving a football-mad environment like Texas but that's exactly what happened in Houston.

The Houston Oilers, an original member of the American Football League, packed up and headed for Nashville after the 1996 season. That left Houston without a pro team for the first time since 1959.

Robert McNair began assembling support to bring the NFL back to Houston, knowing it would take a new stadium to replace the Astrodome. The mission started in 1997 and went through the usual ups and downs. In addition to rallying local support, there was the need to sell the NFL on returning to Houston. The league's first preference was to put a team in southern California, which had been vacant since the Raiders left Los Angeles and the Rams moved out of Anaheim.

But a viable bid failed to materialize from Los Angeles and Houston's well-organized plan was received positively. When it came time for a vote on October 6, 1999, Houston won approval by a unanimous vote.

Then it was down to details in preparation for joining the league in time for the 2002 season. The name was chosen with the idea of making the team regional in scope while still identifying it as a Houston franchise. The logo and colors bore no resemblance to those worn by the Oilers. There was the matter of choosing a staff to lead the franchise through the inevitable growing pains.

Charley Casserly, a George Allen protégé who had worked for the Washington Redskins, was hired to direct the football operations. He chose Dom Capers as his head coach. Capers was a highly-respected defensive tactician and defense is the quickest way for a team to succeed. Capers also had some experience in building a team from scratch, having led the Carolina Panthers when they came into the league in 1995.

FRANCHISE RECORD			
	W	**L**	**T**
Regular Season	9	23	0
Playoffs	0	0	0

HOUSTON TEXANS

1997 — Houston Oilers owner Bud Adams got approval to move the team to Nashville on July 3.

1999 — The NFL approved Houston for an expansion franchise after efforts by Los Angeles to land the 32nd team fell short.

2000 — Charley Casserly, former General Manager of the Washington Redskins, was hired to head the Texans' football operations on January 19.

2000 — On March 9, groundbreaking ceremonies were held for a new football stadium.

2000 — Houston's new football team officially became the Texans on September 6. The other finalists were Apollos and Stallions.

2001 — Dom Capers was hired as the team's first coach on January 21. Capers had also served as the first head coach of the Carolina Panthers when they entered the NFL in 1995.

2001 — Capers hired former Cleveland Browns head coach Chris Palmer as his offensive coordinator.

2001 — The Texans unveiled their uniforms on September 25.

2001 — The team signed its first 10 players on December 29.

2002 — Vic Fangio was hired as the team's first defensive coordinator.

2002 — Tony Boselli of the Jaguars was the first player chosen in the February 18 expansion draft.

2002 — Quarterback David Carr of Fresno State was the first player chosen in the NFL draft.

2002 — The Texans became the first expansion team in 41 years to win its first game, beating the Dallas Cowboys 19-10 on September 8.

INDIANAPOLIS COLTS

The Colts were one of the teams that helped pro football overtake baseball as the No. 1 spectator sport in the United States.

They had their best years in the 1960s, fielding consistently competitive teams led by star players like quarterback Johnny Unitas, running back Lenny Moore and receiver Raymond Berry. In fact, most historians point to the 1958 NFL Championship game between the Colts and New York Giants as the one that ushered pro football into the television era.

Baltimore almost didn't get an NFL franchise. The Baltimore Colts of the All-American Football Conference folded before they got a chance to join the NFL in 1950. In 1953, the league canceled the franchise of the Dallas Texans and gave Baltimore six weeks to sell 15,000 season tickets. The city met that challenge and Carroll Rosenbloom became the owner of the team, which started play that same year.

The 1957 season started a streak of 15 consecutive years with a winning record. Unitas, cast aside by the Pittsburgh Steelers, became the quarterback, and was surrounded by talent on offense. End Gino Marchetti was a fierce, agile pass rusher who led a tough defense. The Colts won NFL titles in 1958 and '59 and competed every year.

The Colts didn't miss a beat when 33-year-old Don Shula replaced Weeb Ewbank as coach in 1963. Baltimore won its division twice and had the unwanted distinction of being the first old-line NFL team to lose a Super Bowl to the American Football League. Ironically, the Colts joined the new American Conference when the leagues merged in 1970, the same year that Shula left for Miami.

Owner Robert Irsay turned his back on Baltimore and moved the franchise to Indianapolis in time for the 1984 season. The Colts have been a frequent playoff qualifier since moving.

After two exceptional offensive performances in the playoffs, the Colts fell to New England in the AFC Championship game in 2003.

FRANCHISE RECORD			
	W	**L**	**T**
Regular Season	364	371	7
Playoffs	12	14	0
NFL Championships	**3** *(1958, 1959, 1968)*		
AFC Championships	**1** *(1970)*		
Super Bowls	**1** *(1970)*		

INDIANAPOLIS COLTS

1953 — The Baltimore Colts joined the NFL.

1957 — The Colts had their first winning season (7-5) to start a streak of 15 consecutive seasons with a winning record.

1958 — The Colts beat the New York Giants 23-17 in overtime to win their first NFL title.

1963 — Don Shula took over as head coach, replacing Weeb Ewbank.

1964 — The favored Colts lost the NFL championship game 27-0 at Cleveland.

1968 — Lineman Art Donovan became the first Colts player elected to the Pro Football Hall of Fame.

1969 — The New York Jets beat the Colts 16-7, marking the first time an AFL team won the Super Bowl.

1969 — Shula left the Colts to become head coach of the Miami Dolphins.

1971 — The Colts beat Dallas 16-13 in the Super Bowl on Jim O'Brien's field goal.

1972 — Owner Carroll Rosenblooom traded the Colts to Robert Irsay, who owned the Los Angeles Rams.

1984 — The Colts moved to Indianapolis on March 28.

2000 — Edgerrin James set a franchise record with 1,709 rushing yards.

2002 — Tony Dungy was hired as head coach on January 22 after six years as Tampa Bay's head coach.

JACKSONVILLE JAGUARS

Getting a National Football League franchise for Jacksonville involved more than a two-minute drill.

In fact, when the Jaguars took the field for the first time in 1995, it was the culmination of a six-year effort to bring pro football to Jacksonville. The effort started a full six months before the NFL even committed to adding two new franchises and almost two years before the league started accepting formal applications.

Civic and business leaders launched the campaign, knowing that Jacksonville would face stiff competition. Among the other cities seeking a team were Charlotte, Memphis, St. Louis and Baltimore. The latter two were markets that had supported the NFL, only to lose the franchise when an owner decided to relocate.

The Jaguars official history notes the exact minute that Jacksonville joined the NFL—4:12 p.m. on November 30, 1993. That was almost two years before the organization would field its first team.

The first order of business was to hire a coach who would set a tone for a new organization. Tom Coughlin, who had engineered a turnaround at Boston College, was chosen. His reputation for structure and discipline was legendary. Pre-game schedules for the team were broken down to fractions of minutes.

The long lead time allowed Jacksonville to build its football staff. NFL free agency allowed the Jaguars to get better players than the marginal talents who would be available in the expansion draft. Some established teams complained that the league had been too generous when the Jaguars went 4-4 within their division in their debut season. It was the best record an expansion team had managed within its division.

By their second season, the Jaguars qualified for the playoffs as quarterback Mark Brunell passed for 4,367 yards.

FRANCHISE RECORD			
	W	**L**	**T**
Regular Season	73	71	0
Playoffs	4	4	0

JACKSONVILLE JAGUARS

1989 — Touchdown Jacksonville! was formed to lead an effort to land an NFL franchise for the city.

1991 — The NFL announced on July 17 that it would accept applications for expansion teams. Jacksonville submitted its proposal on October 17.

1992 — The NFL deferred a decision on expansion due to the lack of a labor agreement with the players.

1993 — Jacksonville was awarded a franchise on November 30.

1994 — Tom Coughlin was hired as head coach on February 21.

1995 — The Jaguars made their first trade on April 21, acquiring quarterback Mark Brunell from Green Bay for two draft picks.

1995 — Offensive tackle Tony Boselli of Southern California was the Jaguars first draft pick.

1995 — The Jaguars beat Houston 17-16 on October 1 for the franchise's first victory.

1996 — The Jaguars defeated Buffalo 30-27 in Jacksonville's first playoff game on December 28.

1998 — Brunell passed for a team-record four touchdowns on November 29.

2000 — Running back Fred Taylor rushed for 1,399 yards.

TENNESSEE TITANS

The Houston Oilers took the first two American Football League championships. By the time the franchise got back to a title game, it had a new name and a new address.

The potent passing combination of quarterback George Blanda and receiver Billy Cannon helped the Oilers win two titles and just miss a third. In 1961, NFL castoff Blanda threw seven touchdown passes in one game and passed for 464 yards in another.

Lean years followed that run of 31-10-1 over the first three years. It wasn't until the late 1970s that the Oilers got back in the postseason. Coach O.A. "Bum" Phillips led a group that include quarterback Dan Pastorini and bruising running back Earl Campbell. The Oilers made the playoffs for three consecutive years from 1978-80 and played in two AFC Championship games. They couldn't get by the Pittsburgh Steelers, though, despite Phillips' bold promise to "kick the door in" the next time his team met the Steelers.

Phillips' colorful years were a highlight of the Oilers' stay in Houston. The Astrodome rocked with the sound of the fight song, "Houston Oilers No. 1" and fans waved "Luv Ya Blue" placards.

Phillips moved on, Campbell wore down and the Oilers missed the playoffs until they started a seven-year run in 1987. Quarterback Warren Moon, a former Canadian League star, led teams that were good but not quite good enough to get to a Super Bowl.

By the late 1990s, Coach Jeff Fisher had assembled a winner around the same time that the Oilers' relationship with Houston was disintegrating. The franchise left Houston for Tennessee and remained the Oilers before making a clean break and being renamed the Titans. The Titans reached Super Bowl XXXIV but came one agonizing yard short of tying the game against the St. Louis Rams and forcing overtime.

Fisher has kept the Titans in contention with an offense built around quarterback Steve McNair and running back Eddie George. Tennessee was 12-4 in 2003.

FRANCHISE RECORD			
	W	**L**	**T**
Regular Season	323	331	6
Playoffs	14	17	0
AFL Championships	**2** *(1960, 1961)*		
AFC Championships	**1** *(1999)*		

TENNESSEE TITANS

1959 — Houston oilman K.S. "Bud" Adams Jr. was granted a franchise on August 3 by the American Football League.

1960 — The Oilers signed No. 1 draft pick Billy Cannon of Louisiana State on January 1.

1961 — With the team off to a 1-3-1 start, Wally Lemm replaced Coach Lou Rymkus, who had led the team to the AFL title a year earlier.

1968 — The Oilers moved from Rice Stadium to the Astrodome, becoming the first pro football team to play indoors and on artificial turf.

1975 — O.A. "Bum" Phillips was hired as head coach on January 25.

1978 — Houston came back from a 23-0 deficit to beat New England 26-23 on November 12.

1984 — Running back Earl Campbell was traded to New Orleans for a first-round draft choice and quarterback Warren Moon was signed as a free agent.

1994 — Jeff Fisher was named head coach on November 14, replacing Jack Pardee.

1996 — NFL owners approved the franchise's move from Houston to Nashville.

1998 — The team played its last game as the Oilers.

2000 — "The Music City Miracle," a kickoff lateral from Frank Wycheck to Kevin Dyson that covered 75 yards for a touchdown allowed the Titans to advance in the playoffs against Buffalo on January 8. Tennessee would go on to lose to St. Louis 23-16 in Super Bowl XXXIV on January 30.

AMERICAN FOOTBALL CONFERENCE

EAST

Buffalo Bills
Miami Dolphins
New England Patriots
New York Jets

BUFFALO BILLS

The history of the Buffalo Bills is summed up in the name of their home field, Ralph Wilson Stadium.

Wilson was awarded an American Football League franchise in 1959 and has owned the Bills since then. The Bills have had a steady parade of marquee players and have been in the playoffs but they haven't won a championship since they claimed the next-to-last AFL title in 1965. The greatest success—and frustration—came during coach Marv Levy's 12-year stay from 1986-97. Levy led the team to four consecutive Super Bowls and the Bills lost all of them.

Much of the success the Bills have enjoyed has come under three coaches—Lou Saban, Chuck Knox and Levy.

Saban led the team to consecutive AFL titles in 1964 and '65, then left the Bills. After just missing a third title (and a berth on the first Super Bowl), the Bills declined, posting a 13-55-2 record over five seasons.

Saban came back to Buffalo and designed an offense to showcase the talents of running back O.J. Simpson. A coaching change midway through the 1976 season again sunk the Bills until Knox led them to a divisional title in 1980. Buffalo again endured tough times that ended shortly after Levy took control of the team.

Levy's teams won the AFC East title five times in six years and set a record by qualifying for the Super Bowl in four consecutive seasons.

The stars of the Bills' AFL days included quarterback Jack Kemp and running back Cookie Gilchrist. Simpson dominated in the '70s and Levy's teams were keyed on offense by quarterback Jim Kelly and running back Thurman Thomas, as well as defensive end Bruce Smith.

The Bills are one northern team that has decided to stay outdoors, despite the sometimes severe weather that hits western New York in winter.

Following a 6-10 season in 2003, the Bills replaced head coach Gregg Williams with Mike Mularkey, who had been Pittsburgh's offensive coordinator.

FRANCHISE RECORD			
	W	**L**	**T**
Regular Season	313	339	8
Playoffs	14	15	0
AFL Championships	**2** *(1964, 1965)*		
AFC Championships	**4** *(1990, 1991, 1992, 1993)*		

BUFFALO BILLS

1959 — Ralph C. Wilson was awarded an American Football League franchise on October 28.

1960 — The Bills lost their first regular season game to the New York Titans, 27-3 on September 11.

1962 — The Bills had their first winning season, finishing 7-6-1.

1962 — Cookie Gilchrist ran for 1,096 yards, becoming the first Bills player to run for 1,000 yards.

1963 — Buffalo made its first playoff appearance, losing 26-8 to the Boston Patriots on December 28.

1964 — A 20-7 victory over San Diego in the AFL Championship Game gave the Bills their first title.

1965 — The Bills again defeated San Diego to take the AFL championship.

1969 — Buffalo made running back O.J. Simpson of USC the first player chosen in the draft.

1973 — Simpson set an NFL record by rushing for 2,003 yards.

1986 — Marv Levy took over as head coach, replacing Hank Bullough.

1991 — The Bills made their first Super Bowl appearance and lost 20-19 to the New York Giants when Scott Norwood's attempt at a game-winning field goal from 47 yards was wide right.

MIAMI DOLPHINS

The Miami Dolphins won Super Bowl VII—but that isn't the number that matters.

The one with which the Dolphins will always be associated is 17-0. That was their record in 1972, when they went 14-0 in the regular season and won two playoff games in advance of beating the Washington Redskins in the Super Bowl. They are the only NFL team to fashion a perfect season and the record has only been threatened once since then—the 1985 Chicago Bears lost only one game en route to a Super Bowl title. Their only defeat came at the hands of the Dolphins in a Monday night game that set ratings records.

The Dolphins became Florida's first pro football franchise in 1965, joining the American Football League as an expansion team. George Wilson coached the team through its first four seasons, during which it steadily added talent.

Don Shula joined the Dolphins as coach in time for the 1970 season and stayed for 26 years, eventually surpassing George Halas' career record for victories. Many of the pieces were in place when Shula took over the team. The Dolphins qualified for the playoffs in his first season, then won the AFC championship for three consecutive years. From 1970-74, the Dolphins dominated the NFL with a 65-15-1 record.

The World Football League didn't last long as an alternative to the NFL but it hurt the Dolphins. Running backs Jim Kiick, Larry Csonka and receiver Paul Warfield all signed contracts with WFL teams and the Dolphins were affected by the disruption.

Shula made a key move in 1983, drafting Dan Marino from the University of Pittsburgh after five quarterbacks had already been taken in the first round. Shula looked past Marino's disappointing senior season and saw a player who was likely to succeed at the pro level.

The Dolphins had two surprises after the 2003 season. They extended the contract of coach Dave Wannstedt and they hired Marino to oversee their football operations.

FRANCHISE RECORD			
	W	**L**	**T**
Regular Season	349	223	4
Playoffs	20	19	0
AFC Championships	**5** *(1971, 1972, 1973, 1982, 1984)*		
Super Bowls	**2** *(1972, 1973)*		

MIAMI DOLPHINS

1965 — Joe Robbie had entertainer Danny Thomas among the investment group that was awarded an AFL franchise on August 16.

1966 — In the Dolphins' first game, Joe Auer returned the opening kickoff 95 yards for a touchdown.

1967 — The Dolphins made Purdue quarterback Bob Griese their first-round draft choice.

1968 — Fullback Larry Csonka of Syracuse was the Dolphins' first-round draft choice.

1970 — Under new coach Don Shula, the Dolphins finished 10-4 for their first winning season.

1972 — The Dolphins played in the Super Bowl for the first time and lost 24-3 to the Dallas Cowboys on January 16.

1973 — Miami capped its 17-0 season by defeating Washington 14-7 in the Super Bowl on January 14.

1983 — University of Pittsburgh quarterback Dan Marino was chosen in the first round of the draft.

1985 — San Francisco beat the Dolphins 38-16 in the Super Bowl on January 20.

1987 — The Dolphins moved from the Orange Bowl to Joe Robbie Stadium, which was later named Pro Player Stadium.

1993 — Shula won his 325th career game, breaking George Halas' record for coaching victories.

1995 — Shula retired after 26 seasons and was replaced by Jimmy Johnson, former coach of the University of Miami and the Dallas Cowboys.

NEW ENGLAND PATRIOTS

The Patriots took years to find a permanent home and decades to win a championship.

But with two Super Bowl titles in three years, they have emerged as the first powerhouse team of the 21st century. The Patriots defeated the Carolina Panthers 32-29 in Super Bowl XXXVIII on Feb. 1, 2004, the second time a last-second Adam Vinatieri field goal produced a championship for coach Bill Belichick's team.

The Patriots were charter members of the American Football League and were then known as the Boston Patriots. Finding the Patriots within Boston was a year-to-year issue in the franchise's first decade, though. They were at Boston University for their first two seasons. They were at Harvard for 1962, then shifted to Fenway Park for a run that lasted from 1963-69. It was back to Boston University for one more season until they changed their name and address in 1971. They became the New England Patriots and moved to Foxboro, Massachusetts, a community about 25 miles from Boston.

The Patriots were playoff contenders in the '60s, although they didn't win an AFL title. They were doormats in the years immediately following the NFL-AFL merger but became contenders again in the late 1970s. They got even better in the 1980s under Raymond Berry, the former Baltimore Colts great who took the team to its first Super Bowl. The Patriots fell apart after Berry left, enduring lean years under Rod Rust and Dick MacPherson.

Their turnaround was engineered by Bill Parcells, who had similarly transformed the New York Giants. The domineering Parcells overhauled the roster and got the Patriots back to the Super Bowl, where they lost to Green Bay. Parcells and owner Robert Kraft clashed, which led to an acrimonious breakup and took Parcells back to New York, this time to lead the Jets. His New England successor, Pete Carroll, couldn't sustain the success, which led to another change.

Belichick, Parcells' former defensive coordinator, led the team to three Super Bowls, winning twice.

FRANCHISE RECORD			
	W	**L**	**T**
Regular Season	314	337	9
Playoffs	13	10	0
AFC Championships	**4** *(1985, 1986, 2001, 2003)*		
Super Bowls	**2** *(2001, 2003)*		

NEW ENGLAND PATRIOTS

1959 — Boston was granted an American Football League franchise on November 16.

1961 — The Patriots posted a winning record (9-4-1) in their second season.

1963 — The Patriots made their first playoff appearance, beating Buffalo 26-8 for the AFL Eastern Division championship.

1966 — Jim Nance became the team's first 1,000-yard rusher with 1,458 yards.

1971 — The team moved to Foxboro, Massachusetts and changed its name to the New England Patriots.

1973 — The Patriots had three first-round draft selections and chose offensive lineman John Hannah, running back Sam Cunningham and receiver Darryl Stingley.

1983 — The team passed on Dan Marino in the first round of the draft and chose quarterback Tony Eason.

1986 — The Patriots reached the Super Bowl for the first time and lost 46-10 to the Chicago Bears.

1991 — Hannah became the first Patriots player to be elected to the Hall of Fame.

1993 — Bill Parcells was hired as Patriots head coach.

1997 — The Patriots returned to the Super Bowl and lost to Green Bay 35-21.

2000 — Bill Belichick became Patriots head coach.

2002 — The Patriots won their first championship, defeating the St. Louis Rams in the Super Bowl 20-17, on Adam Vinatieri's last-second field goal.

2004 — Adam Vinatieri's 41-yard last-second field goal gave the Patriots a 32-29 victory over Carolina in Super Bowl XXXVIII on February 1. New England finished its second championship season with 15 consecutive wins.

NEW YORK JETS

The New York Jets got more than an exceptional quarterback when they invested $400,000 in Joe Namath.

They got credibility in the country's biggest media market.

The Jets had been playing a very distant second fiddle to the Giants, who were established as a contender for the NFL championship. The Jets? They'd already been through a name change, previously called the Titans, and an ownership change from Harry Wismer to Sonny Werblin. In fact, the Titans/Jets front office machinations often seemed to overshadow what was happening on the field.

Things started to change in 1963 and '64. The Jets moved from the dank Polo Grounds in the shadow of Yankee Stadium to brand new Shea Stadium in Queens. They hired coach Weeb Ewbank, who had enjoyed success with the Baltimore Colts. And shortly after the 1964 season ended, the Jets signed Namath, who had come to New York from the unlikely birthplace of Beaver Falls, Pennsylvania by way of Bear Bryant's Alabama program.

In addition to keeping Namath away from the NFL, the Jets acquired a personality who would get publicity for a franchise that needed the help. Namath wore white shoes, he let his hair grow long and he loved being seen at all the hot nightspots around town. The gossip columnists started writing about "Broadway Joe." Namath led the Jets to their only Super Bowl appearance and shocked the world by making good on his prediction to beat the Baltimore Colts. The Jets have spent three decades trying to match that success.

Among coaches who have spent more than one season with the Jets, only Bill Parcells left with a winning record. Parcells departed before the job was done, leaving the Jets to again scramble to regain respectability and be as an important part of the sports scene as they were when Namath was around.

FRANCHISE RECORD			
	W	**L**	**T**
Regular Season	294	358	8
Playoffs	7	9	0
AFL Championships	**1** *(1968)*		
Super Bowls	**1** *(1968)*		

NEW YORK JETS

1959 — The New York Titans joined the American Football League on August 14 as a charter member.

1960 — Receiver Don Maynard, a future Hall of Famer, was the first player to sign with the Titans.

1963 — The franchise was renamed the Jets.

1964 — The Jets used their first draft pick to select Ohio State running back Matt Snell.

1965 — The Jets signed Alabama quarterback Joe Namath for a reported $427,000 on January 2.

1967 — The Jets finished 8-5-1 for their first winning season.

1968 — A 27-23 win over Oakland in the AFL Championship game on December 29 was the Jets' first postseason appearance.

1969 — The Jets beat the Baltimore Colts 16-7 on January 12 and became the first AFL team to win the Super Bowl.

1972 — Namath passed for 496 yards and six touchdowns in a 44-34 over Baltimore on September 24.

1976 — College coaching legend Lou Holtz coached the Jets but resigned after 13 games and a 3-10 record.

1978 — Weeb Ewbank became the first person associated with the Jets to be voted into the Hall of Fame.

1980 — Clark Gaines caught 17 passes on September 21 against San Francisco.

AMERICAN FOOTBALL CONFERENCE

WEST

Denver Broncos
Kansas City Chiefs
Oakland Raiders
San Diego Chargers

DENVER BRONCOS

It took a while for the Denver Broncos to start winning but it's become a habit.

The Bronocs, a charter member of the American Football League, didn't post a winning record until their 14th season. The lack of success led to fan apathy in the early days that almost cost Denver the franchise. Some members of the ownership group wanted to sell the franchise to a group that planned to move it to Atlanta. Other members stepped up to keep the team in Denver and fans responded by almost tripling the Broncos' season ticket base.

What fans saw in the early days wasn't always pretty—including the uniforms. The Broncos debuted wearing second-hand uniforms, which included vertically-striped socks. The fashion faux pas became so associated with the team that a later administration had a public ceremony to burn the socks in the hopes of distancing the Broncos from their dubious past.

Running back Floyd Little was an early star for the Broncos but the team stumbled to a 39-97-4 record during its years in the AFL. Denver's best record in 10 AFL seasons was 7-7 in 1962.

Things finally got better in 1973, when coach John Ralston led Denver to a 7-5-2 record. The Broncos fell below .500 just three times over the next 20 years. They finally made the playoffs in 1977 and represented the American Conference in the Super Bowl four times in the 1970s and '80s. However, they lost all four of those title games.

The fortunes really changed after quarterback John Elway became established as one of the NFL's premier players. Elway, who had been part of three Super Bowl losses, led the Broncos to consecutive Super Bowl championships in 1997 and '98 as Denver defeated Green Bay and Atlanta. Coach Mike Shanahan put together a powerhouse team that went 26-6 over those two seasons and also won all seven of its playoff games.

FRANCHISE RECORD			
	W	**L**	**T**
Regular Season	339	311	10
Playoffs	16	13	0
AFC Championships	**6** *(1977, 1986, 1987, 1989, 1997, 1998)*		
Super Bowls	**2** *(1997, 1998)*		

DENVER BRONCOS

1959 — Denver was granted an American Football League franchise on August 14.

1960 — The Broncos won their first game, beating the Boston Patriots 13-10 on September 9.

1962 — Quarterback Frank Tripucka passed for 447 yards in a 23-20 win over Buffalo on September 15.

1971 — Floyd Little had the first 1,000-yard season in Broncos' history, running for 1,133 yards.

1973 — A 7-5-2 record represented the Broncos' first winning season in the team's 14-year history.

1977 — The Broncos defeated Pittsburgh 34-21 in the franchise's first playoff game.

1978 — Denver made its first Super Bowl appearance, losing 27-10 to the Dallas Cowboys.

1983 — The Broncos played the coldest game in franchise history. The temperature was zero with a wind-chill factor of minus-30 for the game against Kansas City.

1995 — Mike Shanahan took over as head coach on January 31.

1998 — Denver defeated Green Bay 31-24 on January 25 for the Broncos' first championship.

1999 — The Broncos beat Atlanta 34-19 on January 31 for their second consecutive Super Bowl victory.

2001 — INVESCO Field at Mile High opened with a preseason game against New Orleans on August 25 that drew a crowd of 74,063.

KANSAS CITY CHIEFS

When Lamar Hunt couldn't get into the National Football League, he took a radical step to get into professional football.

He formed his own league. Frustrated by his inability to get an NFL franchise, Hunt helped found the American Football League, which began play in 1960. The new league brought franchises to cities that had been unsuccessful in luring the NFL, either by expansion or franchise relocation.

Hunt's team was the Dallas Texans and competed directly with the NFL, which had placed the expansion Cowboys in Dallas the same year. While the Cowboys were still struggling, the Texans developed into one of the early powers of the AFL, winning the league championship in 1962.

That success didn't stop Hunt from moving his team to Kansas City the next year and giving it a new nickname. Hunt believed the AFL would be better off in a market that didn't have an NFL club. The Chiefs won the AFL title again in 1966 and were the league's representative in the first Super Bowl against the Green Bay Packers. They lost that game but were back three years later and knocked off the Minnesota Vikings, marking the second consecutive year in which an AFL team had beaten the NFL. That was the AFL's farewell as the leagues merged the following year and the AFL morphed into the American Conference of the NFL.

It was also the end of the Chiefs success for a long stretch. From 1971 to 1986, Kansas City made just one playoff appearance. The Chiefs lost to Miami in double overtime on Christmas Day.

In the 1990s, coach Marty Schottenheimer restored Kansas City's winning tradition but the Chiefs didn't do well in the playoffs, reaching only one Conference championship game in 1993.

The Chiefs have returned to the playoffs under coach Dick Vermeil. They had a hot start in 2003 and wound up 13-3 before losing to Indianapolis in the playoffs.

FRANCHISE RECORD			
	W	**L**	**T**
Regular Season	349	299	12
Playoffs	8	12	0
AFC Championships	**3** *(1962, 1966, 1969)*		
Super Bowls	**1** *(1969)*		

KANSAS CITY CHIEFS

1959 — The Dallas Texans became a charter member of the American Football League.

1961 — Abner Haynes scored five touchdowns on November 26.

1962 — The Texans beat the Houston Oilers 20-17 in double overtime to win the AFL Championship on December 23.

1963 — The Texans moved to Kansas City and became the Chiefs.

1964 — Quarterback Len Dawson passed for 435 yards and six touchdowns against the Denver Broncos on November 1

1967 — The Green Bay Packers beat the Chiefs 35-10 in the first Super Bowl on January 15.

1970 — The Chiefs, playing their last game as a representative of the AFL, beat Minnesota 23-7 in the Super Bowl.

1973 — Running back Ed Podolak caught a team-record 12 passes on October 7.

1993 — Quarterback Joe Montana signed with the Chiefs after winning three Super Bowl Most Valuable Player awards with San Francisco.

2000 — Elvis Grbac passed for 504 yards on November 5.

2001 — Dick Vermiel came out of retirement on January 12 and became the ninth head coach in franchise history.

OAKLAND RAIDERS

Al Davis is so strongly identified with the Oakland Raiders it's easy to forget he wasn't there from the franchise's start.

Davis didn't join the Raiders until 1963, when he was hired to replace Red Conkright and become the team's fourth head coach in four years. Davis has since become the Raiders owner and has long headed one of the NFL's smallest front offices. At times, the Raiders club directory has consisted of Davis and a handful of hand-picked helpers.

Davis created the Raiders' motto ("Pride and Poise") and their terse, unofficial mission statement—"Just win, baby." His impact on the franchise has been enormous and it's been that way since he first got to Oakland. Davis took over a team that had gone 1-13 under two different coaches in 1962. In his first year the Raiders went 10-4. Aside from a brief stint as AFL Commissioner in 1966, Davis has been with the franchise continuously, steadily taking more responsibility through the years.

Beginning in 1965, the Raiders had winning records in all but one of the next 20 seasons. They won an AFL championship and took three Super Bowls. They are the only team to have been a Super Bowl participant in the 1960s, '70s and '80s. Over the years the Raiders have developed fierce rivalries because of their intense style of play, the success they've had and the often controversial presence of Davis, who is always seen wearing some combination of the Raiders trademark silver, black and white.

From the time Davis took over in 1963 until 1992, the Raiders had a winning percentage of .661, which was the best of any franchise among the major sports. The Raiders played in Los Angeles from 1982-94 because Davis got a better stadium deal there. He moved back to Oakland for the same reason, defeating court challenges from the NFL as he made the trip. The Raiders returned to former glory in 2003 when they again reached the Super Bowl—this time losing to a strong Tampa Bay team, led by Oakland's former head coach, Jon Gruden. But they went from the Super Bowl to a 4-12 season in 2003. That dive, combined with player mutiny, cost coach Bill Callahan his job. Former Redskins coach Norv Turner took over in Oakland.

FRANCHISE RECORD			
	W	**L**	**T**
Regular Season	385	264	11
Playoffs	25	18	0
AFL Championships	**1** *(1967)*		
AFC Championships	**4** *(1976, 1980, 1983, 2002)*		
Super Bowls	**3** *(1976, 1980, 1983)*		

OAKLAND RAIDERS

1960 — The Raiders were granted an American Football League franchise on January 30.

1963 — Al Davis became head coach and the Raiders, who had been 9-33 to that point, went 10-4. Davis was AFL Coach of the Year.

1967 — The Raiders appeared in the playoffs for the first time, beating Houston 40-7 for the AFL Championship on December 31.

1968 — Green Bay beat Oakland 33-14 in the second Super Bowl on January 14.

1969 — John Madden became head coach, replacing John Rauch.

1978 — Madden retired with a 112-39-7 record over 10 seasons and was replaced by Tom Flores, a former Raiders quarterback.

1980 — Center Jim Otto became the first Raiders player to be elected to the Hall of Fame.

1981 — The Raiders became the first wild card team to win a Super Bowl, defeating Philadelphia 27-10 on January 25.

1982 — Southern California running back Marcus Allen was the Raiders' first- round draft choice.

1984 — The Raiders beat Washington 38-9 in the Super Bowl on January 22.

1989 — Art Shell became head coach, becoming the first African-American to hold that position since Fritz Pollard coached the Akron Pros in 1921.

1992 — Al Davis was inducted into the Hall of Fame.

2003 — The Raiders lost Super Bowl XXXVII 48-21 to Tampa Bay on January 26.

SAN DIEGO CHARGERS

For much of their history, the San Diego Chargers have been providing an air show in the beautiful blue skies of southern California.

The Chargers were one of the American Football League's first successful franchises, thanks to an innovative passing attack developed by Hall of Fame coach Sid Gillman.

Hotel magnate Barron Hilton was awarded an AFL franchise for Los Angeles when the league launched in 1960. The Chargers spent just a year there before finding a home in San Diego. Sports editor Jack Murphy, a tireless promoter of San Diego as a place for major league sports, helped convince Hilton to move 120 miles south.

The Chargers were an instant success, winning their division in five of the first six years. They bombed the Boston Patriots 51-10 in the 1963 AFL title game. Receivers Lance Alworth and Keith Lincoln keyed the offense, along with running back Paul Lowe and quarterback John Hadl.

The initial success didn't last, though. Gillman was forced to step down in 1969 for health reasons and the Chargers didn't win another division title until 1979.

The coach who brought them back was as fascinated by the passing game as much as Gillman was. Don Coryell brought a wide-open attack that was quickly dubbed "Air Coryell." Quarterback Dan Fouts ran the offense and piled up statistics that got him and two of his receivers (Charlie Joiner and Kellen Winslow) into the Pro Football Hall of Fame.

Under Coryell, the Chargers won three AFC West titles and went to a pair of Conference Championship games.

Coach Bobby Ross took San Diego to the Super Bowl for the first time, only to lose to the San Francisco 49ers in 1995.

More recent years have seen only modest success. Marty Schottenheimer was hired to get the Chargers back to the postseason.

FRANCHISE RECORD			
	W	**L**	**T**
Regular Season	308	341	11
Playoffs	7	11	0
AFL Championships	**1** *(1963)*		
AFC Championships	**1** *(1994)*		

SAN DIEGO CHARGERS

1959 — The AFL awarded a Los Angeles franchise to Barron Hilton on August 14.

1960 — The Chargers won their first regular season game, defeating the Dallas Texans 21-20 on September 10.

1961 — The AFL approved the Chargers move from Los Angeles to San Diego on February 10.

1963 — Paul Lowe became the franchise's first 1,000-yard rusher with 1,010 yards.

1969 — Sid Gillman was forced to resign as coach because of health issues.

1973 — The Chargers acquired quarterback Johnny Unitas from Baltimore on January 22. He became the first quarterback to top 40,000 career passing yards on September 30.

1978 — Receiver Lance Alworth became the first Chargers player in the Pro Football Hall of Fame.

1980 — Quarterback Dan Fouts had the Chargers' first 400-yard game, passing for 444 yards against the New York Giants on October 19.

1992 — Bobby Ross, formerly of Georgia Tech, was hired as head coach.

1995 — The Chargers upset the Steelers in Pittsburgh in the AFC Championship game, winning 17-13 on January 15.

1995 — The San Francisco 49ers defeated the Chargers 49-26 in Super Bowl XXIX.

2002 — Marty Schottenheimer was hired as the team's 13th head coach on January 29.

2003 — Running back LaDainian Tomlinson became the first player in NFL history to catch at least 100 passes and run for 1,000 yards. He had 100 receptions and 1,645 rushing yards.

NATIONAL FOOTBALL CONFERENCE
NORTH

Chicago Bears
Detroit Lions
Green Bay Packers
Minnesota Vikings

CHICAGO BEARS

There has never been a time when the Chicago Bears weren't part of the National Football League.

Bears founder George Halas was one of the participants at a September 17, 1920 meeting during which the American Professional Football Association was formed. Two years later the group changed its name to the National Football League.

Halas, who was an outstanding athlete, was hired by the Staley Starch Company in 1920 to form a company football team. After just one year, the company gave Halas the team, $5,000 and the right to move from Decatur to Chicago provided he agreed to keep the Staley name for another season. After winning the championship, Halas renamed the team the Bears.

In 1925, he signed Red Grange and took him on a barnstorming tour with the Bears. Grange's presence lent credibility to professional football, which lagged well behind the college game in popularity. Halas would be the driving force behind the operation of the Bears through the 1970s.

The team won two NFL titles in the 1930s and four in the '40s. After winning the 1946 championship, they made the playoffs just twice in 17 years and didn't win another title until 1963.

The Bears fell on hard times for another two decades until the 1985 team rode a ferocious defense to a Super Bowl victory. It came two years after Halas died but the championship season was engineered by coach Mike Ditka, who had played under Halas. Various members of the Halas family have had control of the franchise, keeping it in the family continuously for nine decades. Chicago has a rich football history, reflected by the fact that the Bears have had had more Hall of Fame members than any other team. Among them are a progression of legendary running backs of varying styles—Grange, Bronko Nagurski, Gale Sayers and Walter Payton.

The Bears finished 7-9 in 2003 and changed coaches. Former St. Louis defensive coordinator Lovie Smith replaced Dick Jauron.

FRANCHISE RECORD			
	W	**L**	**T**
Regular Season	641	463	42
Playoffs	14	15	0
NFL Championships	**7** *(1933, 1940, 1941, 1946, 1963, 1965,1985)*		
NFC Championships	**1** *(1985)*		
Super Bowls	**1** *(1985)*		

CHICAGO BEARS

1920 — The Decatur Staleys were made a charter member of the NFL on September 17.

1922 — The franchise name was changed to Bears one year after it moved from Decatur to Chicago.

1922 — The Bears made the NFL's first player transaction by purchasing tackle Ed Healey's contract from the Rock Island Independents for $100 on November 27.

1933 — Bronko Nagurski became the first Bear to rush for 100 yards, running for 124 yards against Portsmouth on Nov. 26.

1934 — Beattie Feathers became the NFL's first 1,000-yard runner, gaining 1,004 yards for the Bears.

1940 — The Bears beat Washington 73-0 in the NFL championship game.

1940 — End Dick Plasman was the last player to appear in a game without a helmet.

1943 — Sid Luckman passed for 433 yards in a game against the New York Giants on November 14.

1963 — George Halas, Red Grange and Nagurski were all members of the Hall of Fame's first class.

1965 — Kansas running Gale Sayers and Illinois linebacker Dick Butkus both joined the Bears.

1967 — Halas retired after 40 years as head coach with 324 career victories.

1985 — The Bears beat New England 46-10 in the Super Bowl for their first championship since 1963.

DETROIT LIONS

The Detroit Lions have sent 11 men to the Pro Football Hall of Fame but it's telling that none of them have been with the team in the last 25 years.

The Lions have had difficulty matching the success they enjoyed in the 1950s when they were one of the NFL's most respected franchises.

The franchise started in 1934 when the Portsmouth (Ohio) Spartans were relocated to Detroit after a radio executive paid $8,000 for the franchise. It took the newly-renamed Lions just two seasons to win their first NFL title. It was also in 1934 that the Lions scheduled a game to be played on Thanksgiving Day, a tradition that has endured through today.

Quarterback Bobby Layne and running back Doak Walker helped lead the Lions to four divisional titles and three NFL championships in the 1950s. They claimed their last title in 1957 and haven't been back to a league championship game since then. From 1957 through 1982, they made the playoffs just twice, qualifying as a wild card entry both times.

The streak ended in 1983 when the team won the NFC Central, a feat they matched in 1991 and 1993. Most of the success came because of running back Barry Sanders, who had record-setting seasons before his abrupt retirement after the 1998 season. The Lions played in the 1991 NFC Championship game, losing to Washington 41-10.

The Lions moved back into the Detroit city limits in 2002. They spent 37 years at Tiger Stadium before moving into a domed stadium in suburban Pontiac, Michigan in 1975. The Lions now play at Ford Field in downtown Detroit.

The Lions have been through a number of administrations and now count on former All Pro linebacker Matt Millen to head their football operations. Millen had been working as a TV analyst since his playing career ended.

Steve Mariucci went 5-11 in his first season as Lions' head coach.

FRANCHISE RECORD			
	W	**L**	**T**
Regular Season	467	510	32
Playoffs	7	10	0
NFL Championships	**4** *(1935, 1952, 1953, 1957)*		

DETROIT LIONS

1934 — The Portsmouth, Ohio Spartans moved to Detroit and become the Lions.

1934 — The Lions established the tradition of a Thanksgiving Day game.

1952 — Detroit won the first of three NFL championships in six years.

1957 — The Lions won the last of their four NFL titles.

1963 — Defensive lineman Alex Karras was suspended for one season and fined $2,000 for placing bets on games.

1964 — William Clay Ford purchased the Lions.

1966 — The Lions had a 99-yard passing play, a completion from Karl Sweetan to Pat Studstill against Baltimore on October 16.

1975 — The Lions moved from Tiger Stadium to the Silverdome in Pontiac, Michigan.

1991 — Barry Sanders became the first Lions player to run for 200 yards in a game, rushing for 220 yards against Minnesota on November 24.

1997 — Sanders set a Lions record for rushing yards in a season by running for 2,053 yards.

1999 — Sanders retired with 15,269 career rushing yards, just 1,457 yards short of Walter Payton's career mark.

2001 — Matt Millen took over as Lions president and CEO.

GREEN BAY PACKERS

Green Bay, Wisconsin is a small dot on the map but it's been an important spot in NFL history.

The Packers were born in 1919 when the Indian Packing Company had an interest in fielding a football team. From those modest beginnings in a relatively small town, the team joined the National Football League in 1921.

Green Bay native Earl (Curly) Lambeau coached the Packers from their inception through 1949. He led the team to six NFL titles in that time. Receiver Don Hutson was among the NFL's first stars. The Packers wouldn't duplicate that success until the 1960s when coach Vince Lombardi came from New York and transformed the Packers into the NFL's premier team.

Lombardi restored order by demanding total authority over the franchise. His systems and ability to recognize talent turned the Packers into a consistent winner and one of the most respected franchises in sports. Other teams tried to get the Lombardi touch by hiring coaches who had served as his assistants.

Eleven members of the '60s Packers were elected to the Hall of Fame. Quarterback Bart Starr led the offense and fierce linebacker Ray Nitschke served the same role on defense. The Packers won the first two Super Bowls but Lombardi retired to the front office for a year, then took over the Washington Redskins as coach and general manager.

The stars faded and Green Bay struggled, even when former stars like Bart Starr and Forrest Gregg came back to fill Lombardi's old role. It was outsider Mike Holmgren who brought back the winning tradition for the NFL's only publicly owned team.

The Packers remain formidable, thanks to a cast headed by Brett Favre, easily the team's best quarterback since Starr. The Packers have been back to the Super Bowl twice, adding one Lombardi Trophy to their collection.

The Packers made the 2003 playoffs when the Arizona Cardinals capped a comeback with a touchdown pass as time expired against the Minnesota Vikings.

FRANCHISE RECORD			
	W	**L**	**T**
Regular Season	602	474	36
Playoffs	24	13	0
NFL Championships	8 *(1936, 1939, 1944, 1961, 1962, 1965, 1966, 1967)*		
NFC Championships	2 *(1996, 1997)*		
Super Bowls	3 *(1966, 1967, 1996)*		

GREEN BAY PACKERS

1921 — The Packers were admitted to the National Football League.

1929 — Green Bay won its first championship.

1935 — Receiver Don Hutson joined the Packers and started a career that would produce a team-record 823 points.

1939 — Andy Uram had a 97-yard run from scrimmage on October 8.

1949 — Tony Canadeo had 1,052 rushing yards, the first Packer to top 1,000 yards.

1959 — Vince Lombardi was hired as head coach

1961 — The Packers won the first of five NFL titles in six years under Lombardi.

1962 — Halfback Paul Hornung was suspended for a season by the NFL for placing bets on games.

1967 — The Packers scored a 34-27 win over the Dallas Cowboys in the NFL Championship game and earned a trip to the first Super Bowl.

1968 — Just weeks after the Packers won their second Super Bowl, Lombardi resigned on January 28.

1992 — Mike Holmgren became the Packers head coach.

1997 — The Packers won their first championship in 29 years, beating New England 35-21 in the Super Bowl on January 26.

MINNESOTA VIKINGS

The Super Bowl is almost always played in some warm weather paradise and maybe that's what threw the Minnesota Vikings.

After winning December and January playoff games in the frozen north, the Vikings had to suddenly shift gears and confront balmy environments like New Orleans and Pasadena.

The Vikings have had an admirable record of success in their five decades but it doesn't include a championship. They went to the Super Bowl four times from 1970-77 and came away empty each time. They haven't been back to the title game since 1977, when they lost to Oakland.

Minnesota was prepared to join the American Football League in 1959 but gave up that opportunity to get an NFL expansion franchise for the 1961 season. The Vikings were led by quarterback Fran Tarkenton, whose scrambling ability seemed to upset coach Norm Van Brocklin as much as it did the defense. They both left in 1967—Tarkenton was traded to the Giants and Van Brocklin resigned. The new management team was General Manager Jim Finks and coach Bud Grant, both of whom came from the Canadian Football League. Finks and the low-key Grant would assemble a team that would contend for two decades.

The Vikings were playoff regulars, winning 11 NFC Central titles in 13 years. They played outdoors at Met Stadium and conquered the harsh elements as well as opponents. Tarkenton came back to run an offense that always featured outstanding running backs—Dave Osborn, Chuck Foreman and reliable Bill Brown. The defense, led by the "Purple People Eater" line that included Jim Marshall, Alan Page and Carl Eller dared opponents to run.

The team seemed to lose some of its mystique when it moved indoors to the Humphrey Metrodome in 1982 but it still had success. The Vikings eventually shifted to a glitzy passing game run by quarterback Warren Moon. Receivers Cris Carter and Randy Moss were All Pros but the Vikings had clearly lost their way as the new century arrived.

FRANCHISE RECORD			
	W	**L**	**T**
Regular Season	354	283	9
Playoffs	17	23	0
NFL Championships	**1** *(1969)*		
NFC Championships	**4** *(1973, 1974, 1976)*		

MINNESOTA VIKINGS

1960 — Minnesota was granted a franchise on January 28, to start play in the 1961 season.

1961 — The Vikings' first win came on September 17 when they beat Chicago 37-13 to start a rivalry that would cover five decades.

1963 — Halfback Tommy Mason became the team's first Pro Bowl selection.

1964 — Minnesota finished 8-5-1 for its first winning season.

1967 — Norm Van Brocklin resigned as coach and was replaced by Bud Grant, coach of the CFL's Winnipeg Blue Bombers. Former NFL quarterback Jim Finks became General Manager.

1968 — The Vikings appeared in the playoffs for the first time, losing to Baltimore 24-14 on December 22.

1970 — Minnesota reached the Super Bowl for the first time but lost 23-7 to the Kansas City Chiefs in the last NFL vs. AFL game.

1977 — The Vikings fell to 0-4 in Super Bowls by losing to Oakland 32-14.

1982 — The team played its first season indoors at the Hubert H. Humphrey Metrodome.

1983 — Grant retired after 17 seasons as head coach.

1985 — Grant returned for the 1985 season to replace Les Steckel, then retired again after a 7-9 season and was replaced by longtime assistant Jerry Burns.

1994 — Grant was elected to the Pro Football Hall of Fame.

2003 — The Vikings started the season 6-0 but were knocked out of the playoff contention by Arizona's last-second comeback in the season finale

NATIONAL FOOTBALL CONFERENCE

SOUTH

Atlanta Falcons
Carolina Panthers
New Orleans Saints
Tampa Bay Buccaneers

ATLANTA FALCONS

Football had been the centerpiece of autumn weekends in Georgia for decades but it wasn't until 1966 that fans got an NFL franchise.

For years groups had no success trying to lure an existing franchise to relocate to the large, untapped southeastern market. Finally, in the summer of 1965, the NFL decided to place a franchise in Atlanta. Insurance executive Rankin Smith paid $8.5 million to join the league in time for the 1966 season.

The response was overwhelming. The Falcons set an NFL record by selling 45,000 season tickets in less than six months. That nearly doubled the previous mark for a new franchise that had been established by the Minnesota Vikings.

Part of the excitement was created by the Falcons' first-round draft pick, Tommy Nobis, a defensive tackle from the University of Texas. The war with the American Football League was still ongoing and the Falcons had to outbid the Houston Oilers to sign Nobis.

The Falcons' first coach was Norb Hecker, who had served on Vince Lombardi's staff at Green Bay. The Falcons started their first season with nine consecutive losses but wound up with three victories, which tied the league record for an expansion franchise.

Norm Van Brocklin led the team to its first winning season in 1971 (7-6-1). In 1977, the Falcons' defense allowed just 129 points over the 14-game season, which established a league record.

There have been a number of basic changes over the years. The Falcons changed the design of their uniforms, replacing red with black as the primary color. They also moved indoors, playing home games at the Georgia Dome after spending their early years at Fulton County Stadium.

The Falcons' best season was 1998, when they went 14-2 in the regular season and made it to the Super Bowl under coach Dan Reeves. They lost to Denver in John Elway's last game.

Reeves' tenure as coach ended with three games left in the 2003 season. He was replaced by Jim Mora, Jr., who had been the 49ers defensive coordinator.

FRANCHISE RECORD			
	W	**L**	**T**
Regular Season	226	344	6
Playoffs	5	7	0
NFC Championships	**1** *(1998)*		

ATLANTA FALCONS

1965 — Atlanta was granted an NFL franchise on June 30.

1965 — The Falcons signed their first draft pick, Outland Trophy winning linebacker Tommy Nobis, on December 14.

1966 — The Falcons played their first game, losing 19-14 to the Los Angeles Rams.

1966 — Junior Coffee ran for 117 yards against Cleveland on October 30, the first 100-yard game for the Falcons.

1966 — Atlanta beat the New York Giants 27-16 on November 20 for the franchise's first victory.

1967 — Nobis became the Falcons' first Pro Bowl player.

1973 — The Falcons finished 9-5, the best mark in the franchise's eight-year history.

1975 — Dave Hampton had the Falcons' first 1,000-yard season, rushing for 1,002 yards.

1978 — The Falcons made their first playoff appearance and beat Philadelphia 14-13 in the NFC Wild Card game.

1981 — Quarterback Steve Bartkowski passed for 416 yards against the Pittsburgh Steelers.

1988 — The Falcons went 14-2 and reached the Super Bowl for the first time. They were defeated 34-19 by Denver at Miami.

CAROLINA PANTHERS

Jerry Richardson spent several seasons playing wide receiver for the old Baltimore Colts, so he understood the value of a good game plan.

That experience served him well when Richardson sought to bring the NFL to the Carolinas. The process took six years from the development of the strategy until the NFL announced Carolina would get one of two expansion franchises for the 1995 season.

Richardson had a successful career in business after his playing career ended. He united other community leaders in the effort to bring pro football to the Carolinas. He brought former NFL owner and coach Mike McCormack into the group as a consultant.

The NFL brought neutral site exhibition games to various locations in the Carolinas for three consecutive years beginning in 1989. Fans considered that an unofficial referendum on the viability of the NFL in the region and made sure the games were sold out.

The expansion field, once 11 cities, was reduced to seven in 1992 and then trimmed to five. Carolina's effort was helped by a solid plan for a new stadium and a brisk sale of personal seat licenses as well as commitments for club seats and luxury suites.

Richardson's planning paid off when Carolina was unanimously awarded the 29th NFL franchise and the first expansion team since 1976, when Seattle and Tampa Bay joined the league.

The NFL had also made an important decision. It made the entry process easier for expansion franchises, allowing them more start-up time. The Panthers also benefited from being able to participate in free agency, an important source of talent that had not been available to past expansion entries.

The first coach was Dom Capers, who had been the defensive coordinator for the Pittsburgh Steelers.

Just two years after a 1-15 season, coach John Fox turned around the franchise and led the Panthers to their first Super Bowl appearance. They lost to New England 32-29 on a last-second field goal in Super Bowl XXXVIII.

FRANCHISE RECORD			
	W	**L**	**T**
Regular Season	64	80	0
Playoffs	4	2	0
NFC Championships	**1** *(2003)*		

CAROLINA PANTHERS

1987 — Former NFL receiver Jerry Richardson began meetings with business leaders in hopes of landing an expansion franchise.

1989 — Richardson Sports announced site selection for a new football stadium.

1992 — Carolina survived as the NFL began to pare the list of expansion candidates.

1993 — Carolina was awarded the 29th NFL franchise on October 26, touching off a fireworks celebration in Charlotte.

1995 — The Panthers and Jacksonville Jaguars participated in the expansion draft on February 15.

1995 — Quarterback Kerry Collins of Penn State became the first player draft by the Panthers.

1995 — The Panthers lost their first regular season game to Atlanta 23-20 in overtime on September 3.

1995 — The Panthers beat the New York Jets 26-15 on October 15 for the franchise's first victory.

1996 — Ericsson Stadium opened for a preseason game against the Chicago Bears.

1996 — The Panthers went 12-4 and qualified for the playoffs.

1999 — Former San Francisco 49ers head coach George Seifert took over the Panthers, replacing Dom Capers.

2002 — New York Giants defensive coordinator John Fox was hired as the Panthers' head coach.

NEW ORLEANS SAINTS

New Orleans has been one of the NFL's favorite sites for the Super Bowl. Nine of the title games have been staged there, probably because the city offers the perfect environment for the week-long party that precedes the big game.

They've never had to worry about inadvertently giving the Saints a home-field advantage by holding the Super Bowl in New Orleans. The team, which began play in 1967, has never even advanced to the conference championship game.

The Saints didn't even finish with a winning record until 1987, their 21st season. Coach Jim Mora led the team to its greatest success after he'd built a reputation as a winner in the USFL. Under Mora, the Saints went to the playoffs four times in six years and won their first divisional championship in 1991.

The coaches who preceded Mora had some good players. They just didn't have enough of them. Quarterback Archie Manning (1971-82) was one of the Saints' early stars. George Rogers had a short but productive stay in New Orleans, gaining more than 4,000 yards from 1981-84.

But New Orleans proved too tough a challenge for coaches who had enjoyed success elsewhere. Hank Stram, Dick Nolan and Bum Phillips were among those who did damage to their career records by trying to coach the Saints. The most celebrated flop was Mike Ditka, who took over the season after Mora was fired. Ditka was brought in to win and create interest. He only accomplished one of those goals. The fiery Ditka got the Saints plenty of publicity but he left with a 15-33 record. His approach made the job more difficult but Jim Haslett, who had been the Pittsburgh Steelers' defensive coordinator, aggressively attacked his first head coaching job.

Haslett has the Saints on the right track, offering hope that the Super Bowl may yet be a home game for the Saints.

The Saints have missed the playoffs for three consecutive seasons. They nearly kept their 2003 hopes alive with an improbable, last-minute, lateral-laden touchdown, but kicker John Carney missed the game-tying extra point.

FRANCHISE RECORD			
	W	**L**	**T**
Regular Season	226	331	5
Playoffs	1	5	0

NEW ORLEANS SAINTS

1966 — New Orleans was awarded an NFL expansion franchise on November 1, which is All Saints Day.

1967 — John Gilliam returned a kickoff 94 yards for a touchdown on the opening play of the Saints' first game on September 17.

1967 — The Saints won for the first time, beating Philadelphia 31-24 on November 5.

1968 — Don McCall became the first Saints player to run for 100 yards, gaining 127 yards against Washington on September 22.

1970 — Tom Dempsey kicked a game-winning 63-yard field goal against Detroit on November 8, setting an NFL record.

1971 — New Orleans chose Mississippi quarterback Archie Manning in the first round of the draft.

1975 — The Saints moved indoors to the new Superdome after eight years in Tulane Stadium.

1979 — Chuck Muncie became the first Saints running back with a 1,000-yard season, rushing for 1,198 yards.

1987 — The Saints played a postseason game for the first time, losing 44-10 to Minnesota in a wild card game.

1996 — Jim Mora, the most successful coach in franchise history, resigned and was replaced by Rick Venturi eight games into the season.

1997 — Mike Ditka became head coach.

2000 — Jim Haslett became the Saints' 13th head coach on February 3.

TAMPA BAY BUCCANEERS

It took the Tampa Bay Buccaneers a while to start winning—almost two full seasons, as a matter of fact.

Once they got started, though, they were on the fast track.

The Buccaneers joined the NFL as an expansion entry (with Seattle) for the 1976 season. They lost all 14 games in that inaugural season. They lost 12 the following season until they returned three interceptions for touchdowns and beat the New Orleans Saints. The Buccaneers won the following week, too.

Ownership hired Southern California coach John McKay to put together a team from scratch. McKay was an ideal choice for two reasons—he had a sharp football mind and he had a biting sense of humor, which was in evidence frequently as the Buccaneers stumbled through those first two seasons.

By their fourth season, the Buccaneers were in the NFC championship game. A 9-0 loss to the Los Angeles Rams kept them from going to the Super Bowl.

McKay built the franchise with defense and that's been a hallmark of the Buccaneers. The lack of offense has also been a problem. Tampa Bay has always been able to prevent points but the Buccaneers have often had problems scoring.

The Buccaneers had a run of success in the 1990s with Tony Dungy as head coach. Dungy, a former defensive coordinator, put together exceptionally tough defenses but he and his staff could never match that success on offense and Tampa Bay struggled in the postseason.

Ownership took a big risk and fired Dungy after the 2001 season. A deal to sign Bill Parcells fell though and the Buccaneers wound up sending cash and a bundle of draft picks to Oakland to acquire Jon Gruden. The investment paid off in January of 2003 when the Buccaneers won their first Super Bowl title.

The Buccaneers failed to follow up on that success, though, falling to 7-9 amid some controversy. Gruden chose to de-activate Keyshawn Johnson, essentially firing the disruptive receiver before the season ended.

FRANCHISE RECORD			
	W	**L**	**T**
Regular Season	167	268	1
Playoffs	6	7	0
NFC Championships	**1** *(2002)*		
Super Bowls	**1** *(2002)*		

TAMPA BAY BUCCANEERS

1974 —Tampa Bay was awarded the NFL's 27th franchise in April with the provision that Tampa Stadium be expanded to 72,000 seats.

1975 — University of Southern California coach John McKay signed a five-year contract to coach the Buccaneers.

1976 — The Buccaneers lost their first game, 20-0 at Houston on September 12, starting a 0-14 season.

1977 — Three interception returns for touchdowns helped the Buccaneers get their first victory, 33-14 at New Orleans on December 11. It ended a 26-game losing streak.

1979 — Ricky Bell became the franchise's first 1,000-yard rusher.

1980 — McKay signed a five-year extension with a provision that he would become team president after its expiration.

1995 — Defensive end Lee Roy Selmon, the Buccaneers' first draft choice in 1976, was elected to the Pro Football Hall of Fame.

1996 — Former Minnesota Vikings defensive coordinator Tony Dungy was hired as head coach on January 22, replacing Sam Wyche.

1998 — The Buccaneers opened Raymond James Stadium with a 27-15 win over Chicago on September 20.

2002 — Jon Gruden became the seventh head coach in franchise history after his rights were secured from Oakland.

2003 — The Buccaneers beat Oakland 48-21 in Super Bowl XXXVII on January 26.

NATIONAL FOOTBALL CONFERENCE

EAST

Dallas Cowboys
New York Giants
Philadelphia Eagles
Washington Redskins

DALLAS COWBOYS

The Dallas Cowboys developed into one of the NFL's most consistent winners but it took them a while to get started.

The Cowboys had an excellent management team with General Manager Tex Schramm and coach Tom Landry. Even they couldn't make much of the castoffs who came to Dallas as part of the expansion draft when the team was launched in 1960. In fact, the Cowboys didn't get their first win until their second season. They did manage a tie in their debut season. By 1965, the Cowboys were a .500 team. A year later they started a streak of 20 consecutive winning seasons and they qualified for the playoffs in 18 of those years. It was around the same time that the Cowboys started to develop a mystique, thanks to their success, regular presence on national television and distinctive silver and blue uniforms with a large star on each side of the helmet. Their widespread fan base eventually led NFL Films to call the Cowboys "America's Team," a distinction the publicity-conscious organization embraced.

The Cowboys made five trips to the Super Bowl and won two of them. The players changed over the 20 years but the constant was Landry, stoic on the sidelines, peering out from under his trademark hat (unless a game was played in a domed stadium).

Some of luster wore off in the late '80s. The Cowboys were 7-9 in 1986, their first losing season in 20 years. Ownership, once a rock of stability for the Cowboys, changed twice in a short period of time. The second change shook the foundation of the team as oilman Jerry Jones decided to replace Landry with University of Miami coach Jimmy Johnson.

Painful as the change was, it re-energized the organization. The Cowboys won three Super Bowls in four years, taking the last title after Barry Switzer had replaced Johnson.

Jones' investment in coach Bill Parcells paid off immediately. Parcells led the Cowboys to a 10-6 record and a wild-card playoff berth. With Parcells now given a chance to reshape the roster, there's hope that Dallas will shortly be a Super Bowl contender again.

FRANCHISE RECORD			
	W	**L**	**T**
Regular Season	377	275	6
Playoffs	32	22	0
NFC Championships	**8** *(1970, 1971, 1975, 1977, 1978, 1992, 1993, 1995)*		
Super Bowls	**5** *(1971, 1977, 1992, 1993, 1995)*		

DALLAS COWBOYS

1960 — Dallas was granted an expansion franchise on January 28, to begin play later that year.

1961 — Defensive tackle Bob Lilly of TCU was the team's first draft pick and a future Hall of Famer.

1961 — The Cowboys won their first game, beating the Pittsburgh Steelers 27-24 on September 17.

1964 — With his original five-year contract about to expire, coach Tom Landry was given a 10-year contract despite failing to post a winning record.

1966 — After five losing seasons and one at .500, the Cowboys went 10-3-1 for their first winning season.

1967 — Dallas made its first playoff appearance, losing 34-27 to Green Bay in the NFL Championship game on January 1.

1969 — Don Perkins became the last of the original Cowboys to retire.

1971 — The Cowboys made their first Super Bowl appearance, losing 16-13 to Baltimore on January 17.

1972 — Dallas won its first Super Bowl, beating Miami 24-3 on January 16.

1989 — New owner Jerry Jones fired Landry and hired Jimmy Johnson to replace him.

1994 — Barry Switzer replaced Johnson, who left after clashing with Jones.

2002 — Emmitt Smith became the NFL's all-time leader in rushing yards, breaking Walter Payton's record of 16,726.

NEW YORK GIANTS

It's hard to believe but the New York Giants were not part of the National Football League when it formed in 1920.

Tim Mara bought the franchise for just $500 in 1925. Of course, he had to invest another $25,000 that year to keep the team in business. His commitment assured the NFL of having a team in the nation's biggest city.

Three seasons into their NFL history, the Giants were champions. They won the 1927 title and were a constant threat under coach Steve Owen. The Giants were strong through the late 1950s and early 1960s. They won the NFL championship in 1956 and took six Eastern Conference championships in eight years from 1956-63. The team failed to adequately replace its aging stars and fell upon hard times that lasted nearly 20 years. For a time, they weren't even really the New York Giants. They left their familiar turf at Yankee Stadium and played in the Yale Bowl until their new home in East Rutherford, New Jersey was ready. The Giants' decline in the late '60s coincided with the rival Jets' rise across town.

The Giants' fortunes changed when Bill Parcells came in as head coach in 1983. Parcells barely survived a bad debut season but soon turned the team around. The Giants finished in first place in 1986 and went on to win the Super Bowl over Denver, their first league championship since 1956. They won again in 1990, beating Buffalo in what proved to be Parcells' last game as coach.

The Giants sagged under former Parcells assistant Ray Handley but improved under Dan Reeves. Jim Fassel got the team back to the Super Bowl in 2000, where it lost to the Baltimore Ravens.

The Giants remain one of the NFL's most storied franchises and have honored 11 players by retiring their numbers.

After a dispirited 4-12 season, Jim Fassel was fired and replaced by Tom Coughlin, who acquired a reputation as a disciplinarian when he coached Jacksonville.

FRANCHISE RECORD			
	W	**L**	**T**
Regular Season	571	477	33
Playoffs	16	21	0
NFL Championships	**3** *(1934, 1938, 1956)*		
NFC Championships	**3** *(1986, 1990, 2000)*		
Super Bowls	**2** *(1986, 1990)*		

NEW YORK GIANTS

1925 — Tim Mara was granted an NFL franchise for New York on August 1.

1927 — The Giants won their first NFL championship with an 11-1-1 record.

1933 — Harry Newman ran for 108 yards against the Boston Redskins on October 8, the Giants' first 100-yard game.

1952 — The Giants used their first draft pick to select Southern California's Frank Gifford.

1953 — Steve Owen ended a 24-year coaching career with a 153-108-17 record.

1962 — Y.A. Tittle passed for 505 yards and an NFL-record seven touchdowns against the Washington Redskins on October 28. Del Shofner had 269 receiving yards.

1965 — Tittle announced his retirement on January 22.

1971 — Quarterback Fran Tarkenton requested a trade after a 4-10 season and was dealt back to Minnesota.

1979 — Quarterback Phil Simms of Morehead State was the Giants' first-round draft choice.

1981 — North Carolina linebacker Lawrence Taylor was chosen on the first round of the draft.

1987 — The Giants made their first Super Bowl appearance and beat the Denver Broncos 39-20 on January 25.

1991 — The Giants beat Buffalo 20-19 in the Super Bowl on January 27.

PHILADELPHIA EAGLES

This puts the Philadelphia Eagles' championship drought in perspective: The last time they won an NFL title, the hero of the game was the NFL's last full-time two-way player.

Linebacker Chuck Bednarik made a game-saving open-field tackle on Green Bay's Jim Taylor in the 1960 NFL title game and preserved the Eagles' 17-13 victory over the Packers.

It may be hard to believe it's been that long since the Eagles claimed a championship because they've had some good teams in the interim. Although they've reached the postseason with some regularity, they've only been to one Super Bowl. They lost 27-10 to the Oakland Raiders in Super Bowl XV in January of 1981.

The franchise was launched in 1933 when Bert Bell and Lud Wray paid $2,500 for the existing Frankford Yellowjackets. Ten years later, the manpower shortages of World War II forced the Eagles and cross-state Pittsburgh Steelers to merge for a season. The combination was referred to both as "Phil-Pitt" and the "Steagles." Philadelphia's Greasy Neale and Walt Kiesling of the Steelers co-coached the squad to a 5-4-1 record.

Neale had his own team back the following year and led the Eagles to their first success. Running back Steve Van Buren, tackle Alex Wojciechowicz and end Pete Pihos were among the stars, joined by Bednarik in 1949. The Eagles were one of the NFL's powers for six years, taking league titles in 1948 and '49.

Coach Buck Shaw and quarterback Norm Van Brocklin helped the Eagles win the title in 1960. Philadelphia just missed the postseason in 1961, then didn't have a playoff game for 18 years.

Coach Dick Vermeil's team made the playoffs in 1978, his third year on the job. In recent years, Coach Andy Reid has shaped the Eagles into a contender with a tough defense and quarterback Donovan McNabb.

The Eagles again fell short of the Super Bowl in 2003, losing the NFC Championship game for the third consecutive year.

FRANCHISE RECORD			
	W	**L**	**T**
Regular Season	437	493	24
Playoffs	14	15	0
NFL Championships	**3** *(1948, 1949, 1960)*		
NFC Championships	**1** *(1980)*		

PHILADELPHIA EAGLES

1933 — Bert Bell and Lud Wray bought the Frankford Yellowjackets franchise for $2,500 and it became the Eagles.

1935 — Bell proposed a draft of college players, which was adopted for the 1936 season.

1939 — The Eagles lost to the Brooklyn Dodgers 23-14 in the first televised football game. NBC broadcast the game.

1943 — The Eagles and Pittsburgh Steelers merged to form the "Steagles" as a means to deal with personnel shortages brought on by World War II.

1947 — Philadelphia played for the NFL title for the first time but lost 28-21 to the Chicago Cardinals.

1948 — The Eagles won their first championship, beating the Cardinals 7-0 in a snowstorm.

1949 — A 14-0 win over the Los Angeles Rams gave the Eagles their second consecutive NFL title.

1960 — Led by NFL Most Valuable Player Norm Van Brocklin, the Eagles came from behind to beat Green Bay 17-13 and win the NFL championship.

1971 — The team moved to Veterans Stadium.

1980 — After a 12-4 regular season, the Eagles reached the Super Bowl for the first time and lost 27-10 to Oakland.

1986 — Buddy Ryan became head coach.

2000 — The Eagles reversed their previous year's record, went 11-5 and reached the NFC playoffs under second-year coach Andy Reid.

WASHINGTON REDSKINS

The Redskins have been part of Washington for so long that it's easy to forget they didn't start there.

Their history began in 1932 when George Preston Marshall headed a group that purchased the NFL's inactive franchise in Boston. They were called the Braves, sharing the name with the baseball team that played on the same field. When they moved to Fenway Park after one season, they became the Redskins.

The relationship with Boston was rocky. Disappointed by fan support in 1936, Marshall transferred the team's championship game against Green Bay from Boston to the Polo Grounds in New York. By the next season, the Redskins were calling Washington home and they gave Boston ample reason to miss them. They won the 1937 NFL championship behind quarterback Sammy Baugh, making for a spectacular debut in Washington.

The Redskins would win again in 1942 but that was followed by a long dry spell. Washington struggled through the 1950s and '60s. They appeared to be on the right track in 1969 when Vince Lombardi signed on as head coach and led the team to a winning season. But Lombardi was only able to serve one year before he succumbed to cancer.

Former Los Angeles Rams Coach George Allen moved east and his energetic approach and fondness for experienced players kept the Redskins in contention, even though they didn't win a Super Bowl.

The most glorious days of the franchise came in the 1980s when Joe Gibbs was hired as head coach and won three Super Bowls with three different starting quarterbacks. Gibbs installed a solid program and a no-frills offense that relied on the power blocking of a line that embraced the nickname "The Hogs."

Steve Spurrier from the University of Florida is the latest head coach to tackle the challenge of making the Redskins winners again.

Spurrier's transition from college to pro football failed badly. The Redskins shocked the NFL by luring Joe Gibbs out of an 11-year retirement to take over as head coach of the team he led to three Super Bowl titles.

FRANCHISE RECORD			
	W	**L**	**T**
Regular Season	499	452	27
Playoffs	22	15	0
NFL Championships	**2** *(1937, 1942)*		
NFC Championships	**5** *(1972, 1982, 1983, 1987, 1991)*		
Super Bowls	**3** *(1982, 1987, 1991)*		

WASHINGTON REDSKINS

1932 — George Preston Marshall purchased the Boston franchise on July 9.

1937 — The Redskins got approval to move from Boston to Washington on February13.

1955 — Washington scored 21 points in 2 minutes and 17 seconds and beat the Philadelphia Eagles 31-30.

1961 — The Redskins played their first game in new D.C. Stadium, losing 24-21 to the New York Giants.

1964 — Washington shook the NFL with two major trades, acquiring quarterback Sonny Jurgensen from Philadelphia and linebacker Sam Huff from the New York Giants.

1966 — Hall of Fame quarterback Otto Graham was hired as the Redskins' coach and general manager on January 25.

1969 — After one season in the Green Bay Packers front office, Vince Lombardi returned to coaching with the Redskins on January 7.

1970 — Lombardi died of cancer in New York on September 3.

1971 — George Allen, formerly of the Los Angeles Rams, became the head coach and general manager. He led the team to its first playoff game in 26 years.

1981 — Joe Gibbs was hired as the team's 17th head coach.

1993 — Gibbs resigned on March 5 after three Super Bowls and a 140-65 record.

2002 — Steve Spurrier signed as head coach after a successful career at the University of Florida.

NATIONAL FOOTBALL CONFERENCE

WEST

Arizona Cardinals

St. Louis Rams

San Francisco 49ers

Seattle Seahawks

ARIZONA CARDINALS

The Cardinals have been a constant in the NFL even though their address has changed frequently.

The history of the franchise stretches back to 1898 when the Chicago-based team was known as the Morgan Athletic Club. They became the Cardinals a few years later in deference to the color of their uniforms.

The NFL's predecessor, the American Football Professional Association, began in 1920 and established a Chicago franchise called the Tigers to compete with the Cardinals. The Cardinals won a one-game "loser leave town" showdown 6-0 and stayed.

Charles W. Bidwell bought the team in 1932 and his heirs still own the franchise. Under Bidwell ownership, the Cardinals won the NFL title in 1947.

The Cardinals moved to St. Louis in 1960, creating some confusion with the baseball team of the same name. The football Cardinals, though, were anxious to have their own market so they weren't the "second" franchise to the much more successful Bears in Chicago. George Halas' Bears were one of the NFL's powerhouse franchises at the time. The Cardinals had some winning seasons in the 1960s but never seriously competed for a championship in a league dominated at the time by Green Bay and Dallas.

The franchise packed its gear for another move in 1988 and headed to Phoenix. The Cardinals were frustrated by their inability to get a new stadium in St. Louis and were also a distant second among the city's baseball-mad sports fans.

Despite their long history, the Cardinals haven't enjoyed much success. Their career record is well below .500 and they have only two championships to their credit, the last coming in 1947. They didn't win a postseason game between 1947 and 1988.

The Cardinals' best player was probably defensive back Larry Wilson, whose No. 8 has been retired. Wilson also served his old team as General Manager.

Former Vikings coach Dennis Green is the latest to take on the challenge of rebuilding the Cardinals. He succeeded Dave McGinnis as head coach.

FRANCHISE RECORD			
	W	**L**	**T**
Regular Season	440	617	39
Playoffs	2	5	0
NFL Championships	**1** *(1947)*		

ARIZONA CARDINALS

1920 — The Chicago Cardinals joined the NFL as a charter franchise on September 17.

1922 — The Cardinals had their first winning season, finishing 8-3.

1923 — The Cardinals beat the Rochester Jeffersons 60-0 for the most lopsided victory in franchise history.

1929 — Fullback Ernie Nevers scored an NFL-record 40 points against the Chicago Bears on November 28. He had six touchdowns and four PATs.

1932 — William Bidwell purchased the franchise, beginning eight decades of family ownership.

1939 — Center Phil Dougherty and end Gaynell Tinsley became the Cardinals' first Pro Bowl selections.

1947 — With Charley Trippi leading the "Dream Backfield," the Cardinals won the NFL title, beating Philadelphia 28-21.

1960 — Bidwell moved the Cardinals from Chicago to St. Louis.

1963 — Nevers was a charter inductee to the Hall of Fame.

1965 — Future Hall of Fame defensive back Larry Wilson returned an interception 96 yards for a touchdown against the Cleveland Browns on December 19.

1988 — Team moved to Phoenix.

1994 — Franchise name was changed from Phoenix to Arizona Cardinals.

ST. LOUIS RAMS

The Rams' franchise has deep roots in the NFL but they're spread across the country.

The team started in Cleveland, moved west to stops in Los Angeles and Anaheim, then switched to its current location in St. Louis.

The Cleveland Rams started play in 1937, disbanded temporarily in 1943, then returned and eventually moved west in 1946. The first winning season in franchise history was 1945, which also led to the NFL title with a 15-14 win over Washington in the championship game.

Upon reaching Los Angeles, the Rams made history by making Kenny Washington and Woody Strode the first African-American players under NFL contract since 1933. Moving to Los Angeles meant the Rams were competing directly with the Los Angeles Dons of the All-American Football Conference.

When that league folded, the Rams had the city to themselves and unveiled a spectacular brand of football that highlighted the passing game. The Rams won four Western Division titles in seven years as quarterback Norm Van Brocklin hooked up with receivers Tom Fears and Elroy "Crazy Legs" Hirsch. The Rams' division championship in 1955 would prove to be their last until 1967, though.

George Allen, a former George Halas assistant in Chicago, arrived in Los Angeles and helped restore the Rams to contending status. In five years, his teams were 44-19-4 without winning a championship. In 1973 the Rams started a streak of seven consecutive division championships. It began under Coach Chuck Knox and continued with Ray Malavasi. The Rams made it to Super Bowl XIV but lost to the Pittsburgh Steelers.

The Rams moved further south to Anaheim before they abandoned California and moved to St. Louis in 1995. They enjoyed great success in short order, winning Super Bowl XXXIV over Tennessee after a dream season by quarterback Kurt Warner. They played in Super Bowl XXXVI two years later but were defeated by New England.

FRANCHISE RECORD			
	W	**L**	**T**
Regular Season	476	415	20
Playoffs	18	23	0
NFL Championships	**2** *(1945, 1951)*		
NFC Championships	**3** *(1979, 1999, 2001)*		
Super Bowls	**1** *(1999)*		

ST. LOUIS RAMS

1945 — The Rams made their first postseason appearance, defeating Washington 15-14 for the NFL championship.

1946 — The Rams received approval on January 11 to move from Cleveland to Los Angeles.

1950 — The Rams beat Baltimore 70-27 on October 22.

1951 — The Rams won their second NFL championship, defeating Cleveland 24-17.

1962 — Dick Bass ran for 1,033 yards for the first 1,000-yard season in franchise history.

1965 — Quarterback Bob Waterfield became the first Rams player to be elected to the Pro Football Hall of Fame.

1966 — George Allen replaced Harland Svare as head coach.

1971 — Former UCLA head coach Tommy Prothro replaced George Allen.

1980 — The Rams moved to Anaheim Stadium, playing the first of 15 seasons there.

1984 — Running back Eric Dickerson set an NFL single-season rushing record by gaining 2,105 yards in his second year as a pro.

1995 — The Rams played and won their first game in St. Louis, defeating New Orleans 17-13.

1999 — Mike Jones' tackle preserved the Rams' 23-16 victory over the Tennessee Titans in Super Bowl XXXIV.

SAN FRANCISCO 49ERS

San Francisco, already famous for the 1849 Gold Rush, also became the destination for the western migration of professional sports.

The 49ers joined the All America Football Conference when it launched in 1946, becoming the first major league professional franchise on the west coast. Owner Anthony Morabito, who had made his money with a lumber hauling company, correctly foresaw the coming of convenient coast-to-coast air travel and convinced AAFC founder Arch Ward to put a franchise in San Francisco.

The club took its name from the famous Gold Rush and did well in the AAFC's four seasons, finishing as a runner-up to the Cleveland Browns each year. The Browns, 49ers and Baltimore Colts joined the NFL for the 1950 season after the AAFC folded. The 49ers were competitive for most of the 1950s but couldn't manage a championship. They started a distinguished line of quarterbacks with Stanford's Frankie Albert, followed by Y.A. Tittle and John Brodie.

In fact, the 49ers always had impressive individual stars, especially on offense. They featured running backs Hugh McElhenny, Joe Perry and John Henry Johnson and massive tackle Bob St. Clair. But it would take time for the 49ers to develop as contenders. They won division titles from 1970-72 but were knocked out each year by the Dallas Cowboys.

The franchise struggled until Bill Walsh from Stanford was hired as coach in 1979 and overhauled the entire organization. Backed by the financial support of owner Edward DeBartolo, Jr., Walsh was able to construct the team of the 1980s, which would win four Super Bowls in the decade. For 15 years, the 49ers were the winningest franchise in any professional sport. An offense constructed around quarterback Joe Montana and receiver Jerry Rice also helped revolutionize schemes throughout the NFL.

FRANCHISE RECORD			
	W	**L**	**T**
Regular Season	432	333	13
Playoffs	25	17	0
NFC Championships	**5** *(1981, 1984, 1988, 1989, 1994)*		
Super Bowls	**5** *(1981, 1984, 1988, 1989, 1994)*		

SAN FRANCISCO 49ERS

1946 — The 49ers were formed as a charter franchise of the All-America Football Conference.

1950 — Upon the demise of the AAFC, the 49ers joined the National Football League and were 3-9 in their first season.

1957 — Franchise founder Anthony Morabito died of heart failure during the team's game against Chicago on October 27.

1960 — 49ers Coach Howard W. (Red) Hickey brought the shotgun offense back to the NFL.

1970 — Quarterback John Brodie was named the NFL's Most Valuable Player after he led the 49ers to a 10-3-1 record.

1971 — The team abandoned ancient Kezar Stadium and played its first game at Candlestick Park, a 20-13 loss to the Los Angeles Rams on October 10.

1977 — The Edward DeBartolo family of Youngstown, Ohio, purchased the franchise on March 31, marking the 49ers' first change in ownership.

1978 — Bill Walsh of Stanford was hired as head coach after the team had gone through two head coaches in a 2-14 season.

1979 — In the draft on May 3, the 49ers chose Notre Dame quarterback Joe Montana on the third round.

1982 — The 49ers claimed their first championship by defeating the Cincinnati Bengals 26-21 in Super Bowl XVI.

1995 — San Francisco became the first franchise to win five Super Bowls with a 49-26 defeat of San Diego on January 29.

1997 — Steve Mariucci from the University of California was named head coach on January 16 and led the 49ers to a 13-3 record.

SEATTLE SEAHAWKS

The NFL came to Seattle in 1976, the culmination of a nearly 20-year effort to lure a franchise to the Pacific Northwest.

The Seahawks entered the league as an expansion franchise along with the Tampa Bay Buccaneers, the first time the league added two new teams simultaneously. Picking from castoffs made available by the established teams, the Seahawks won only two games in their first season. Still, that gave them a two-game edge on the Buccaneers, who went 0-14 in their first season. Seattle improved to 5-9 in its second season, then had consecutive 9-7 records.

Despite that quick progress and early promise, the Seahawks have enjoyed only mild success through their history. They've won two division championships and made five playoff appearances during their existence.

Their greatest success came under Chuck Knox, who signed with the Seahawks in 1983 after coaching the Los Angeles Rams and Buffalo Bills. Sparked by rookie running back Curt Warner's 1,449 yards, the Seahawks made the 1983 playoffs as a wild card. They defeated Denver and Miami and made it to the NFC Championship game, where they lost 30-14 to the Los Angeles Raiders.

Knox left by mutual consent after the 1991 season. Tom Flores failed to match the success he'd had with the Raiders and Dennis Erickson couldn't find the same formula that had made him a winner at the collegiate level.

The Seahawks' biggest star was receiver Steve Largent, who was the NFL career leader in receptions and yards at the time of his retirement. Largent was picked up in a trade from Houston in the Seahawks' inaugural season and was the first Seattle player to reach the Hall of Fame.

In recent years, former Green Bay Packers coach Mike Holmgren has been charged with the responsibility of making the Seahawks a Super Bowl contender.

The Seahawks made the playoffs as a wild card after a 10-6 season in 2003.

FRANCHISE RECORD			
	W	**L**	**T**
Regular Season	205	231	0
Playoffs	3	6	0

SEATTLE SEAHAWKS

1974 — The NFL on June 4 approved an expansion franchise for Seattle, to start play in 1976.

1976 — Minnesota Vikings defensive line coach Jack Patera was hired as the Seahawks first head coach on January 3.

1982 — Mike McCormack was named interim head coach after Patera was fired on October 13.

1983 — Chuck Knox was named head coach on January 26 and the Seahawks reached the playoffs for the first time.

1986 — The Seahawks won a lottery for the first pick in the supplemental draft and chose Oklahoma linebacker Brian Bosworth.

1987 — Steve Largent caught six passes in a 41-20 loss at Kansas City on December 27 and became the NFL's all-time leader with 751 career receptions.

1988 — Largent became the career leader in receiving yards on September 18 when he passed the Charlie Joiner's total of 12,146 in a game at San Diego.

1991 — Knox departed on December 27 after nine years and a record of 80-63-0, just eight months after he had signed a two-year extension.

1994 — Falling tiles in the Kingdome on July 19 forced the Seahawks to play five home games outdoors at the University of Washington's Husky Stadium.

1995 — Largent became the first Seahawks player elected to the Pro Football Hall of Fame.

1999 — The Seahawks traded a draft choice to Green Bay to secure the services of Mike Holmgren, who became head coach and general manager.

2001 — The Seahawks switched from the West Division in the AFC to the same division in the NFC. That reversed a move that was made after the team's first season.

THE
PLAYERS

A–Z

HERB ADDERLEY

Full Name: **Herbert A. Adderley**

Date of Birth: **June 8, 1939, Philadelphia, PA**

College: **Michigan State**

NFL Teams: **Green Bay Packers, Dallas Cowboys**

Position: **Defensive Back**

Ht: **6-0**

Wt: **205**

"I'm just thankful he plays for the Packers."
—Green Bay Hall of Fame quarterback Bart Starr

Herb Adderley represented one of Coach Vince Lombardi's few errors in talent evaluation.

Lombardi didn't make a mistake drafting Adderley on the first round from Michigan State in 1961; rather, his miscalculation was in picking a position for Adderley. Lombardi insisted that Adderley was a flanker until he came to realize his aggressive nature made him perfect for cornerback.

The switch was made and Adderley fashioned a Hall of Fame career on the defensive side of the ball. Like secondary mate Willie Wood, he was mentored by Emlen Tunnell, the New York Giants' Hall of Fame defensive back who finished his career with the Packers. Like Wood, he was an apt student.

Adderley got his chance when the Packers lost two defensive backs to injuries in the same game. Lombardi scanned his sideline and called on Adderley, whom he considered one of the team's best athletes. Despite his inexperience, Adderley held his own and his defensive career was born.

Over 12 years, he intercepted 48 passes for 1,046 yards and seven touchdowns. Three of those touchdown returns came in 1965 and that still stands as a Packers season record. Adderley was also a dangerous special teams player who returned 120 kickoffs for 3,080 yards. He became the first player to score a defensive touchdown in the Super Bowl. He ran back an interception of Daryle Lamonica's pass 60 yards in Super Bowl II to help the Packers beat the Oakland Raiders. It was the only time an interception was returned for a score in the first 10 Super Bowls.

The Packers traded Adderley to Dallas just before the start of the 1970 season and he spent three years with the Cowboys. He led Dallas with six interceptions in 1971. Thanks to the move, he played in four of the first six Super Bowls. Adderley, though, said he always considered himself a Packer and never wore his championship ring from the Cowboys.

Adderley was voted into the Pro Football Hall of Fame in 1980.

CAREER TOTALS							
G	Int	Yds	Avg	FR	Sacks	Total TD	Points
164	48	1046	21.8	14	0.0	9	54

TROY AIKMAN

Full name: **Troy Kenneth Aikman**	Position: **Quarterback**
Date of Birth: **Nov. 21, 1966, West Covina, CA**	Ht: **6-4**
College: **UCLA**	Wt: **220**
NFL Teams: **Dallas Cowboys**	

"Every season we have Troy at quarterback we have a chance to go to the Super Bowl."—Dallas Cowboys owner Jerry Jones.

When Coach Jimmy Johnson tackled the enormous task of reviving the Dallas Cowboys, he knew he needed a franchise quarterback.

Fortunately, the Cowboys had the No. 1 pick in the 1989 draft and Troy Aikman was in the talent pool. Aikman had finished his college career as the No. 3 passer in NCAA history and was a classic pro-style quarterback. He was the player around whom Johnson would build the Dallas offense. The Cowboys were 1-15 in Aikman's first season. He was the first rookie to start a season opener at quarterback for Dallas since Roger Staubach had done it 20 years earlier. There was marked improvement in 1990 as the Cowboys finished 7-9. They were 11-5 the following season and qualified for the playoffs.

By Aikman's fourth year, the Cowboys were Super Bowl champions and he was the game's Most Valuable Player after completing 73.3 percent of his passes against Buffalo. Dallas won the Super Bowl again the next season.

After a year away, Dallas won its third Super Bowl, defeating Pittsburgh, which had beaten the Cowboys twice in the 1970s. Aikman passed for 3,304 yards in 1995 with 16 touchdowns and had a stretch of 156 pass attempts without an interception.

He was the winningest quarterback of the decade and had an 11-5 record as a starter in postseason games. Accumulated injuries became a growing concern, though, and Aikman, after sustaining 10 concussions in 12 seasons, opted to retire at age 34, holding the Dallas team record for passing yards with 32,942.

He became involved in NASCAR ownership and also serves as a television analyst on NFL games for CBS.

CAREER TOTALS

G	Att	Cmp	Pct.	Yds	TD	Y/A	Lg	Int
165	**4715**	**2898**	**61.5**	**32942**	**165**	**6.99**	**90t**	**141**
Rush	Yds	Avg	TD	Lg	Total TD	Points	Rating	
327	**1016**	**3.1**	**9**	**25**	**9**	**54**	**81.6**	

MARCUS ALLEN

Full name: **Marcus LeMarr Allen**	Position: **Running Back**
Date of Birth: **March 26, 1960, San Diego, CA**	Ht: **6-2**
College: **Southern California**	Wt: **210**
NFL Teams: **Los Angeles Raiders, Kansas City Chiefs**	

"I'm proud of the records but it's the people I've worked with who have really made the game for me."—Marcus Allen

Marcus Allen saw both sides of the Los Angeles Raiders-Kansas City Chiefs rivalry and he had particularly intense passion once he switched teams.

Allen was comfortably entrenched with the Raiders when a dispute with owner Al Davis led to a reduced role and, ultimately, his departure from Los Angeles.

He went from Super Bowl XVIII's Most Valuable Player to virtual anonymity with the Raiders and was never quite able to grasp why the relationship soured as badly as it did. Allen was still a productive player, as he demonstrated in the five years he spent with the Chiefs.

Allen played defense in high school until his senior year when he became a running back. He was considered too slow, which prompted him to work with a track coach to improve his running technique and his speed. Allen started as a defensive back at Southern California before coaches cast him as a blocking back for Heisman Trophy winner Charles White. Blocking backs often have low-profile roles but Allen moved up to become the featured back in USC's offense.

After helping White win a Heisman, he won the trophy on his own in 1981. The Raiders took him on the first round of the draft and he was the NFL's Rookie of the Year. He was the fastest to reach 10,000 career-rushing yards.

Allen had 11 years with L.A., none better than 1985 when he rushed for 1,759 yards and was the NFL's player of the year. He ultimately was supplanted by multi-sport star Bo Jackson. Allen served a secondary role until he left Los Angeles and signed with the Chiefs for the 1993 season.

He wound up with 145 touchdowns, third in NFL history, and was the all-time running back leader in games with 222. Allen also threw six touchdown passes on halfback option plays. He played in six Pro Bowls and was voted into the Pro Football Hall of Fame in 2003.

CAREER TOTALS							
G	Rush	Yds	Avg	TD	Lg		
222	**3022**	**12243**	**4.1**	**123**	**61t**		
Rec	Yds	Avg	TD	Lg	Total TD	Points	
587	**5411**	**9.2**	**21**	**92**	**145**	**872**	

LANCE ALWORTH

Full name: **Lance Dwight Alworth**	Position: **Receiver**
Date of Birth: **August 3, 1940, Houston, TX**	Ht: **6-0**
College: **Arkansas**	Wt: **184**
NFL Teams: **San Diego Chargers, Dallas Cowboys**	

"When the ball was thrown, it was mine."—Lance Alworth

What kind of nickname is "Bambi" for a football player?

In Lance Alworth's case, a perfect one.

Alworth was thin and had a loping stride that led to the unusual nickname. He had the hands to catch the ball and the speed to do something after the reception.

"You could see right away that he was going to be a superstar," said Al Davis, who was a San Diego Chargers assistant coach when Alworth was drafted by that franchise in 1962.

In fact, Alworth was one of the first superstars of the American Football League. To challenge the established NFL, the AFL needed some glitz and Alworth provided that. He'd catch passes in traffic, he'd break away from would-be tacklers and he'd consistently make big plays. He averaged 18.9 yards per catch.

"He had the greatest hands I've ever seen," Chargers coach Sid Gillman said. "Nobody could jump and catch a ball like Lance. He was in a class by himself."

Alworth was pursued by a number of baseball teams but opted for football. He played at Arkansas and was drafted by both leagues. The Chargers took him on the second round but he was the ninth player selected. The San Francisco Giants took him on the first round, eighth overall.

Alworth chose the Chargers, where he had a perfect fit with Gillman, an offensive innovator. He had 10 catches as a rookie despite missing the last 10 games with a knee injury. In 1963, Alworth caught nine passes against Kansas City for 232 yards and a pair of touchdowns.

Any doubts about his toughness were dispelled in 1966 when he played with a fractured bone in his right hand and a broken left wrist. He had both injuries heavily taped.

Alworth was an All-AFL player from 1963-69 and caught passes in 96 consecutive games.

The Chargers traded him to Dallas for the 1971 season. He ended his career primarily as a blocker for the Cowboys but did earn a Super Bowl ring. In 1978, Alworth became the first AFL player voted to the Hall of Fame.

CAREER TOTALS						
G	Rec	Yds	Avg	TD	Lg	
136	**542**	**10266**	**18.9**	**85**	**80t**	
Rush	Yds	Avg	TD	Lg	Total TD	Points
24	**129**	**5.4**	**2**	**21**	**87**	**524**

LEM BARNEY

Full name: **Lemuel Jackson Barney**
Date of Birth: **September 8, 1945, Gulfport, MS**
College: **Jackson State**
NFL Teams: **Detroit Lions**

Position: **Defensive Back**
Ht: **6-0**
Wt: **190**

"He's unbelievable. I wish I had two others just like him. I'd play one next to him on defense and use the other on offense."—Lions head coach Joe Schmidt

The Detroit Lions were faced with the enormous task of replacing cornerback Dick "Night Train" Lane in 1967.

The player who succeeded him wound up joining Lane in the Hall of Fame.

Lem Barney didn't take long to make a solid first impression when he stepped into Lane's old spot. In his first game, he picked off a pass by Green Bay's Bart Starr and returned it 24 yards for a touchdown. It was the kickoff to a spectacular rookie season that saw him intercept 10 passes to tie for the league lead. He finished with a flourish, ending the season by intercepting three Minnesota passes in one quarter, returning one of them 71 yards for a touchdown. He scored three touchdowns that season but had only one scored against him. He disregarded Schmidt's modest expectations for his rookie season.

Schmidt had said in training camp there was a "pretty slight" chance Barney would start, noting, "It takes a little longer to learn how to play cornerback than almost any other position."

Barney believed in the "Five P" system that had been taught by one of his coaches—"Proper preparation prevents poor performance." Barney was a complete player. He was also a productive return man on punts and kickoffs and he served as the Lions emergency punter in parts of two seasons.

He was a big-play specialist, too. Of his 11 career touchdowns, seven came on plays that covered at least 40 yards.

Packers receiver Carroll Dale said, "The only way to beat him is to be perfect."

Barney spent his entire 11-year career with Detroit, playing on teams that were good enough to contend but not good enough to win—or even get to a conference title game. Upon his election to the Hall of Fame in 1992, he said, "I never had a chance to be a champion. Now I feel like I am a champion."

CAREER TOTALS

G	Int	Yds	Avg	FR	Sacks	Total TD	Points
140	56	1077	19.2	17	0.0	11	66

SAMMY BAUGH

Full name: **Sammy Adrian Baugh**	Position: **Quarterback**
Date of Birth: **March 17, 1914, Temple, TX**	Ht: **6-2**
College: **Texas Christian**	Wt: **180**
NFL Teams: **Washington Redskins**	

"There's nobody any better than Sam Baugh was in pro football."
—Hall of Fame receiver Don Maynard

Pro football was a dull game dominated by defense in the early days.

Then Sammy Baugh came along.

Baugh helped lead an offensive revolution that made the game more interesting and made the league realize that fans wanted to see scoreboards light up. He revolutionized the game with his willingness to pass on first down or any other situation. Before that, most teams only threw the ball when they had no other choice.

Baugh came to the Washington Redskins in 1937 after leading Texas Christian University to a couple of wins in bowl games. Although he was more of a city boy, Redskins owner George Preston Marshall promoted him as a gun slinging cowboy and Baugh fulfilled Marshall's order to buy a Stetson hat before he left Texas for Washington.

He didn't become a quarterback until his fifth season but once he got the nod "Slingin' Sammy's" unconventional sidearm style soon became the basis for Washington's offense. His accuracy was honed by his habit of throwing the ball through tires he hung from tree branches. The most famous story relating to his fabled accuracy came when a coach outlined a route for a receiver and told Baugh, "Whenever he gets to this point, you hit him in the eye." Baugh is supposed to have said, "Which eye?"

Baugh was an All-Pro selection seven times, led the league in passing six times and helped the Redskins to a pair of NFL titles. He was also an exceptional punter and grabbed 28 interceptions as a defensive back.

He starred in a couple of movies, including "King of the Texas Rangers." Baugh retired in 1952 and coached at Hardin-Simmons University. He was the first coach of the New York Titans (later Jets) and later coached the Houston Oilers briefly. Baugh was part of the Hall of Fame's first class in 1963.

CAREER TOTALS								
G	Att	Cmp	Pct.	Yds	TD	Y/A	Lg	Int
165	2995	1693	56.5	21886	187	7.31	86t	203
Rush	Yds	Avg	TD	Lg	Total TD	Points	Rating	
324	325	1.0	9	34	9	55	72.2	

CHUCK BEDNARIK

Full name: **Charles Philip Bednarik**
Date of Birth: **May 1, 1925, Bethlehem, PA**
College: **Pennsylvania**
NFL Teams: **Philadelphia Eagles**

Position: **Linebacker/Center**
Ht: **6-3**
Wt: **233**

"A linebacker is like an animal. He's like a lion or tiger and he goes after prey. That's a linebacker."—Chuck Bednarik

Chuck Bednarik was inescapable for opponents of the Philadelphia Eagles.

For much of his career, he played on both sides of the ball, the last NFL player to play a significant role on both offense and defense. He cleared defenders out as a center and he jarred ball carriers with his tackles as a linebacker.

He made the All-NFL team at both positions. For as much as he played, he was amazingly durable, missing just three games in his 14-year career.

He played more minutes than most of his contemporaries, yet his career is best remembered for two moments. Both came in 1960, his final season. During a game late in the regular season, he drilled New York Giants running back Frank Gifford. The hit was so devastating that Gifford suffered a concussion and missed the entire next season.

His other famous tackle was a fitting way to end his career. The Eagles were protecting a 17-13 lead late in the 1960 championship game against Green Bay. The Packers threw a swing pass to Jim Taylor but Bednarik was able to stop him just short of the goal line as time ran out.

In the title game, Bednarik played 135 of 138 plays. The only three he sat out were Green Bay's kickoffs.

Bednarik had almost retired after the 1956 season, frustrated by the Eagles' 3-8-1 record. He came back and played mostly center. He pondered retirement again after 1959 but came back for one last season at age 35. That was also the year he went back to two-way duty because injuries created a need.

The man nicknamed "Concrete Charlie" was ready for any challenge, having survived 30 combat missions during World War II. Bednarik's tough-guy image was authentic. In the 1990s, Deion Sanders was playing both ways as a receiver and cornerback and reporters sought comment from Bednarik on the game's new 60-minute man.

"He's a good football player but he can't tackle," Bednarik said. "He couldn't tackle my wife."

CAREER TOTALS
G
169

RAYMOND BERRY

Full name: **Raymond Emmett Berry**
Date of Birth: **Feb. 27, 1933, Corpus Christi, TX**
College: **Southern Methodist**
NFL Teams: **Baltimore Colts**

Position: **Wide Receiver**
Ht: **6-2**
Wt: **187**

"He was one of a kind."—Baltimore Colts Hall of Fame guard Art Donovan

On Sundays, Raymond Berry caught passes from the best quarterback in the game, Johnny Unitas.

Every other day, he'd catch them from anybody willing to throw him the football. Berry worked so long and hard in practice that he'd outlast most of the other players. He'd continue to run patterns and rely on equipment men or grounds crew workers to throw to him. Legend has it that he even had his wife throw him passes in their back yard.

The drill was always the same—Berry wanted to 'look' the ball into his hands, making sure he caught it and held it. In the off season, he would practice running with a football in his hands, just to get accustomed to the feeling of keeping his balance while hanging on to the ball. He fumbled only once in his career.

That attention to detail made Berry one of the most reliable receivers in the NFL for 13 seasons. He was the most unlikely star. At Southern Methodist, he had scored one touchdown in three years. One of his legs was slightly shorter than the other and he had to wear special shoes to compensate for the difference. He was laced into a brace to protect a bad back. He was one of the first players to wear contact lenses, which he needed to correct poor vision.

Colts coach Weeb Ewbank had a fondness for players with good practice habits. Berry's hard work and sure hands didn't go unnoticed so he stayed with the team as a 20th round draft pick. Berry became a starter in his third year, 1957, and led the NFL with 800 receiving yards.

Berry's best game was the legendary 1958 NFL Championship game, when he caught 12 passes for 178 yards in the overtime defeat of the New York Giants.

Berry retired after the 1967 season and started a coaching career that lasted 20 years and included a 51-41 record with New England. He was elected to the Hall of Fame in 1973.

CAREER TOTALS						
G	Rec	Yds	Avg	TD	Lg	
154	631	9275	14.7	68	70t	
Rush	Yds	Avg	TD	Lg	Total TD	Points
0	0	-	0	-	68	408

FRED BILETNIKOFF

Full name: **Frederick S. Biletnikoff**	Position: **Wide Receiver**
Date of Birth: **February 23, 1943, Erie, PA**	Ht: **6-1**
College: **Florida State**	Wt: **190**
NFL Teams: **Oakland Raiders**	

"He can catch anything he can touch."

—John Madden

Fred Biletnikoff was slower and smaller than many of the defensive backs who covered him. But that wasn't enough to stop him from lasting 14 seasons in a career that ended up in the Hall of Fame. John Madden, his coach for part of his time with the Oakland Raiders, called him a "self-made player."

"Some receivers catch 15 or 20 passes in practice," Madden said. "Fred will catch 100."

Biletnikoff ran precise routes and was blessed with quarterbacks who liked to throw the ball and were very good at it. Daryle Lamonica's arrival in Oakland helped Biletnikoff establish himself and Ken Stabler helped him become a star.

The Raiders never had a losing season during Biletnikoff's career. One reason was the undersized but reliable receiver who managed to get open and make the difficult catches. It was the only aspect of football that ever interested him.

"I would be lost if I were ever told to do anything on a football field except catch passes," Biletnikoff once said.

He came to the Raiders in the 1965 draft, spurning an offer from the Detroit Lions. He didn't become a starter until the second half of his rookie season. He lost 1966 to a knee injury but was a starter again by the fourth game of 1967. He stayed in the lineup until his retirement after the 1978 season.

Biletnikoff was known for his intensity. He developed ulcers at a young age and needed time to decompress after games. He was also famous for loading his hands with "stickum," a pine tar-based substance that provided a better grip on the ball.

Biletnikoff had 10 straight seasons with at least 40 catches and was the Most Valuable Player of Super Bowl XI when Oakland beat Minnesota. He later became an assistant coach with the Raiders.

CAREER TOTALS

G	Rec	Yds	Avg	TD	Lg	
190	589	8974	15.2	76	82	
Rush	Yds	Avg	TD	Lg	Total TD	Points
0	0	-	0	-	77	462

GEORGE BLANDA

Full name: **George Frederick Blanda**	Position: **Quarterback/Kicker**
Date of Birth: **Sept. 17, 1927, Youngwood, PA**	Ht: **6-2**
College: **Kentucky**	Wt: **215**
NFL Teams: **Chicago Bears, Baltimore Colts,**	
Houston Oilers, Oakland Raiders	

"I really believe George Blanda is the greatest clutch player I have ever seen in pro football."—Oakland Raiders owner Al Davis

George Blanda's career spanned 26 years over four decades but it seemed as though he saved the best for last.

Blanda was a 12th round draft pick of the Chicago Bears in 1949 and spent one season there before moving on to the Baltimore Colts for one year. He went back to Chicago and settled in for a decade-long run as the Bears' starting quarterback. He also doubled as the team's kicker and balked when the Bears wanted to limit him to that role.

Blanda's disenchantment with the Bears came at the time when the fledgling American Football League was looking to fill its rosters with experienced players. Blanda signed on with Houston, leading them to the first two AFL titles. His run with Houston lasted until 1966, when the Oilers were convinced the 39-year-old Blanda was at the end of the line.

Al Davis claimed him on waivers for the Raiders, a move that worked out spectacularly well for both parties. Blanda, then 43, was pressed into emergency duty at quarterback in 1970 and was responsible for last-minute heroics in five consecutive games.

Against Pittsburgh, he threw for three touchdowns and kicked a field goal to lead a comeback win. His 48-yard field goal against Kansas City with three seconds remaining gave the Raiders a tie. He threw a touchdown pass and kicked a 52-yard field goal to beat Cleveland. His touchdown pass was responsible for a victory over Denver and he kicked a game-winning field goal against San Diego.

Twelve years after the Bears thought he was strictly a kicker and four years after the Oilers were sure he was washed up, Blanda was the biggest story in the NFL.

Blanda finally retired in 1976, just before his 49th birthday. He was voted into the Pro Football Hall of Fame in 1981.

CAREER TOTALS								
G	Att	Cmp	Pct.	Yds	TD	Y/A	Lg	Int
340	4007	1911	47.7	26920	236	6.72	94t	277
Rush	Yds	Avg	TD	Lg	Total TD	Points	Rating	
135	344	2.5	9	19	9	2002	60.6	

TERRY BRADSHAW

Full name: **Terry Paxton Bradshaw**

Date of Birth: **Sept. 2, 1948, Shreveport, LA**

College: **Louisiana Tech**

NFL Teams: **Pittsburgh Steelers**

Position: **Quarterback**

Ht: **6-3**

Wt: **210**

"My nature was attack, throw it deep. Anybody can throw wide. Let's go deep."—Terry Bradshaw

There were a lot of people in Pittsburgh who didn't think Bradshaw had any business playing quarterback. Some of the doubters wore Steelers uniforms.

Bradshaw ended up in the Hall of Fame but the path wasn't easy. He spent the first five years of his professional career in a three-way quarterback controversy with Terry Hanratty and Joe Gilliam, both of whom had supporters on the team.

In fact, as late as 1974 Bradshaw was on the bench and Gilliam was the starter. Some people thought Bradshaw should have been a running back with Hanratty calling the signals. Fortunately, that thought wasn't shared by anyone on the coaching staff.

Bradshaw took over midway through the 1974 season and executed the Steelers' run-first offense, which was fueled by Franco Harris and a smart and quick offensive line. Bradshaw didn't begin to assert himself until the Steelers' second run of consecutive Super Bowls, in 1978 and '79. By then, rules had been changed to help the passing game and Bradshaw loved to go downfield to Lynn Swann and John Stallworth. In the midst of their run of four championships in six years, the Steelers made the transition to a passing offense and the cannon-armed Bradshaw bombed opponents into submission. He capped a 14-2 regular season with four touchdown passes in Super Bowl XIII against the Dallas Cowboys.

Bradshaw endured constant shots at his intellect, including Dallas linebacker Thomas Henderson's famous pre-Super Bowl observation that Bradshaw "couldn't spell cat if you spotted him the 'c' and the 'a'."

A naïve country boy when he arrived in Pittsburgh as the first pick in the 1970 draft, Bradshaw was smart enough to exploit that image for his own gain. He became a singer and an actor. He appeared in commercials and successfully parlayed the outsized bumpkin personality into a lucrative career as a broadcaster.

CAREER TOTALS

G	Att	Cmp	Pct.	Yds	TD	Y/A Lg	Int
168	3901	2025	51.9	27989	212	7.17	90t
Rush	Yds	Avg	TD	Lg	Total TD	Points	Rating
210	444	2257	5.1	32 39	32	192	70.9

JIM BROWN

Full name: **James Nathaniel Brown**
Date of Birth: **February 17, 1936, St. Simons, GA**
College: **Syracuse**
NFL Teams: **Cleveland Browns**

Position: **Running Back**
Ht: **6-2**
Wt: **232**

"The best way to tackle Jim Brown is hang on and wait for help."
—Jim Steffen of the Washington Redskins.

Other backs have rushed for more yards than Jim Brown did but no one has overtaken his reputation as the best running back in NFL history.

It was inevitable that Brown's career rushing total of 12,312 yards would fall. The NFL expanded to a 16-game schedule (Teams played only 12 games, then 14 per year during Brown's career) and he stayed just nine seasons, retiring at age 29 to pursue an acting career.

He set the standard. In his final season, 1965, Brown ran for 1,544 yards, an average of 5.3 yards per carry. That still stands as the second-best rushing season in Browns history and Brown still owns the six best seasons in team history.

Brown was Cleveland's first-round draft choice in 1957, an All-American from Syracuse who would lead the NFL in rushing for eight of his first nine seasons. Brown had amazing mental toughness. He played most of the 1962 season with a sprained left wrist and played despite a broken toe the following year. Brown did his best to avoid the trainers' room.

"If you were a marked man like I was, then your attitude was you had to be tough," he told author Terry Pluto. "You had to take the pain. To be the kind of runner I wanted to be, you needed a strong mind."

Teammate Dick Modzelewski had played for the New York Giants and said players there had nicknamed Brown "Superman."

Brown had to walk on at Syracuse until a track coach gave him a scholarship. Five NFL teams passed on Brown before the Browns spent their first draft pick on him. It took one exhibition game for coach Paul Brown to decide Brown was his starting fullback.

An ill-advised ultimatum from owner Art Modell may have hastened Brown's retirement. He was late for training camp because of filming and Modell pressured him to get back to Cleveland. Instead, Brown chose to leave the game at the height of his career.

			CAREER TOTALS			
G	Rush	Yds	Avg	TD	Lg	
118	**2359**	**12312**	**5.2**	**106**	**80t**	
Rec	Yds	Avg	TD	Lg	Total TD	Points
262	**2499**	**9.5**	**20**	**83t**	**126**	**756**

ROOSEVELT BROWN

Full name: **Roosevelt Brown Jr.**	Position: **Offensive Line**
Date of Birth: **Oct. 20, 1932, Charlottesville, VA**	Ht: **6-3**
College: **Morgan State**	Wt: **255**
NFL Teams: **New York Giants**	

"He was my favorite, my idol. Everything I learned, I picked up from him."
—Hall of Fame tackle Jim Parker

Roosevelt Brown came to camp as a 27th round draft pick and never once worried about getting cut by the New York Giants.

Incredible confidence? No, blissful naiveté.

Brown was so unaware of the ways of pro football that he didn't realize he was in danger of being cut. He thought being drafted and being invited to training camp meant he had a spot on the team.

As it turned out, he was correct. Brown was a 13-year starter for the Giants, providing protection for quarterback Y.A. Tittle and opening running lanes for backs like Frank Gifford and Alex Webster.

Because he'd been smart enough to skip grades in school, Brown was only 20 years old in his rookie season. He was drafted only because someone on the Giants staff had noticed his name on a Black All-American team in a newspaper. The Giants took a chance on the big man from tiny Morgan State and were rewarded with a player who anchored their offensive line through some successful seasons.

Brown was raw when he reported to the Giants. He didn't even know the proper stance for a lineman. He had never seen a pro football game, although he did recall listening to one of the NFL championship games on the radio.

He was 6-foot-3 and his weight hovered between 255 and 270 pounds. But Brown had more than just size on his side. He was quick to learn and he was quick to react, dropping back to pass block while his speed allowed him to get outside to lead a running back on a sweep.

Brown played in nine Pro Bowls and helped the Giants stay at or near the top of the standings. He missed only three games in his career.

Brown was forced to retire during training camp in 1966 because of phlebitis. He was voted into the Hall of Fame in 1975 and continued his relationship with the Giants by serving the team as a scout.

CAREER TOTALS		
G		
162		

WILLIE BROWN

Full name: **William Ferdie Brown**
Date of Birth: **Dec. 12, 1940, Yazoo City, MS**
College: **Grambling**
NFL Teams: **Houston Oilers, Denver Broncos, Oakland Raiders**

Position: **Cornerback**
Ht: **6-1**
Wt: **210**

"You can waste a lot of moves on Willie."—Hall of Fame receiver Lance Alworth

Playing against Willie Brown was an intensely personal experience.

There was no escaping Brown, whose specialty was extremely close coverage. Some say Brown invented the idea of "bump and run" coverage; others insist he merely perfected the technique.

From his cornerback position, Brown would engage the receiver near the line of scrimmage, then continue to stay within bumping distance as the receiver made his way downfield on the pattern.

Brown was among a handful of exceptional defensive backs who became so proficient at the method that the NFL changed its rules. The bump and run was taking offense out of the game, so the NFL decreed that defensive backs couldn't make contact with receivers beyond five yards of the line of scrimmage.

Brown had the ability to read a receiver and resist the fakes that would fool lesser defenders. He was fast, mobile and aggressive and quickly excelled at a position he had never played before entering professional football.

His career path was filled with obstacles. Brown was not drafted out of Grambling but signed on with the Houston Oilers as a free agent. They cut him in camp and he then hooked on with the Denver Broncos. He became a starter six games into his rookie season of 1963. In short order, he began to get matched up against the opponent's best receiver.

Brown wound up with the Raiders in 1967 and found a home in Oakland. His 12-year playing career was the start of a 31-year connection to the team.

He played in two Super Bowls with the Raiders and had a 75-yard interception return for a touchdown in Super Bowl XI. He had sure hands and picked off 54 passes in his career.

After his retirement in 1978, Brown served the Raiders as an assistant coach and remains on the team's staff as the Director of Squad Development.

Brown won election to the Pro Football Hall of Fame in 1984.

CAREER TOTALS							
G	Int	Yds	TD				
204	54	472	2	-	-	-	-

BUCK BUCHANAN

Full name:**Junious Buchanan**	Position: **Defensive Line**
Date of Birth: **Sept. 10, 1940, Gainesville, AL**	Ht: **6-7**
Died: **July 16, 1992**	Wt: **279**
College: **Grambling**	
NFL Teams: **Kansas City Chiefs**	

"You don't imagine a guy 6-foot-8 and 300 pounds being so quick. You'd go to hit him and it was like hitting a ghost."—Hall of Fame guard Gene Upshaw

Buck Buchanan was a big part of the Kansas City Chiefs defense. A very big part.

Officially, Junious Buchanan was listed at 6-foot-7 and 274 pounds but pardon Upshaw for thinking he was even bigger than that. As large he was was, Buchanan was also rangy and quick, which meant problems for any lineman assigned to block him.

A six-time All Pro, Buchanan was the forerunner of today's agile defensive tackles. Normally players who fit his profile were placed at defensive end so they could have a freer path on the pass rush. But Kansas City coach Hank Stram was an innovator and quickly moved Buchanan to defensive tackle.

In fact, Stram changed the game by teaming Buchanan with Curley Culp at the other tackle spot. That gave the Chiefs two fast, capable players at the position at a time when most tackles were lumbering hulks. It caused confusion. Minnesota Vikings All Pro center Mick Tinglehoff was overwhelmed by Buchanan and Culp in Super Bowl IV.

The Chiefs made Buchanan the first player chosen in the 1963 American Football League draft. The New York Giants selected him on the 19th round of the NFL draft. The Chiefs' evaluation was on the mark. Buchanan had been a standout at Grambling.

Buchanan's long arms allowed him to interfere with a quarterback's vision and trajectory —he was credited with batting down 16 passes in 1967. In 13 years, Buchanan missed only one game. He got into the record books by recording the first sack in Super Bowl history.

After his retirement in 1975, Buchanan was an assistant coach in the NFL before returning to Kansas City to launch several businesses. He was voted into the Hall of Fame in 1990 and succumbed to lung cancer two years later.

Today, the Buck Buchanan Award is given to the outstanding defensive player competing at the Division I-AA level.

CAREER TOTALS							
G	Sacks	FR	Int	Yds	Avg	Total TD	Points
182	0.0	3	3	37	12.3	0	2

DICK BUTKUS

Full name: **Richard Marvin Butkus**	Position: **Linebacker**
Date of Birth: **December 9, 1942, Chicago, IL**	Ht: **6-3**
College: **Illinois**	Wt: **244**
NFL Teams: **Chicago Bears**	

"I'd rather go one-on-one with a grizzly bear. I prayed that I would get up every time Butkus hit me."—MacArthur Lane, Packers running back

Dick Butkus was the meanest man on the field because he worked at it.

After his playing career ended, Butkus admitted that in addition to studying opponents and their tendencies, some of his preparation time was devoted to working up rage.

"I would manufacture things to make me mad," he said. "If someone on the other team was laughing, I'd pretend he was laughing at the Bears."

Had his opponents known that was happening, they wouldn't even have smiled. Butkus cultivated his image, once telling a reporter, "I wouldn't ever set out to hurt anyone deliberately unless it was, you know, important…like a league game or something."

Butkus was a two-time All-American at the University of Illinois who came to the Chicago Bears in a 1965 first-round draft bonanza that also netted them Gale Sayers. The Bears already had a standout middle linebacker in veteran Bill George.

"The second I saw him on the field I knew my playing days were over," George said of Butkus.

In his NFL debut, Butkus made 11 unassisted tackles against the San Francisco 49ers. He recovered six fumbles as a rookie. He would lead the Bears in tackles for eight consecutive years. He was also skilled in stripping the ball. In 119 career games, Butkus had 25 fumble recoveries and 22 interceptions.

Butkus came from Chicago's tough South Side and embodied the Bears' "Monsters of the Midway" tradition. The Bears teams he played on weren't championship contenders but he made the Pro Bowl eight times. In 1970, NFL coaches voted him the one player they would like to use as the foundation for a franchise.

Knee injuries caught up with Butkus and he had to take himself out of a game in 1973 because of the pain. That was his last NFL season.

The award given to the outstanding linebacker in college football is named for Butkus. He was elected to the Hall of Fame in 1979 and became an actor after leaving the game.

CAREER TOTALS							
G	Sacks	FR	Int	Yds	Avg	Total TD	Points
119	0.0	25	22	166	7.5	1	10

EARL CAMPBELL

Full name: **Earl Christian Campbell**

Date of Birth: **March 29, 1955, Tyler, TX**

College: **Texas**

NFL Teams: **Houston Oilers, New Orleans Saints**

Position: **Running Back**

Ht: **5-11**

Wt: **233**

"I wouldn't say Earl is in a class by himself but I'll tell you one thing—it doesn't take them long to call the roll."—Bum Phillips

Bum Phillips wasn't just Earl Campbell's coach, he was his biggest booster, too.

Shortly before the 1978 draft, Phillips sent tight end Jimmy Giles and a bundle of prime draft picks to Tampa Bay to secure the overall No. 1 pick. There was no doubt about which player he would select.

He wanted Campbell, a native of Tyler, Texas who went on to become the University of Texas' first Heisman Trophy winner. The Oilers needed to create some excitement and nothing would do that like a native son who was also a gifted player.

Campbell immediately established himself as a force in the NFL. In a Monday night game against Miami, he gained 199 yards and was exactly what the Oilers needed to step up and challenge the powerful Pittsburgh Steelers.

"(Quarterback) Dan Pastorini has some weapons to fight with," Phillips said. "He used to be like a sword fighter with a pocket knife. Now he has his sword."

Or sledgehammer. Campbell's power came from 34-inch thighs that let him run over people. Oakland defensive back Jack Tatum, one of the NFL's most feared hitters, once lined Campbell up for a tackle. Campbell ran into Tatum and knocked him over. Players said the collision sounded like a train wreck.

Campbell was good from the start but he got better as he learned more of the game's subtleties, such as reading his blocks. His best season was 1980 when he ran for 1,934 yards and topped 200 yards in four games. Once Phillips was fired, things soured in Houston. Campbell was traded to New Orleans, where Phillips had become head coach of the Saints.

They couldn't recreate the magic they had in Houston and Campbell retired after eight seasons and 9,407 yards. He went into the Hall of Fame in 1991 with Phillips serving as his presenter.

CAREER TOTALS

G	Rush	Yds	Avg	TD	Lg	
115	2187	9407	4.3	74	81t	
Rec	Yds	Avg	TD	Lg	Total TD	Points
121	806	6.7	0	66	74	444

WILLIE DAVIS

Full name: **William Delford Davis**
Date of Birth: **July 24, 1934, Lisbon, LA**
College: **Grambling**
NFL Teams: **Cleveland Browns, Green Bay Packers**

Position: **Defensive Line**
Ht: **6-3**
Wt: **243**

"I was willing to work hard. I was willing to do all the things necessary to be a winner."—Willie Davis

Willie Davis thought his pro football career was over when he was traded to Green Bay. Actually, it was just beginning.

He was an overachiever, a 17th round draft pick who had spent two years in the Army and reported to the Cleveland Browns as a 24-year-old rookie. He was the last Browns player to play full-time on both offense and defense. He contributed on both lines for the Browns.

When Packers coach Vince Lombardi evaluated Davis, he saw a defensive player who had the ability to be a standout because he had speed, agility and size.

"Give me a man with any two of those dimensions and he'll be OK," Lombardi said. "But give him all three and he'll be great."

Davis was. He was a regular at defensive end for the Packers' powerhouse teams of the 1960s, a five-time All-Pro who never missed a game.

His career almost ended after Cleveland. Davis was driving when he heard the news that the Browns had traded him to Green Bay for a marginal wide receiver. Stung by the feeling of rejection, Davis wasn't sure he would report to the Packers. He was contemplating retirement until he talked to Lombardi.

"There was never any doubt I wanted to play for the man," Davis said.

He flourished in Green Bay as the Packers dominated the NFL through much of the 1960s.

"He's the quickest defensive end in the business," Chicago Bears quarterback Bill Wade said. "He's not the strongest or the biggest but he's always in there."

Davis was just as driven off the field. He got his Masters degree in business at the University of Chicago, working in the off season. When his classroom work faltered and he considered abandoning his pursuit of the degree, Lombardi again provided the motivation.

"I've never known Willie Davis to be a quitter," Lombardi said.

Davis retired after the 1969 season and made millions in business. He was elected to the Pro Football Hall of Fame in 1981.

CAREER TOTALS							
G	Sacks	FR	Int	Yds	Avg	Total TD	Points
162	0.0	22	2	21	10.5	2	16

ERIC DICKERSON

Full name: **Eric Demetric Dickerson**
Date of Birth: **September 2, 1960, Sealy, TX**
College: **Southern Methodist**
NFL Teams: **Los Angeles Rams, Indianapolis Colts, Los Angeles Raiders, Atlanta Falcons**

Position: **Running Back**
Ht: **6-3**
Wt: **220**

"You have to make up your mind when you go on the field that you are the best."—Eric Dickerson

Eric Dickerson played 11 seasons in the NFL but probably secured his Hall of Fame credentials after just four years.

He had a spectacular rookie the season, the first of four solid years that would see him gain a minimum of 1,000 yards in each and have three seasons with at least 1,800 yards.

Dickerson had been a spectacular college player at Southern Methodist as part of the school's "Pony Express" backfield. The Los Angeles Rams took him with the second overall pick in the 1983 draft and Dickerson was an immediate sensation.

He set rookie records with 390 attempts, 1,808 yards and 18 touchdowns. He easily won Rookie of the Year honors.

His second year was even more impressive as he broke O.J. Simpson's record for yards in a season with 2,105. He had 12 games with at least 100 yards en route to the record. In 1985, Dickerson rushed for 1,234 yards and ran for 248 yards in a playoff game against Dallas.

Dickerson was built for power and speed. He ran with a gliding gait and was an unusual sight on the field, decked out in goggles and a tinted face shield.

His career took a major turn in 1987 when he played just three games with the Rams before a contract impasse led to a trade to the Indianapolis Colts. In just nine games with the Colts, Dickerson piled up 1,011 yards for a season total of 1,288.

In 1989, Dickerson became the first player with seven straight seasons with at least 1,000 rushing yards. He also became the fastest to accumulate 10,000 yards on the ground, needing just 91 games to reach that milestone.

Dickerson played in six Pro Bowls and his 13,259 yards were second on the career list when he retired after the 1993 season. He returned to Los Angeles to play for the Raiders for a season and finished his career with the Atlanta Falcons.

CAREER TOTALS							
G	Rush	Yds	Avg	TD	Lg		
146	2996	13259	4.4	90	85t		
Rec	Yds	Avg	TD	Lg	Total TD	Points	
281	2137	7.6	6	50t	96	576	

MIKE DITKA

Full name:**Michael Keller Ditka**
Date of Birth: **October 18, 1939, Carnegie, PA**
College: **Pittsburgh**
NFL Teams: **Chicago Bears, Philadelphia Eagles, Dallas Cowboys**

Position: **Tight End**
Ht: **6-3**
Wt: **228**

"I just try to hit the other guy before he hits me."—Mike Ditka

He came from Aliquippa, Pa., where the Jones & Laughlin mill hunkered down alongside the Ohio River. The men who worked there were as tough as the steel they manufactured.

Ditka escaped the mill but the toughness and work ethic of Aliquippa were an indelible part of his character. He played tight end with the mentality of a defensive player. He was difficult to tackle because he was big, strong and aggressive. Ditka's stiff arm dropped many defensive backs. It was all part of Ditka's strike-first theory.

"If I hit him hard enough, maybe he won't want to hit back," he reasoned.

Ditka considered attending Notre Dame and Penn State but chose to stay close to home at the University of Pittsburgh, partly because he was interested in attending dental school.

Both professional leagues wanted Ditka when he left Pitt. The NFL's Chicago Bears and the Houston Oilers of the American Football League both made him a first-round draft pick. Ditka chose the Bears and Chicago became his adopted home.

He was named Rookie of the Year in 1961 and quickly established himself on a veteran-laden Bears team. Linebacker Bill George called Ditka, "the best rookie I've ever seen."

There were considerations for using Ditka at linebacker or fullback but it was decided he should play tight end. He had good hands, could gain yards after the catch and block on plays when he didn't get the ball.

Ditka made five straight Pro Bowls and was an important part of the Bears' 1963 championship team. His reckless style led to knee injuries and ultimately a dispute with Bears coach George Halas. Ditka was traded to Philadelphia, where he spent two unhappy seasons, before he revived his career with the Dallas Cowboys.

Ditka started a coaching career as an assistant to Tom Landry in Dallas, then returned to Chicago as head coach of the Bears. His 1985 team claimed the Bears' first title since 1963.

Ditka was voted into the Pro Football Hall of Fame in 1988.

CAREER TOTALS						
G	Rec	Yds	Avg	TD	Lg	
158	**427**	**5812**	**13.6**	**43**	**76t**	
Rush	Yds	Avg	TD	Lg	Total TD	Points
2	**2**	**1.0**	**0**	**11**	**45**	**270**

TONY DORSETT

Full name: **Anthony Drew Dorsett**
Date of Birth: **April 7, 1954, Rochester, PA**
College: **Pittsburgh**
NFL Teams: **Dallas Cowboys, Denver Broncos**

Position: **Running Back**
Ht: **5-11**
Wt: **191**

"He'll see a narrow opening and suddenly be gone right through it before you know it."—Tom Landry

The Cowboys thought so much of Tony Dorsett that they manipulated the 1977 draft to make sure they got him.

The Seattle Seahawks had the second pick in the draft but traded it to Dallas for a bundle of draft choices. The deal made sense at both ends—the second-year Seahawks needed a lot of help and Dallas needed Dorsett.

The match was perfect for Dorsett, too. Instead of being the focal point of a bad team's offense, he was one of many weapons for the contending Cowboys. He got to run behind an experienced offensive line and since he was one of many offensive options, he wasn't overworked. Dorsett played at around 190 pounds so keeping him strong and healthy was an important consideration.

He came from Hopewell, Pennsylvania and stayed home to attend the University of Pittsburgh, helping Coach Johnny Majors re-establish football at the school. Pitt went undefeated in 1976 to win the national championship and Dorsett won the Heisman Trophy in his senior year.

Dorsett had a smooth running style and breakaway speed. His tremendous balance gave him the ability to make sharp cuts. As a rookie he ran for 1,007 yards with 12 touchdowns and capped the season with a Super Bowl victory.

Dorsett was a consistent performer for the Cowboys for 11 seasons. He rushed for 12,739 yards and caught 398 passes for another 3,554 yards. Landry and the coaching staff designed schemes that highlighted Dorsett's talents but didn't overexpose him.

Dorsett played a final season with the Denver Broncos. He was voted to the Hall of Fame in 1994 and his name has lived on for another generation. His son, Anthony, has played defensive back for several NFL teams.

CAREER TOTALS							
G	Rush	Yds	Avg	TD	Lg		
173	2936	12739	4.3	77	99t		
Rec	Yds	Avg	TD	Lg	Total TD	Points	
398	3554	8.9	13	91t	91	546	

BRETT FAVRE

Full name: **Brett Lorenzo Favre**	Position: **Quarterback**
Date of Birth: **October 10, 1969, Gulfport, MS**	Ht: **6-2**
College: **Southern Mississippi**	Wt: **225**
NFL Teams: **Atlanta Falcons, Green Bay Packers**	

"I've never seen such a talent. I think he could throw better lying down than I could standing up."—Hall of Fame Green Bay Packers quarterback Bart Starr

The Atlanta Falcons used a second-round draft pick to get Brett Favre and traded him for a No. 1 choice, so it should have been a good deal.

It wasn't.

The Falcons wound up giving away a future Hall of Famer, the one quarterback who would help return the Green Bay Packers to their glory days of the 1960s.

It wasn't the first time someone had underestimated Favre. When he came out of high school, the only Division I-A school to offer him a scholarship was Southern Mississippi—and the coaches there projected him as a defensive back.

Instead, Favre became the guy who would make life miserable for defensive backs. He started as the No. 7 quarterback but quickly moved up. In his second college game, Favre replaced the starter and took over the job in his third game as a freshman.

Favre endured some hardship just before his senior season. He was in a serious automobile accident that resulted in 30 inches of his intestine being removed. Remarkably, he was back playing within five weeks of the accident.

He appeared in just two games with the Falcons before his move to Green Bay. The trade to the Packers turned out to be a perfect fit. He took over from Don Majkowski during the 1992 season, his first in Green Bay, and quickly established himself as the starter. At just 23, he was the youngest quarterback ever to start in the Pro Bowl.

Favre became the first three-time NFL Most Valuable Player and had a stretch of five consecutive years with at least 30 touchdown passes. On January 26, 1997, he helped Green Bay win its first Super Bowl in nearly 30 years, passing for 246 yards and two touchdowns.

Favre contemplated retirement after the Packers' loss to Atlanta in the wild card round of the 2002 playoffs. He shook off that disappointment and decided to continue his career.

CAREER TOTALS								
G	Att	Cmp	Pct.	Yds	TD	Y/A	Lg	Int
193	6464	3960	61.3	45646	346	7.06	99t	209
Rush	Yds	Avg	TD	Lg	Total TD	Points	Rating	
469	1647	3.5	12	40	12	72	86.9	

DAN FOUTS

Full name: **Daniel Francis Fouts**

Date of Birth: **June 10, 1951, San Francisco, CA**

College: **Oregon**

NFL Teams: **San Diego Chargers**

Position: **Quarterback**

Ht: **6-3**

Wt: **210**

"Dan Fouts was the master of finding the receiver who was open."

—San Diego Chargers assistant coach Al Saunders

The San Diego Chargers were "Air Coryell" and Dan Fouts was the pilot.

Coach Don Coryell went to San Diego and brought back some of the early flavor of the old American Football League with a wide-open passing attack. It was a dream system for a quarterback, especially when the Chargers built a corps of receivers that included Charlie Joiner, John Jefferson, Wes Chandler and tight end Kellen Winslow.

"When Coryell came, it was bombs away," Fouts said.

Fouts was a third-round draft choice from Oregon who joined the Chargers in 1973 as a rookie understudy to veteran legend Johnny Unitas. When it became apparent that Unitas was at the end of his career, the Chargers installed Fouts as the starter.

Unitas had become the NFL's first 40,000-yard passer during his one season with San Diego. Fouts would eventually pass that milestone himself and finish his career with 43,040 passing yards. For three years, from 1979-81, Fouts passed for more than 4,000 yards in each season. He had 51 games with at least 300 yards and topped 3,000 yards in six different seasons.

Fouts had grown up around pro football. His father, Bob, was the play-by-play voice of the San Francisco 49ers and Dan served his father as a statistician and worked for the 49ers as a ballboy.

Fouts' big break came when the Unitas-led Chargers fell behind 38-0 to Pittsburgh on Oct. 7, 1973. San Diego switched to Fouts and the final score was 38-21. In his first three years, though, the Chargers were just 9-32-1.

The addition of Bill Walsh as offensive coordinator helped and things turned around when Coryell took over. Fouts wasn't especially mobile but he had a quick release and a knack for finding the open man.

Fouts retired after the 1987 season and was voted into the Hall of Fame in 1993.

CAREER TOTALS								
G	Att	Cmp	Pct.	Yds	TD	Y/A	Lg	Int
181	5604	3297	58.8	43040	254	7.68	81t	242
Rush	Yds	Avg	TD	Lg	Total TD	Points	Rating	
224	476	2.1	13	32	13	78	80.2	

OTTO GRAHAM

Full name: **Otto Everett Graham Jr.**
Date of Birth: **December 6, 1921, Waukegan, IL**
College: **Northwestern**
NFL Teams: **Cleveland Browns**

Position: **Quarterback**
Ht: **6-1**
Wt: **195**

"The test of a quarterback is where his team finishes. By that standard, Otto was the best of them all."—Paul Brown

They called him "Otto-matic," a play on his first name and a tribute to his consistency.

The Cleveland Browns won 10 divisional titles in 10 years with Otto Graham as their quarterback. He was an All Pro player in nine of those 10 years. Graham was a tailback in college but switched to quarterback when he became a pro.

Graham was a record-setter from the start. He was born in Waukegan, Illinois and weighed in at 14 pounds and 12 ounces, which set a state mark for the largest baby. He developed into precisely the type of player made for Paul Brown's offense. Brown was drawn to Graham for his decision-making capabilities and his scrambling ability.

Graham didn't have the strongest throwing arm but he was incredibly accurate and had uncommon poise. He could stand in against a pass rush and wait the extra second for a receiver to become open. He could run out of the pocket and still make a play.

From 1946-49, the Browns went 47-4-3 and won four consecutive All-American Football Conference titles. When the Browns joined the NFL in 1950, their first game was against the defending champion Philadelphia Eagles. Graham made his presence felt by throwing for a touchdown on his first NFL pass attempt.

"I could throw a pass to a spot as well as anyone who ever lived," Graham said. "That's a God-given talent. I could never stand back and flick the ball 60 yards downfield like Dan Marino."

In his 10 years, Graham never missed a game because of injury. During his career, the Browns were 105-17-4.

Graham later coached at the Coast Guard Academy and came back to the NFL to coach the Washington Redskins from 1966-69. His No. 14 was retired by the Browns and he was elected to the Hall of Fame in 1965.

CAREER TOTALS

G	Att	Cmp	Pct.	Yds	TD	Y/A	Lg	Int
126	2626	1464	55.8	23584	174	8.98	81t	135
Rush	Yds	Avg	TD	Lg	Total TD	Points	Rating	
325	882	2.7	33	36	34	204	86.6	

RED GRANGE

Full name: **Harold Edward Grange**	Position: **Running Back**
Date of Birth: **June 13, 1903, Forksville, PA**	Ht: **6-0**
Died: **January 28, 1991**	Wt: **184**
College: **Illinois**	
NFL Teams: **Chicago Bears, New York Yankees**	

"They built my accomplishments way out of proportion. I never got the idea I was a tremendous big shot."—Red Grange.

Harold (Red) Grange was professional football's first star. He came along at a time when America's interest in the game was focused on the college level.

Grange was a national figure, thanks to his amazing accomplishments with the University of Illinois. On October 18, 1924, he scored four touchdowns in just 12 minutes. In another game, he returned the opening kickoff 95 yards for a touchdown, scored on four other runs and threw a touchdown pass. The exploits of the "Galloping Ghost" were regularly part of movie newsreels. Grange was an All-American for three consecutive years.

Immediately after the 1925 college season ended, the Chicago Bears' George Halas huddled with Grange and his agent, C.C. Pyle. They came up with a contract agreement that was reported to be worth $3,000 per game and a percentage of the gate. Grange debuted in the Bears' scoreless tie against the Chicago Cardinals on Thanksgiving Day.

Halas knew that Grange was the big name who could put pro football on the map and he was correct. He booked a barnstorming tour that took Grange and the Bears all over the country, playing 19 games in 67 days. They drew 65,000 to the Polo Grounds in New York for a game against the Giants.

Pyle was a savvy promoter who maximized Grange's star power. He even did some rudimentary merchandising, attaching Grange's name to consumer products.

Grange did not return for the 1926 season after failing to reach terms with the Bears. Grange and Pyle formed the American Football League and took the New York franchise, named the Yankees. The League folded after one year and the Yankees joined the NFL. Grange sat out the 1928 season with a knee injury, then came back to the Bears in 1929.

The knee injury affected his ability to run the ball but Grange still excelled at defensive back. Grange was in the Hall of Fame's charter class in 1963.

CAREER TOTALS							
G	Rush	Yds	Avg	TD	Lg		
96	**170**	**569**	**3.3**	**16**	**-**		
Rec	Yds	Avg	TD	Lg	Total TD	Points	
16	**288**	**18.0**	**10**	**-**	**26**	**157**	

DARRELL GREEN

Full name: **Darrell Ray Green**
Date of Birth: **February 15, 1960, Houston, TX**
College: **Texas A&M-Kingsville**
NFL Teams: **Washington Redskins**

Position: **Defensive Back**
Ht: **5-9**
Wt: **187**

"I thought he was going to be too small...until I saw him run."
—Washington Redskins Coach Richie Petitbon

Darrell Green outran his shortcomings.

Any doubts about his ability to play cornerback at 5-foot-9 and 184 pounds vanished when Green took off down the field. He was a blur, able to keep up with any receiver in the league.

Green's reputation was made in the first regular season game of his rookie year. The Redskins were playing the Dallas Cowboys, their No. 1 rival. Tony Dorsett, then one of the top backs in the NFL, took off on a long run. Dorsett appeared to be headed for a touchdown and Green's pursuit seemed to be the admirable effort of a naïve rookie. But Green caught Dorsett from behind and hauled him down at the 6-yard line, no doubt shocking Dorsett.

That single play established Green as one of the fastest players in the NFL. That designation would become official later when Green won four fastest-man competitions.

He combined speed with technique to throw a blanket over some of the best receivers in the game. Redskins General Manager Charley Casserly called Green the best defensive back in the NFL after watching how his coverage disrupted offenses week after week.

Green got his chance to start as a rookie when veteran Jeris White was injured. White never got the spot back.

Green played in seven Pro Bowls and he played the position with a high degree of class and professionalism. He never taunted opponents and he never talked trash. He just did his job better than just about every other defensive back in the league.

He maintained that level of play for a long time, too. Green remained in the starting lineup until he was 40 and played through the 2002 season, when he was 42. In his last two years, he'd been reduced to playing on third down and special teams.

Green had an emotional on-field ceremony at his last game and will no doubt be preparing a speech for the Hall of Fame as soon as he's eligible.

CAREER TOTALS							
G	Int	Yds	Avg	FR	Sacks	Total TD	Points
295	54	621	11.5	10	1.0	8	48

JOE GREENE

Full name: **Charles Edward Greene**

Date of Birth: **September 24, 1946, Temple, TX**

College: **North Texas**

NFL Teams: **Pittsburgh Steelers**

Position: **Defensive Line**

Ht: **6-4**

Wt: **275**

"I never ran into anyone who wanted to play more and be better more than Joe."—Chuck Noll

He was "Joe Who?" on the day the Pittsburgh Steelers made him their first choice in the 1969 draft. Little wonder, considering the defensive tackle from North Texas State wasn't exactly a household name. The feeling of disenchantment was mutual.

"Pittsburgh was the last place I wanted to go," Greene admitted later.

Little wonder there, either, considering the Steelers had just gone 2-11-1, a season bad enough to get their coach fired and replaced by Noll, fresh from a job assisting Don Shula with the Baltimore Colts.

Ten years later, though, the Steelers were about to win their fourth Super Bowl in 10 years. Everyone knew who Joe Greene was and Greene knew that Pittsburgh had turned out to be the perfect place for him. Franchise founder Art Rooney fostered a comfortable family atmosphere and Noll made the right moves to turn the Steelers into the NFL's team of the '70s.

The first step toward that distinction was the drafting of Greene, whom Noll described as "a fort on foot." At 6-foot-4 and 275 pounds, Greene moved people out of his way and attacked quarterbacks. In short order the Steelers were able to surround him with similarly talented players and the "Steel Curtain" defense that would carry the team through its first two championships was in place.

"When the Steelers were playing, it was like Jaws was in the water," Greene said.

Mean Joe Greene picked up a nickname he never liked when his college team became known as the "Mean Green" for the color of its uniforms. His protests aside, Greene lived up the name, especially in his early years. His bursts of temper, fueled by the frustration of losing, got him ejected from games until Noll urged him to channel his aggressiveness in a more positive manner.

Greene appeared in 10 Pro Bowls and retired in 1981. He was elected to the Hall of Fame in 1987 and has worked as an assistant coach for several NFL teams, including the Steelers.

CAREER TOTALS							
G	Sacks	FR	Int	Yds	Avg	Total TD	Points
181	0.0	16	1	26	26.0	0	0

FORREST GREGG

Full name:**Alvis Forrest Gregg**	Position: **Offensive Lineman**
Date of Birth: **October 18, 1933, Birthright, TX**	Ht: **6-4**
College: **Southern Methodist**	Wt: **249**
NFL Teams: **Green Bay Packers, Dallas Cowboys**	

"The best player I ever coached,"—Vince Lombardi

Consider the magnitude of that statement, given all the talented players Lombardi had while building a dynasty in Green Bay.

Maybe Gregg was destined to be Lombardi's favorite, just like he was destined to follow Lombardi's path and become the Packers' head coach.

Gregg wasn't the biggest player at 6-foot-4 and 249 pounds. Nor was he the strongest. He compensated by studying his opponents and developing blocking techniques that would make him effective. Perhaps it was devotion to the craft that so impressed Lombardi.

Gregg was born in Birthright, Texas and played at Southern Methodist University. The Packers drafted him on the second round in 1956, three years before Lombardi would arrive in Green Bay.

He played 188 consecutive games from 1956-71. Gregg was an All-NFL player for eight years from 1960-67. He played in nine Pro Bowls. His career coincided with the Lombardi era, when the coach made the Packers into a powerhouse that set the standard in the NFL.

Gregg studied film on the NFL's best linemen, focusing particularly on Jim Parker of the Baltimore Colts and the New York Giants' Roosevelt Brown. He made wise choices since both players would wind up in the Hall of Fame. He noticed their footwork was the key. Gregg developed an ability to be light on his feet and get into proper position quickly. He used finesse to beat opponents rather than trying to constantly overpower them.

Twice during his career he had to temporarily switch to guard because of a need created by injuries. Gregg graded out well at the new position, even though playing guard carried different responsibilities.

Gregg retired after playing in 1970 with Green Bay. He was persuaded to come back the next season by the Dallas Cowboys. He finished his career as a member of the Cowboys' Super Bowl team.

Gregg launched a coaching career that took him to three NFL stops—Cleveland (1975-77), Cincinnati (1980-83) and Green Bay (1984-87). He later coached SMU when the school re-established football after NCAA sanctions had shut down the program.

CAREER TOTALS				
G				
193				

LOU GROZA

Full name: **Louis Ray Groza**
Date of Birth: **Jan. 25, 1924, Martin's Ferry, OH**
Died: **November 29, 2000**
College: **Ohio State**
NFL Teams: **Cleveland Browns**

Position: **Offensive Line/Kicker**
Ht: **6-3**
Wt: **250**

"Lou won more games in clutch situations with his kicking than any player in the game's history."—Hall of Fame coach Paul Brown

Lou Groza's career with the Cleveland Browns covered parts of three decades and saw him on hand for just about every success the franchise had.

Groza joined the Browns in 1946, when they were still part of the All American Football Conference and stayed through 1967, the year the NFL staged the first Super Bowl against the champion of the American Football League. He was there for all eight Browns titles—four in the AAFC and four more in the NFL. He was a teammate of all 12 of the Browns who are in the Hall of Fame.

He actually had two separate careers with the Browns. From 1946 through 1959, he played on the offensive line and served as the team's kicker. After a back injury knocked him out for the 1960 season, he became a full-time kicker.

Browns coach Paul Brown gave him the nickname "The Toe." After he won a game, Brown said, "Lou 'The Toe-za' Groza," which was shortened. Despite his success as a kicker, Groza liked to remind people that he was a full-time player first and that he went into the Hall of Fame as a lineman.

Groza came from Martins Ferry, Ohio, where his introduction to sports came from his older brother. His brother taught him to kick and Groza used to practice by booting footballs over telephone wires that stretched across the street.

Groza served in World War II, then went to Ohio State. He joined the Browns as a 22-year-old rookie when the franchise was launched. His most memorable moment came when he won the 1950 NFL Championship game with a last-second field goal.

His straight-on style produced 640 extra points and 233 field goals, both of which stand as Browns records. He also has the franchise records for most seasons and points. The Browns' training complex is at 76 Lou Groza Boulevard in Berea, Ohio, a tribute to the team's senior Hall of Famer and his uniform number.

CAREER TOTALS							
G	FGA	FGM	Pct.	XPA	XPM	Pct.	Points
268	481	264	54.9	833	810	97.2	1608

JOHN HANNAH

Full name: **John Allen Hannah**	Position: **Offensive Line**
Date of Birth: **April 4, 1951, Canton, GA**	Ht: **6-2**
College: **Alabama**	Wt: **265**
NFL Teams: **New England Patriots**	

"The best offensive lineman I ever coached."—Alabama coach Bear Bryant

Football was the Hannah family business.

Father Herb was an outstanding player at Alabama and spent a season with the New York Giants. Younger brother Charley spent 12 seasons in the NFL with the Bucs and Raiders.

The best of them all was John Hannah, one of three players drafted in the first round in 1973 by the New England Patriots. That single round got the Patriots two outstanding players (running back Sam Cunningham and receiver Darryl Stingley) and one who was good enough to make the Hall of Fame—John Hannah.

Hannah, who played for 13 years, was considered the premier guard of his time. He was an effective pass protector and he had the speed and agility to lead the blocking on sweeps. Jim Ringo, who coached the Patriots' linemen, compared Hannah favorably to a couple of his Green Bay teammates from the Packers' dynasty days of the 1960s.

"John has better pulling speed than Jerry Kramer and Fuzzy Thurston, even though he's 20 pounds heavier than either of them," Ringo said.

Hannah was a two-time All-American at Alabama and an All Pro for 10 consecutive years with the Patriots. His legendary work ethic was forged at Alabama, where he followed his father.

"Bear Bryant taught us how to win," Hannah said. "He told us a game is usually decided by only four or five plays. You never know when the plays are coming so you have to be ready on every play."

Hannah worked on getting his temper under control after a couple of outbursts that embarrassed him during his rookie season. He conquered that problem but would contend with injuries for much of his career. He only missed five games in 13 years but he played through many injuries.

"To be great you have to forget about pain," he once said.

The Patriots reached the Super Bowl for the first time in what turned out to be Hannah's last season. That summer, he underwent surgery on both of his shoulders and decided to retire before the start of the new season.

CAREER TOTALS
G
183

FRANCO HARRIS

Full name: **Franco Harris**	Position: **Running Back**
Date of Birth: **March 5, 1950, Fort Dix, NJ**	Ht: **6-2**
College: **Penn State**	Wt: **225**
NFL Teams: **Pittsburgh Steelers, Seattle Seahawks**	

"Franco was the differcnoc. He gave us confidence. With him carrying the football, we knew we could play with anybody."—Joe Greene

People sometimes tried to link Franco Harris' mellow personality to a lack of desire on the football field. That was a big mistake.

Harris was a notoriously poor practice player who was spectacularly unimpressive in training camp as a rookie with the Steelers. But when the game started, Harris was as intense as any player and his fervor increased as the stakes rose.

Harris was the fullback at Penn State when halfback Lydell Mitchell was piling up yards. Even though Harris gained 2,002 yards over three college seasons, he was perceived as something of an underachiever, a player who didn't have the inner fire needed to be great.

The Steelers chose him in the first round in 1972 with the 13th overall pick. Steelers legend holds that head coach Chuck Noll wanted Robert Newhouse but was overruled by the scouting staff. Newhouse went to Dallas while Harris went to the Hall of Fame on the first ballot.

Harris was a sensation as a Steelers rookie. The team reached the postseason for the first time and Harris was a big part of an offense geared almost exclusively to the running game. He was the son of a black army officer and his Italian war bride, which inspired a fan club. "Franco's Italian Army" made Harris a folk hero in Pittsburgh.

Two days before Christmas in 1972, Harris was involved in the greatest play in NFL history. He picked off a deflected Terry Bradshaw pass and ran for the winning touchdown against the Oakland Raiders in a playoff game. It came to be known as "The Immaculate Reception."

Harris had eight 1,000-yard seasons, including six in a row. That streak went from 1974-79, which coincided with the Steelers' four Super Bowl victories. He was the Most Valuable Player of Super Bowl IX after rushing for 158 yards against Minnesota. He ran for 343 yards in three 1974 postseason games.

Harris left the Steelers in a contract dispute and spent his last year with Seattle.

CAREER TOTALS						
G	Rush	Yds	Avg	TD	Lg	
172	2949	12120	4.1	91	-	
Rec	Yds	Avg	TD	Lg	Total TD	Points
307	2287	7.4	9	-	100	600

MIKE HAYNES

Full name: **Michael James Haynes**	Position: **Cornerback**
Date of Birth: **July 1, 1953**	Ht: **6-2**
College: **Arizona State**	Wt: **195**
NFL Teams: **New England Patriots, Los Angeles Raiders**	

"Mike Haynes played man-to-man better than anyone."

—Oakland Raiders Hall of Fame cornerback Willie Brown

Conventional wisdom holds that a team should always attack the least experienced player in the secondary.

That strategy was practiced against Mike Haynes, even though he was a first-round draft choice of the New England Patriots. After he intercepted eight passes, opponents got the idea this was one time conventional wisdom wasn't so wise.

Haynes demonstrated early that he was a special player. No defensive back had been taken as early in the draft since 1963.

Haynes had been a standout at Arizona State University where Coach Frank Kush quickly discovered what a luxury he had. He could always assign Haynes to the opposing team's best receiver for one-on-one coverage. That left the safety free to help the other cornerback or blitz.

His performance in a high-profile program led the Patriots to make Haynes the fifth player taken overall in the 1976 draft. He had the speed, reflexes and range to make the adjustment to the pro game. In addition to his work in the secondary, he was also an effective punt returner. His 608 return yards led the American Conference in 1976. The Patriots had never had a punt returned for a touchdown until Haynes arrived in New England. He had returns of 89 and 62 yards for touchdowns in his first season.

Haynes intercepted seven passes within four weeks as a rookie. Opponents decided to stay away from Haynes' side of the field. New England coach Chuck Fairbanks recalled a stretch of three weeks where only one pass was thrown in Haynes' direction.

The secret to his success was watching the receiver's belt buckle: By focusing on the center of gravity, he wouldn't get fooled by all the false signals a receiver tried to send.

Haynes played out his option in New England and went to the Raiders in 1983 for the last seven seasons of his career. He added a Super Bowl interception to his long list of accomplishments.

Haynes was voted into the Hall of Fame in 1997.

CAREER TOTALS							
G	Int	Yds	TD	PR	Yds	TD	Points
177	46	688	2	112	1168	2	30

TED HENDRICKS

Full name: **Theodore Paul Hendricks**

Date of Birth: **November 1, 1947, Guatemala**

College: **Miami (FL)**

NFL Teams: **Baltimore Colts, Green Bay Packers, Oakland Raiders, Los Angeles Raiders**

Position: **Linebacker**

Ht: **6-7**

Wt: **222**

"Great players make great plays and I can't think of any defensive player who made more big plays for us than Ted Hendricks."

—Oakland Raiders coach John Madden

Sometimes the measure of Ted Hendricks' impact was in the number of tackles he didn't make.

When he was a standout defensive end at the University of Miami, Penn State's Joe Paterno once directed 14 consecutive offensive plays away from Hendricks. That was the kind of fear and respect he commanded among teams who had seen his ability to dominate games.

Hendricks had freakish size for a linebacker—at 6-foot-7, he is still the tallest player to handle the position in the NFL. He used that size to great advantage since he could get in the way of passes that would sail over more conventionally sized linebackers. He was also credited with blocking 25 kicks in his 15-year career. His tall, gangly frame and aggressive play earned him the nickname "The Mad Stork."

Born in Guatemala, Hendricks came to Florida at an early age and was a multi-sport star, excelling at track, basketball and baseball in addition to football. He landed at the University of Miami, where he was a physics major who relaxed by solving complex math problems.

The Baltimore Colts drafted him in the second round in 1969 and he became a starter midway through his rookie season. When he signed a future contract with the upstart World Football League, the Colts dealt him to Green Bay. Hendricks spent one season with the Packers. By the time he was supposed to switch leagues, the WFL didn't exist any more and he was an NFL free agent.

He signed with the Raiders and was a key part of their defense. In all, he played in four Super Bowls—one with the Colts and three with the Raiders. He also appeared in seven conference championship games. Fittingly, his last pro game was Super Bowl XVIII.

The Miami Quarterback Club annually gives the Ted Hendricks award to college football's best defensive end. Hendricks was elected to the Hall of Fame in 1990.

CAREER TOTALS

G	Sacks	FR	Int	Yds	Avg	Total TD	Points
215	9.0	16	26	332	12.8	4	32

ELROY (CRAZY LEGS) HIRSCH

Full name: **Elroy Leon Hirsch**
Date of Birth: **June 17, 1923, Wausau, WI**
Died: **January 28, 2004**
College: **Wisconsin**
NFL Teams: **Los Angeles Rams**

Position: **Wide Receiver**
Ht: **6-2**
Wt: **190**

"He ran like a demented duck. His crazy legs were gyrating in six different directions all at the same time during a 61-yard touchdown run."
—*Chicago Daily News* writer Francis Powers

With that bit of colorful newspaper hyperbole, Elroy Hirsch forever became "Crazy Legs," a nickname that would stick with him even when he wore a suit and tie during a long career as Wisconsin's athletic director.

The flashy name was a symbol of what players were doing to the staid NFL. Most teams featured running offenses that were efficient but weren't necessarily interesting to watch. Some teams were relying more on passing but none took it to the extreme that the Los Angeles Rams did. Maybe their offense reflected their Hollywood surroundings. The Rams didn't just play winning football, they put on a show.

Hirsch was perfectly suited for the Rams' strategy. He had the speed of a sprinter and he had a running back's ability to evade tacklers. The Rams came to realize how dangerous he was when he led the College All-Stars to a victory over the NFL champion Rams in 1946.

Hirsch teamed effectively with Tom Fears and they were the main cogs in the Rams' innovative three-end offense that debuted in 1949.

Because of his attention-getting nickname, the Rams' success and their proximity to the film-making capital of the world, Hirsch even found work in the movies during his time with Los Angeles but the moonlighting didn't affect his production on the football field. In 1951, he had 17 touchdown receptions. He set NFL receiving records with his performance that season: 66 receptions and 1,495 yards as he led Los Angeles to the NFL title.

Hirsch played through 1957, then started a second career in athletic administration. He spent a year as the Rams general manager, then later headed the athletic department at Wisconsin, one of his two alma maters.

Hirsch was voted into the Pro Football Hall of Fame in 1968.

CAREER TOTALS							
G	Rec	Yds	Avg	TD	Lg		
127	387	7029	18.2	60	91t		
Rush	Yds	Avg	TD	Lg	Total TD	Points	
207	687	3.3	4	51	64	393	

KEN HOUSTON

Full name: **Kenneth Ray Houston**	Position: **Defensive Back**
Date of Birth: **November 12, 1944, Lufkin, Texas**	Ht: **6-3**
College: **Prairie View**	Wt: **197**
NFL Teams: **Houston Oilers, Washington Redskins**	

"How many times do you have a chance to watch the best there ever was at a position? Washington has had eight years to appreciate Kenny."

—Washington Redskins coach George Allen

There was no doubt George Allen thought highly of Ken Houston.

Allen traded five players, including two regulars, to the Houston Oilers to acquire Houston in 1973. Houston was a six-year veteran who had been a standout for the Oilers, exactly the kind of proven player Allen always wanted.

The deal worked out better for Washington than it did for Houston. The Oilers only got one player of any consequence in the trade while Houston helped solidify the Redskins secondary for a series of title runs.

Houston was a lanky player who wasn't taken until the ninth round in 1967. Although he played safety, his unique talents made him an in-between defensive back. He had the skills to cover receivers one-on-one but his experience at linebacker in college also allowed him to provide run support.

In 1971, Houston had an NFL-record nine interceptions and returned four of them for touchdowns. He intercepted 49 passes in his career and returned them for 898 yards and nine touchdowns. He also scored on a returned blocked field goal, a fumble recovery and a punt return. Houston played in 10 Pro Bowls.

He made his impact very early in his career with Washington. The Redskins were playing the rival Dallas Cowboys on *Monday Night Football* on Oct. 8, 1973. Houston stopped Cowboys' running back Walt Garrison at the 1-yard line on a fourth-and-goal play from the 6 with 24 seconds left. His tackle prevented the Cowboys from scoring the tying touchdown and preserved Washington's 14-7 lead. The single play became a defining moment in his career.

"The minute you say Kenny Houston, people say Walt Garrison," Houston said.

During his playing career, Houston won the Byron "Whizzer" White Humanitarian Award. Now there is a similar award named for Houston as a tribute to his work off the field.

He was voted into the Pro Football Hall of Fame in 1986.

CAREER TOTALS							
G	Int	Yds	Avg	FR	Sacks	Total TD	Points
196	49	898	18.3	21	0.0	12	72

SAM HUFF

Full name: **Robert Lee Huff**	Position: **Linebacker**
Date of Birth: **Oct. 4, 1934, Edna Gas, WV**	Ht: **6-1**
College: **West Virginia**	Wt: **230**
NFL Teams: **New York Giants, Washington Redskins**	

"I wanted to rattle a guy's teeth."—Sam Huff

Tom Landry and Vince Lombardi were instrumental figures in Sam Huff's NFL career.

That was ironic because both coaches would end up as opponents, spending considerable time creating game plans designed to cope with Huff's presence on defense.

Landry and Lombardi were assistants on the New York Giants staff when Huff arrived in 1956 as the team's third-round draft pick. At 6-foot-1 and 230 pounds, he was too small for the defensive line. There were questions about whether he was quick enough for linebacker.

Landry decided to slot him at middle linebacker, which was a spot for aggressive players who could make good decisions quickly. The Giants switched to the 4-3 defense in Huff's rookie season. Lombardi's contribution? He tracked down Huff at the airport when the rookie tried to leave his first training camp, convinced he wouldn't make the team. He came back at Lombardi's urging and settled in for a Hall of Fame career.

"Sam really wrote the book on how to play middle linebacker in the 4-3 defense," teammate Andy Robustelli said.

Huff had been a two-way standout at West Virginia University. His fierce style was backed with plenty of study. Jim Brown once said Huff was "addicted to detail."

Being in the nation's media capital helped make Huff a household name. In 1959, CBS put a microphone on him during games and assembled a documentary "The Violent World of Sam Huff" that was narrated by Walter Cronkite. The Giants were among the NFL's elite teams at the time and Giants fans rocked Yankee Stadium by repeatedly chanting Huff's name when he made tackles.

Huff played in six NFL title games and five Pro Bowls. In 1964, he was 29 and seemingly at the peak of his career. He was shocked to learn he'd been traded to the Washington Redskins. He played four more seasons with the Redskins, then retired after 1967. He came back in 1969 as a player and assistant coach after Lombardi took over the Redskins, showing loyalty to the man who saved his career 13 years earlier.

CAREER TOTALS							
G	Sacks	FR	Int	Yds	Avg	Total TD	Points
168	0.0	17	30	381	12.7	5	30

DON HUTSON

Full name: **Donald Montgomery Hutson**	Position: **Receiver**
Date of Birth: **January 31, 1913, Pine Bluff, AR**	Ht: **6-1**
Died: **June 26, 1997**	Wt: **180**
College: **Alabama**	
NFL Teams: **Green Bay Packers**	

"He had all the moves. He invented the moves."

—Green Bay teammate Larry Canadeo

At a time when most teams didn't pass the football, Don Hutson became the prototypical NFL wide receiver. He was swift and lanky, possessed of moves that could get him separation from defenders to catch the passes and avoid their tackles.

In his second game with the Green Bay Packers, Huston showed how the NFL was changing. The defense was geared to stop Johnny (Blood) McNally, the Packers' running threat. Instead, the play was a pass to Hutson that went for an 83-yard touchdown.

Hutson earned a partial baseball scholarship to Alabama and walked on for a spot on the football team. The coaches discovered Hutson's skills were made for the receiver position.

"It looked like he was going as fast as possible when all of a sudden he'd put on an extra burst of speed and be gone," Alabama coach Bear Bryant said.

In the pros, most passes were either inspired by desperation or a desire to take the other team by surprise. Once they had Hutson, the Packers made passing part of their normal plan. The secret to his success was his hard work.

"For every pass I catch in a game, I caught a thousand in practice," Hutson said.

Hutson was the NFL's receiving leader in eight seasons and was an All-NFL player in nine of his 11 years. He was the league's Most Valuable Player in 1941 and '42.

On October 7, 1945, Hutson caught four touchdown passes in one quarter. With five extra points (he was also a placekicker) he scored 29 points in a quarter.

Following his retirement, Hutson joined the Packers coaching staff and later served as a director. Today, the team's indoor training facility bears the name of the man who bewildered opponents and became the league's first great receiver.

Said Pittsburgh coach Walt Kiesling, "No one man can cover Don Hutson. The way you play Hutson is you double-team him—or shoot him."

CAREER TOTALS							
G	Rec	Yds	Avg	TD	Lg		
116	488	7991	16.4	99	75t		
Rush	Yds	Avg	TD	Lg	Total TD	Points	
62	284	4.6	3	27	105	823	

CHARLIE JOINER

Full name: **Charles Joiner Jr.**	Position: **Wide Receiver**
Date of Birth: **October 14, 1947, Many, LA**	Ht: **5-11**
College: **Grambling**	Wt: **180**
NFL Teams: **Houston Oilers, Cincinnati Bengals, San Diego Chargers**	

"The most intelligent, the smartest, calculating receiver the game has ever known."—Hall of Fame coach Bill Walsh

The San Diego Chargers represented the third stop in Charlie Joiner's 18-year NFL career.

It was by far the most enjoyable and not just because of the winter warmth and sunshine of Southern California.

Joiner found himself working with a coach who loved the passing game in Don Coryell and a quarterback (Dan Fouts) who had an unerring knack for finding the open receiver. So Joiner, who had enjoyed a solid career to that point, probably established his Hall of Fame credentials thanks to "Air Coryell," the nickname that the San Diego passing offense was assigned.

At an inch under six feet and just 180 pounds, Joiner was small in a world where receivers seemed to get bigger every year. He had exceptional speed and used a repertoire of great moves to overcome any physical disadvantage against bigger defensive backs.

In fact, nothing pleased him more than studying film and finding a new way to beat an opposing cornerback. "He loved the technical part of the game," said Hall of Fame coach Joe Gibbs, who had been San Diego's offensive coordinator. "He was a totally dedicated guy, a great producer."

Joiner was drafted on the fourth round by Houston in 1969. The Oilers saw him as a defensive back and his limited playing time was on that side of the ball. He also returned kicks.

He moved to Cincinnati in 1972 and stayed for four seasons. He found his place in San Diego, where he spent the final 11 years of his career. He had 50 or more receptions in seven of those seasons and topped 70 catches three times. He was known for running pass routes with precision.

Joiner played in three Pro Bowls and missed just one game in his last 13 years. He continued to play despite chronic knee problems and was named San Diego's most inspirational player seven times. He retired at age 39 in 1986 and was elected to the Hall of Fame in 1996.

CAREER TOTALS

G	Rec	Yds	Avg	TD	Lg		
239	750	12146	16.2	65	-		
Rush	Yds	Avg	TD	Lg	Total TD	Points	
8	22	2.8	0	-	65	390	

DEACON JONES

Full name: **David D. Jones**	Position: **Defensive Line**
Date of Birth: **December 9, 1938, Eatonville, FL**	Ht: **6-5**
College: **Mississippi Valley State**	Wt: **254**
NFL Teams: **Los Angeles Rams, San Diego Chargers, Washington Redskins**	

"You haven't lived until you've had your bell rung by Deacon a few times."
—Hall of Fame offensive lineman Ron Mix

Dave (Deacon) Jones regularly led the NFL in quarterback sacks and colorful comments.

Start with the term "sack." Jones claims to have originated it, borrowing the word from his history classes.

"Like you sack a city," he explained. "You devastate it."

Devastate was a good word to associate with a former 14th round draft pick from Mississippi Valley State. He named himself "Deacon" to get attention that his common given name didn't allow, then proceeded to make himself the focal point on the football field. Jones played defensive end for 14 years and three teams, slashing his way past offensive lineman. He felled a lot of them with his head slap, a technique so brutal it was eventually outlawed. Jones titled his autobiography, "Head Slap."

He said, "I didn't invent the head slap, just like Rembrandt didn't invent painting. But I perfected it. I put the fear of God into the whole league."

His other calling cards were strong legs, quickness and a fierce desire to get to the quarterback. He was the leader of the Los Angeles Rams "Fearsome Foursome," which included Merlin Olsen, Roosevelt Grier and Lamar Lundy.

"We set the pace," Jones said. "We started the trend. We proved that a defensive line can control the game."

Jones spent 11 years with the Rams, two with San Diego and finished with one season in Washington. Sacks didn't become an official statistic until 1969 so some of his best work is not officially recorded. But that's not his career regret.

"I'd kill more quarterbacks," he said. "That's the only thing I could do differently. I couldn't be any nastier. I couldn't have any more intent. The only thing I could do is execute better."

Jones, who retired after 1974, said he's not impressed by the modern NFL.

"They protect everybody now," he grumbled. "The game is not wide open. A lot of the toughness has been taken out of the game."

CAREER TOTALS							
G	Sacks	FR	Int	Yds	Avg	Total TD	Points
191	0.0	15	2	50	25.0	0	5

PAUL KRAUSE

Full name: **Paul James Krause**	Position: **Defensive Back**
Date of Birth: **February 19, 1942, Flint, MI**	Ht: **6-3**
College: **Iowa**	Wt: **199**
NFL Teams: **Washington Redskins, Minnesota Vikings**	

"Paul had the game down to a science. He could turn a game around."
—Vikings coach Bud Grant

Paul Krause grew up in Flint, Michigan, idolizing Mickey Mantle and dreaming of playing center field in the major leagues.

He played center field but he didn't do it on a baseball field.

As a free safety, Krause had responsibility for covering the middle of the field, reading the quarterback and trying to get to the spot the ball was headed. Football people have a term for that assignment.

"We wanted him to act as our center fielder," Bud Grant said. "He could read a quarterback as well as any defensive back."

Krause was a multiple sport athlete who was likely headed for baseball if it hadn't been for a shoulder injury he sustained while playing football. Krause liked baseball better than football and a number of major league teams were offering him bonuses to sign. The shoulder injury took away his ability to throw so he turned to football and became a two-way star at the University of Iowa.

The Washington Redskins drafted him on the second round in 1964 and installed him as a starter. He led the NFL with 12 interceptions and played in the first of his eight Pro Bowls. Krause had a streak of seven games with interceptions. He was runner-up to teammate Charley Taylor in rookie of the year voting.

The Redskins traded him to Minnesota in 1968 for linebacker Marlin McKeever and a second-round draft choice. Krause's career flourished with the Vikings, who had one of the best defenses in the game. Minnesota's line was so strong against the run that Krause rarely had to get involved in that aspect of the game. He was free to play center field.

His 81 career interceptions broke Emlen Tunnell's NFL record of 79 and the 53 he had for the Vikings are that team's record. In his first year with the Vikings, Krause had interceptions in six consecutive games. Krause, who missed only two games in his 16 seasons, gained 1,185 yards on interception returns. He was elected to the Hall of Fame in 1998.

CAREER TOTALS							
G	Int	Yds	Avg	FR	Sacks	Total TD	Points
226	81	1185	14.6	19	0.0	6	36

JACK LAMBERT

Full name: **John Harold Lambert**

Date of Birth: **July 8, 1952, Mantua, OH**

College: **Kent State**

NFL Teams: **Pittsburgh Steelers**

Position: **Linebacker**

Ht: **6-4**

Wt: **220**

"Jack was a full-time competitor and that's what made him stand out."

—Pittsburgh Steelers Coach Chuck Noll

He was a fearsome sight on the football field—piercing eyes, missing front teeth, snarl clearly visible behind the facemask, blood stains blotted on his gold uniform pants.

It was scary enough watching Jack Lambert on television so just imagine what it was like to line up against him.

Lambert had more going for him than a motor that constantly ran at full speed. He was fast and athletic, a student of the game who dutifully prepared.

The Steelers took Lambert from Kent State on the second round of a 1974 draft that directly helped them win four Super Bowls. Shortly after he was drafted, Lambert took the initiative to show up at the Steelers offices without being required to report. He wanted to get a head start on learning the defense.

He was instantly installed as a starter, playing between Andy Russell and Jack Ham to form one of the league's best linebacking trios.

For all the obvious big hits, one of the secrets to Lambert's success was his amazing range. The Steelers were able to put him in coverage 30 yards downfield, the kind of assignment very few run-stuffing middle linebackers of that era could handle.

Lambert intercepted 28 passes, recovered 15 fumbles and played in nine consecutive Pro Bowls from 1975-83. He called the signals for one of the most dominating defenses in NFL history. He also set a tone that could intimidate opponents.

Away from the field, Lambert was quiet and intensely private but when it came time to play he was the perfect fit for Pittsburgh, a town that embraced smash-mouth football long before anyone ever thought of that term. He was fierce competitor who was always quick to respond whenever an opponent tried to take liberties with any Steeler.

As he said in his 1990 Hall of Fame enshrinement speech, "If I could start my life all over again, I would be a professional football player...and you damn well better believe I would be a Pittsburgh Steeler."

CAREER TOTALS							
G	Sacks	FR	Int	Yds	Avg	Total TD	Points
146	8.0	17	28	243	8.7	0	0

DICK (NIGHT TRAIN) LANE

Full name: **Richard Lane**

Date of Birth: **April 16, 1927, Austin, TX**

Died: **January 29, 2003**

College: **Scottsbluff J.C.**

NFL Teams: **Los Angeles Rams, Chicago**

Cardinals, Detroit Lions

Position: **Defensive Back**

Ht: **6-3**

Wt: **194**

"Train will always be the Godfather of cornerbacks."

—Hall of Fame member Lem Barney

Night Train Lane had everything a team wanted in a cornerback, starting with his attitude.

Lane was a gambler who would take risks to make big plays. The fact he's in the Hall of Fame shows he knew how to play the odds. His trademark clothesline-style tackle—the "Night Train Necktie"—was judged to be too brutal by the NFL, which outlawed it.

That didn't slow down Lane, who was still one of the game's most fierce tacklers. At 6-foot-3 and 195 pounds, he was bigger than most of the receivers he covered. He had an unerring sense for the ball, too. In his rookie year, he set an NFL record by intercepting 14 passes. That was in a 12-game season. The record stood, even though the NFL eventually expanded the schedule to 16 games.

Lane overcame tough circumstances. He was abandoned as a child and adopted at age three. He didn't go to college but instead played at a junior college. He spent four years in the Army and then went to work in an aircraft factory. When he tired of that job, he asked the Los Angeles Rams for a tryout. Lane wound up playing 15 seasons with the Rams, Chicago Cardinals and Detroit Lions. He intercepted 68 passes, returned them for 1,207 yards and impressed almost everyone he played against.

"I played with him and against him and he's the best I've ever seen," Pat Summerall said.

When Weeb Ewbank coached the Baltimore Colts, he ordered Johnny Unitas to avoid throwing passes to Lane's side of the field.

"Night Train Lane was the best defensive back to ever play the game," Green Bay's Herb Adderley said.

Lane was married for a time to singer Dinah Washington. After football, he worked as the road manager for comedian Redd Foxx and had a couple of college coaching jobs.

His mellifluous nickname came about because he visited a teammate's room in training camp when the song "Night Train" was on the phonograph.

CAREER TOTALS

G	Int	Yds	Avg	FR	Sacks	Total TD	Points
157	68	1207	17.8	11	0.0	8	50

WILLIE LANIER

Full name: **William Edward Lanier**	Position: **Linebacker**
Date of Birth: **August 21, 1945, Clover, VA**	Ht: **6-1**
College: **Morgan State**	Wt: **245**
NFL Teams: **Kansas City Chiefs**	

"His destiny was to be the prototype linebacker of his era."

—Kansas City Chiefs owner Lamar Hunt

Willie Lanier was always easy to spot on the football field. You just had to look for the ball and chances are Lanier would be there.

He was a fierce middle linebacker for the Kansas City Chiefs and always seemed to be involved in the play. He was the Chiefs' defensive leader, a man whose hard-hitting tackles earned him the nickname "Contact" from teammates.

Was it what like to be tackled by Lanier? Hewritt Dixon of the Oakland Raiders, the Chiefs' traditional rivals, had a colorful description of the experience:

"It really wasn't much," Dixon told reporters. "Part of me landed one place and the rest of me landed somewhere else. I pulled myself together and went on just like a mountain had never fallen on me."

Another reason Lanier was easy to spot was the big roll padding he wore around the neck of his jersey. That was a concession to head and neck injuries he'd sustained over his career. But even with those problems, Lanier only missed five games in 11 years.

He became a linebacker in high school after a coach noticed his exceptional ability to move laterally. The position was perfect for Lanier, especially playing in the middle. He was constantly involved and he loved the action. He had good hands and enjoyed the challenge of providing pass coverage. He intercepted 27 passes and recovered 15 fumbles.

Lanier had another nickname—"Honey Bear"—which reflected his easy-going, thoughtful nature away from the football field.

He made up his mind that he wanted to attend Morgan State and he went there, even though no scholarship was available. Lanier financed his first semester with loans and a work-study program, then earned the scholarship.

The Chiefs chose him on the second round of the 1967 draft and he quickly worked his way into the lineup. He played in six Pro Bowls and was elected to the Pro Football Hall of Fame in 1986.

CAREER TOTALS							
G	Sacks	FR	Int	Yds	Avg	Total TD	Points
149	0.0	18	27	440	16.3	2	14

STEVE LARGENT

Full name: **Stephen Michael Largent**	Position: **Receiver**
Date of Birth: **September 28, 1954, Tulsa, OK**	Ht: **5-11**
College: **Tulsa**	Wt: **184**
NFL Teams: **Seattle Seahawks**	

"He manipulates defensive backs. He dissects them."—teammate Kenny Easley.

Steve Largent's football career was almost over before it started. Largent reported for tryouts at his high school but became discouraged when he saw 150 candidates there, many of them bigger and faster than he was. He decided to give up his hope of playing for the varsity.

His mother encouraged him to stick with it, a bit of parental advice that had an impact on the NFL record books. Largent's sure hands and ability to get open helped him to 819 receptions over 14 seasons with the Seattle Seahawks. He earned election to the Pro Football Hall of Fame in 1995.

Largent's pro career got off to a rough start, too. He was drafted in the fourth round in 1976 by Houston. The Oilers didn't have a spot for him but Seattle assistant Jerry Rhome had coached Largent in college at Tulsa and recommended that the Seahawks deal for him.

Largent caught 54 passes as a rookie with the expansion Seahawks, the first of 10 seasons in which he would catch at least 50 passes. There were six years when he had at least 70 receptions.

Consistency was his trademark. Largent set an NFL record by catching passes in 177 consecutive games. He led the NFL in receiving twice and played in seven Pro Bowls.

Oakland Raiders defensive back Lester Hayes called Largent "the master of tomfoolery." Largent was never as fast or big as other NFL receivers, so he had to rely on technique. He would study defensive backs, looking for any edge he could find.

Seahawks GM Mike McCormack always believed that Largent promoted the idea that he didn't have exceptional size or speed so opponents who would then underrate his ability.

Seattle Coach Chuck Knox offered this assessment of Largent's attributes: "He has lateral quickness, great balance, body control, tremendous hand/eye coordination and great hands."

After football, Largent served two terms in the U.S. House of Representatives and unsuccessfully ran for governor of Oklahoma.

CAREER TOTALS

G	Rec	Yds	Avg	TD	Lg	
200	**819**	**13089**	**16.0**	**100**	**74t**	
Rush	Yds	Avg	TD	Lg	Total TD	Points
17	**83**	**4.9**	**1**	**21**	**101**	**608**

BOB LILLY

Full name: **Robert Lewis Lilly**	Position: **Defensive Line**
Date of Birth: **July 26, 1939, Olney, TX**	Ht: **6-5**
College: **Texas Christian**	Wt: **260**
NFL Teams: **Dallas Cowboys, Los Angeles Rams**	

"A player like Bob Lilly comes along once in a coach's lifetime."—Tom Landry

Bob Lilly was the Dallas Cowboys' first draft choice ever and that was appropriate.

No one symbolized the franchise more than Lilly, a Texas native who played collegiate football at Texas Christian and spent his entire 14-year NFL career with the Cowboys.

Lilly missed only one game in his career and was there for the Cowboys' transition from ragged expansion outfit to "America's Team," a powerhouse with an aura that helped cultivate a national fan base.

He was a fixture at defensive tackle, although he played end for two seasons. Lilly was big (6-foot-5 and 260 pounds) but extremely agile. He was quick and Landry said he had the ability to consistently break through a first block. Playing against Lilly almost always meant a double-team strategy was required and that freed another Cowboys player to make plays.

One of the reasons Landry held him in such regard was Lilly's intelligence and ability to absorb new concepts. When the Cowboys debuted their Flex defense, Lilly was able to handle the unconventional strategy that allowed the Cowboys to maximize their personnel.

Lilly was one of the players most likely spend extra time studying game films and developing techniques specific to one opponent. He had ability and size but he also had a plan every time he stepped on the field.

"He knew before the snap where the ball was going all the time," said Marion Campbell, a former Cowboys assistant coach. "He was a big-time playmaker who made things happen."

The most famous play of Lilly's long career came in the Super Bowl against the Miami Dolphins. Lilly and teammate Larry Cole broke through the line and chased quarterback Bob Griese, sacking him for a loss of 29 yards.

Lilly retired after the 1974 season and became the first Cowboys player to be elected to the Hall of Fame in 1980. His was also the first name placed on the Cowboys' Ring of Honor at Texas Stadium. Lilly went on to publish a book of his photographs called "Reflections."

CAREER TOTALS							
G	Sacks	FR	Int	Yds	Avg	Total TD	Points
196	0.0	18	1	17	17.0	4	24

RONNIE LOTT

Full name: **Ronald Mandel Lott**
Date of Birth: **May 8, 1959, Albuquerque, NM**
College: **Southern California**
NFL Teams: **San Francisco 49ers, Los Angeles Raiders, New York Jets**

Position: **Defensive Back**
Ht: **6-1**
Wt: **203**

"He's like a middle linebacker playing safety. He's devastating. He may dominate the secondary better than anyone I've ever seen."
—Dallas Cowboys Coach Tom Landry

Ronnie Lott played for three different teams and played three different positions. The one constant was his excellence.

Lott was an All Pro player at three different positions—cornerback, strong safety and free safety—and a big reason why the San Francisco 49ers were the dominant team of the 1990s.

As 49ers president Carmen Policy explained it, "If Joe Montana was the heart of the team, then Ronnie Lott was the backbone."

Lott was the 49ers top draft pick in 1981, the eighth player chosen in the draft. He was a cornerback at Southern California and left corner was where Lott started with the 49ers. He was an immediate starter and finished second to New York Giants linebacker Lawrence Taylor in the Rookie of the Year voting.

His arrival coincided with the building program Coach Bill Walsh had launched. Lott was one of three rookie starters in the secondary that season, yet the 49ers went on to win their first Super Bowl.

Lott spent three more seasons at cornerback, then moved to safety. The theory—which proved to be true—was that Lott would be even more effective placed in a role where he was free to roam more of the field. He was a fierce tackler and had a habit of involving himself in the play. The position change was something of a gamble but the move worked.

In 1986 Lott intercepted 10 passes to tie a San Francisco franchise record. Lott collected three more Super Bowl championship rings with the 49ers before he left for the Los Angeles Raiders in 1991. He spent two seasons there, then moved east and ended his career with the New York Jets, playing for two years.

Lott had five seasons with at least 100 tackles, twice led the NFL in interceptions and was named to 10 Pro Bowl squads.

He was voted into the Hall of Fame in 2000.

CAREER TOTALS							
G	Int	Yds	Avg	FR	Sacks	Total TD	Points
192	63	730	11.6	17	8.5	5	30

SID LUCKMAN

Full name: **Sidney Luckman**	Position: **Quarterback**
Date of Birth: **November 21, 1916, Brooklyn, NY**	Ht: **6-0**
Died: **July 5, 1998**	Wt: **197**
College: **Columbia**	
NFL Teams: **Chicago Bears**	

"Sid made himself a great quarterback. No one else did it for him."
—George Halas

It may have taken Sid Luckman a while to get used to the quarterback position but he excelled once he grasped the basics.

Luckman was the player Halas wanted to run the Bears offense in an age when the forward pass was becoming an important part of the NFL game. The Pittsburgh Steelers drafted the Brooklyn-born Luckman from Columbia in 1939 and immediately traded him to Chicago.

He wasn't the classic quarterback type. At 6-foot and 195 pounds, he had a stocky build. Luckman initially had trouble adjusting to the responsibilities of the T-formation quarterback. He moved to halfback and stayed there for much of his rookie season. He spent time learning the quarterback position and eventually took over, which is why Halas described him as a self-made player.

"He worked hard, staying up nights studying and he really learned the T," Halas said.

Luckman and Washington's Sammy Baugh were at the forefront of the passing explosion. Fans loved the new wide-open game after years of watching football that was characterized by three yards and a cloud of dust.

Luckman was with the Bears from 1939-50 and the team failed to contend in just one of those seasons. During his stay, Chicago won four NFL championships, the first coming in 1940. That was the year of the famous 73-0 Bears win over Baugh's Redskins in the championship game.

On November 14, 1945, Luckman was honored with a day in his native New York City before a game against the Giants at the Polo Grounds. He made sure it was a memorable experience for all concerned, throwing for seven touchdowns. In the 1945 championship game against the Redskins, Luckman threw five touchdown passes.

Luckman was voted into the Hall of Fame in 1965.

CAREER TOTALS								
G	Att	Cmp	Pct.	Yds	TD	Y/A	Lg	Int
128	1744	904	51.8	14686	137	8.42	86t	132
Rush	Yds	Avg	TD	Lg	Total TD	Points	Rating	
204	-239	-1.2	4	40t	6	37	75.0	

JOHN MACKEY

Full name: **John Mackey**	Position: **Tight End**
Date of Birth: **Sept. 24, 1941, New York, NY**	Ht: **6-3**
College: **Syracuse**	Wt: **222**
NFL Teams: **Baltimore Colts, San Diego Chargers**	

"I'd catch the ball and just be ready to hurt someone."—John Mackey

John Mackey had the hands and speed of wide receiver and the body of an offensive lineman.

No wonder he's credited with being the prototype for the modern tight end.

Mackey had the ability to outrun the linebackers who tried to cover him and the strength to run over the defensive backs who tried to tackle him. Until then, most tight ends had been adjunct offensive linemen, blockers who could catch the occasional short pass.

New York City native Mackey, 6-foot-3 and 222 pounds, changed that. He was part of the Baltimore Colts teams that were regular contenders in the 1960s and a favorite large target for quarterbacks Johnny Unitas and Earl Morrall.

Mackey grew up idolizing Jim Brown, which influenced his decision to attend Syracuse. Once his college career ended, Mackey dreamed of playing for his hometown team. He was the ultimate New Yorker, born in a taxi on the way to the hospital. But the Giants passed and the Colts took Mackey on the second round of the draft, the 19th player chosen overall. Happy as he was in Baltimore, the Giants' snub stuck with him. Once, after catching a touchdown pass against the Giants, Mackey held the ball aloft and shouted to New York coach Allie Sherman, "Why didn't you draft me?"

That kind of aggressiveness helped Mackey on and off the field. In 1966, Mackey scored six touchdowns that covered at least 50 yards, partly because of his ability to fight off would-be tacklers.

Off the field, he was the president of the NFL Players Association and was at the forefront of fighting to get players a better system that included some form of true free agency. Mackey's efforts resulted in the temporary rescinding of the "Rozelle Rule," which held that teams losing free agents were entitled to compensation from the player's new team. The controversy may have been a factor in his waiting until 1992 for Hall of Fame induction, his 15th year of eligibility.

CAREER TOTALS

G	Rec	Yds	Avg	TD	Lg	
139	**331**	**5236**	**15.8**	**38**	**89t**	
Rush	Yds	Avg	TD	Lg	Total TD	Points
19	**127**	**6.7**	**0**	**33**	**38**	**228**

GINO MARCHETTI

Full name: **Gino John Marchetti**

Date of Birth: **January 2, 1927, Smithers, WV**

College: **San Francisco**

NFL Teams: **Dallas Texans, Baltimore Colts**

Position: **Defensive Line**

Ht: **6-4**

Wt: **245**

"It's a waste of time to run around this guy's end. It's a lost play. You don't bother to try it."—Hall of Fame coach Sid Gillman

Gino Marchetti became a football player almost by accident, yet still managed to fashion a Hall of Fame career with the Baltimore Colts.

He played defensive end from 1952-64 and came back briefly in 1966. He was selected for 11 consecutive Pro Bowls and was frequently the target of double-team blocking because of his ability to get to the quarterback.

Marchetti was born in West Virginia but his family soon moved to northern California in search of better opportunities. He served in combat during World War II and played semi-pro football after he returned home. A recruiter from Modesto Junior College spotted him and invited him to tag along on a visit the school had arranged for Marchetti's brother and a family friend.

From that modest beginning, he advanced to the University of San Francisco and was a standout for coach Joe Kuharich. He was drafted by the Dallas Texans and played one season there before the franchise moved to Baltimore and became the Colts. He played offensive tackle—a position he disliked—until the Colts new head coach Weeb Ewbank shifted him to defensive end.

Marchetti was made for the position. He was rangy and exceptionally tough to block. He was quick off the ball and confessed later that he was probably offside on a lot of plays because he'd penetrated the neutral zone before the ball was snapped. Marchetti had incredibly strong hands and could often toss aside blockers.

Marchetti was tough, too. He once played a half with a separated shoulder and came back to the lineup just two weeks after he'd undergone an appendectomy.

He retired in 1964 but returned for four games in November of 1966 when the Colts were depleted by injuries. At the advice of owner Carroll Rosenbloom, Marchetti was one of several players who invested in fast-food restaurants. The company he started wound up selling for more than $48 million. Later, Marchetti took up competitive fishing.

CAREER TOTALS							
G	Sacks	FR	Int	Yds	Avg	Total TD	Points
161	0.0	13	1	1	1.0	3	20

DAN MARINO

Full name: **Daniel Constantine Marion**
Date of Birth: **Sept. 15, 1961, Pittsburgh, PA**
College: **Pittsburgh**
NFL Teams: **Miami Dolphins**

Position: **Quarterback**
Ht: **6-4**
Wt: **224**

"I don't think Dan believes there's anything he can't do. So far he's been right."—Miami Dolphins receiver Jimmy Cefalo.

Dan Marino is a prime example of what an inexact science NFL scouting is.

He was part of the rich quarterback crop from the 1983 draft and, incredibly, he was the last of the six first-round quarterbacks to be chosen. John Elway was the first overall pick and Jim Kelly was the third of quarterbacks drafted. But Todd Blackledge (Kansas City), Tony Eason (New England) and Ken O'Brien (New York Jets) were all chosen before Marino was.

Asked why the Jets took O'Brien instead of Marino, personnel director Mike Hickey said, "He's a better football player. He has a better arm." Marino spent the next 17 years reminding the Jets of their error.

Some teams were scared away by Marino's disappointing senior season at the University of Pittsburgh. The Dolphins looked at his entire career and saw a big, strong-armed quarterback who compensated for a lack of mobility with an incredibly quick release. Marino was also a confident leader who didn't hesitate to jump on teammates for lackadaisical play.

His assault on the record book began with his first professional start on Oct. 9, 1983 when he passed for 322 yards and three touchdowns. He became the first rookie quarterback to start in the Pro Bowl and was even better the next year, leading the Dolphins all the way to the Super Bowl.

He reached 100 touchdowns faster than anyone. He was also the quickest to reach 200. Marino was the first passer with 50,000 yards and the first with 7,000 passes. An nine-time Pro Bowl selection, he flourished under a pass-first system that coach Don Shula devised. The Dolphins rarely supported him with a running game but Marino still succeeded.

Marino never returned to the Super Bowl. Injuries slowed him later in his career and he chose to retire as a Dolphin, spurning an offer from the Minnesota Vikings. More than 55,000 people attended his farewell tribute in Miami.

CAREER TOTALS								
G	Att	Cmp	Pct.	Yds	TD	Y/A	Lg	Int
242	8358	4967	59.4	61361	420	7.34	85t	252
Rush	Yds	Avg	TD	Lg	Total TD	Points	Rating	
301	87	0.3	9	15	9	54	86.4	

JOE MONTANA

Full name: **Joseph Clifford Montana**

Date of Birth: **June 11, 1956, New Eagle, PA**

College: **Notre Dame**

NFL Teams: **San Francisco 49ers, Kansas City Chiefs**

Position: **Quarterback**

Ht: **6-2**

Wt: **205**

"If you have to win a game or score a touchdown or win a championship, the only guy to get is Joe Montana."—former teammate Randy Cross

People in his hometown of Monongahela, Pennsylvania still talk about Joe Montana's games at Ringgold High School. Of course, they talk about Montana, the basketball player.

He excelled in basketball, baseball and football. His San Francisco 49ers coach Bill Walsh would call Montana one of the best athletes he'd ever seen. As a high school senior, Montana was offered a basketball scholarship by North Carolina State and baseball scouts were watching him closely, too.

Montana was good enough to earn a football scholarship to Notre Dame but wasn't good enough to start right away. The Fighting Irish stockpile talent and Montana was No. 7 on the depth chart when he arrived at South Bend. He became the starter in his junior year.

Then again, his career would be characterized by misjudgments of his talent. The 49ers drafted him in the third round. Montana wasn't tall and he wasn't exceptionally fast. He had a strong arm, great football sense and the poise to calmly confront tough situations with confidence.

One of the favorite stories among the 49ers came from the 1989 Super Bowl when San Francisco trailed the Cincinnati Bengals by three points with 3:20 left. The story holds that Montana called a teammate over and showed him where actor John Candy was sitting.

Montana led 31 come-from-behind fourth quarter wins. He pulled games out often enough that the unlikely wins came to be called "Montana Magic." He was with the 49ers for three Super Bowls and 11 playoff seasons. He left San Francisco after 1992 and spent his last two years with the Kansas City Chiefs. Montana retired after the 1994 season.

"It started to become a job," he said. "I still enjoyed Sundays but the other part was difficult."

Montana was elected to the Hall of Fame in 2002.

CAREER TOTALS

G	Att	Cmp	Pct.	Yds	TD	Y/A	Lg	Int
192	5391	3409	63.2	40551	273	7.52	96t	139
Rush	Yds	Avg	TD	Lg	Total TD	Points	Rating	
457	1676	3.7	20	21	20	120	92.3	

MARION MOTLEY

Full name: **Marion Motley**

Date of Birth: **June 5, 1920, Leesburg, GA**

Died: **June 27, 1999**

College: **Nevada, South Carolina State**

NFL Teams: **Cleveland Browns, Pittsburgh Steelers**

Position: **Running Back**

Ht: **6-1**

Wt: **238**

"No one ever cared more about his team and whether it won or lost, rather than caring about how many yards he gained."—Paul Brown

In many ways, Marion Motley was professional football's version of Jackie Robinson.

He was one of the league's first black players and the first black to be elected to the Hall of Fame. Like his baseball counterpart Robinson, that distinction came with indignities and hostility. Motley and Bill Willis joined the Cleveland Browns at the same time as Paul Brown quietly broke an unofficial color line that had been in effect for 30 years. Some players deliberately stepped on their hands or otherwise tried to rough them up when Willis and Motley found themselves at the bottom of the pile after a tackle.

Motley could handle rough tactics. He was solidly built at 6-foot-1 and 238 pounds and was a exceptional pass blocker. "He was pretty big," Browns center Frank Gatski said. "And he was pretty bad." When Motley wasn't carrying the ball, his role on the Browns was to stay in the backfield and protect quarterback Otto Graham from blitzes. Motley did the job so well that he came to be known as Graham's personal bodyguard.

He did more than that, though. Motley led the NFL in rushing in 1950, the Browns' first year in the NFL after the All-American Football Conference had ended. That helped answer some of the questions about the quality of personnel in the "other" league.

Motley had played for Brown at the Great Lakes Naval Training Center. He turned down a chance to play football for a more secure job in a mill. Later, though, he tried out for the Browns and was a rookie at age 26.

He quickly became famous for running the draw play, using his size to power through defenses. Motley also played linebacker and Brown maintained he merited All Pro consideration there, too. Motley retired after the 1953 season, then tried a brief comeback with Pittsburgh as a linebacker in 1955. He was elected to the Hall of Fame in 1968.

CAREER TOTALS						
G	Rush	Yds	Avg	TD	Lg	
106	828	4720	5.7	31	69t	
Rec	Yds	Avg	TD	Lg	Total TD	Points
85	1107	13.0	7	68t	38	228

ANTHONY MUNOZ

Full name: **Michael Anthony Munoz**	Position: **Offensive Line**
Date of Birth: **August 19, 1958, Ontario, CA**	Ht: **6-6**
College: **Southern California**	Wt: **285**
NFL Teams: **Cincinnati Bengals**	

"I thought he was special from the beginning. It turned out he was."
—Former Cincinnati Bengals coach Forrest Gregg

Forrest Gregg, himself a Hall of Fame offensive lineman, quickly learned how good Munoz was.

When the Bengals were considering drafting Munoz on the first round, Gregg went to the Southern California campus to conduct a personal workout. When the coach picked himself off the turf, he certified Munoz as worthy of the first pick.

In addition to his massive size, Munoz had a solid work ethic. After knee surgery he came home and jumped rope on one leg to maintain his conditioning. Munoz's starting position was guaranteed but he never took his job for granted.

"He played like he was always trying to work his way into a starting slot," teammate Max Montoya said.

Munoz played in 11 consecutive Pro Bowls and was the NFL's offensive lineman of the year three times. He had massive legs but quick feet and was agile despite three knee surgeries. His tremendous strength helped him clear lanes for running backs and protect his quarterbacks.

Because of knee injuries, Munoz played only one full game in his senior season at USC. Still, the Bengals didn't hesitate to call his name when their turn came in the 1980 draft.

"The guy was so big and so good it was a joke," Bengals founder Paul Brown said.

Munoz wasn't allowed to play Pop Warner football in his native California because he was too big. He was a standout baseball pitcher and chose USC because the coaching staff was willing to let him substitute varsity baseball for spring football practice. Munoz pitched for USC's national championship baseball team as a sophomore. It was the only year he was able to play baseball. Knee problems prevented him from playing in other seasons.

Munoz was also used by the Bengals as a receiver on tackle-eligible plays. He had four career touchdown receptions.

The bad knees and pounding of the NFL caught up with him after 13 seasons and Munoz played his last game in 1992. He was elected to the Hall of Fame in 1998.

CAREER TOTALS
G
185

BRONKO NAGURSKI

Full name: **Bronislaw Nagurski**

Date of Birth: **Nov. 3, 1908, Rainy River, Ontario**

Died: **January 7, 1990**

College: **Minnesota**

NFL Teams: **Chicago Bears**

Position: **Running Back**

Ht: **6-2**

Wt: **226**

"There's only one way to defense Nagurski—shoot him before he leaves the locker room."—New York Giants coach Steve Owen

Bronko Nagurski was bigger than most of the linemen who blocked for him.

Coach Owen once said of him, "He was the only back I ever saw run his own interference."

Nagurski was 6-foot-2 and 225 pounds with broad shoulders and huge hands (he wore a size 19 ½ ring). When he got going, defenses had to deal with those shoulders and knees that were churning. To say he was hard to bring down was an understatement.

"When you hit him at the ankles, it was almost like getting an electric shock," Red Grange said. "If you hit him above the ankles, you were likely to get killed."

Nagurski didn't feature a lot of shifty moves because he didn't need them. He moved forward and used his power to get past tacklers. When he didn't carry the ball, he was a blocker. His blocking was one reason Beattie Feathers had the NFL's first 1,000-yard rushing season in 1934.

Nagurski was born in Rainy River, Ontario but grew up across the border in International Falls, Minnesota. He went to the University of Minnesota, where he was a running back and linebacker. He quickly developed a reputation as a tough tackler. But for all his brute force, Nagurski helped bring the forward pass into the pro game. Before he came along, a player had to be five yards behind the line of scrimmage in order to pass the ball.

Nagurski debuted with the Chicago Bears in 1930 and was an all-NFL player from 1932-34. He threw two touchdown passes that helped the Bears win the 1933 title.

Nagurski retired after the 1937 season when the Bears refused to raise his salary from $5,000 to $6,500. He entered the world of professional wrestling with some success before coming back to the Bears as a tackle in 1943 at age 35, helping the team win another title.

Today the best defensive player in college football is given the Bronko Nagurski Award. He was elected to the Hall of Fame in 1963.

CAREER TOTALS						
G	Rush	Yds	Avg	TD	Lg	
97	633	2778	4.4	25	-	
Rec	Yds	Avg	TD	Lg	Total TD	Points
11	134	12.2	0	-	25	154

JOE NAMATH

Full name: **Joseph William Namath**
Date of Birth: **May 31, 1943, Beaver Falls, PA**
College: **Alabama**
NFL Teams: **New York Jets, Los Angeles Rams**

Position: **Quarterback**
Ht: **6-2**
Wt: **200**

"Namath has the presence of a star."—New York Jets owner Sonny Werblin

He came from Beaver Falls, Pennsylvania via Alabama but he was truly Broadway Joe.

Joe Namath was a player made for the stage of New York, a flamboyant quarterback who helped put the Jets and the American Football League on the map. Namath came out of football-rich western Pennsylvania and headed for Alabama and the program run by the legendary Paul (Bear) Bryant. Both professional leagues had tagged him as a future star. The Jets drafted him on the first round, as did the St. Louis Cardinals of the NFL.

The Jets won with a contract package worth a record-setting $427,000. But the Jets were competing against the Giants, one of the NFL's flagship franchises, and they needed to create excitement. Werblin, who came from show business, correctly guessed that Namath would do that.

Namath was seen at all the hot night spots around Manhattan. He wore white shoes on the field at a time when Johnny Unitas was still wearing black high tops. He had a television show. The Jets sold 2,800 season tickets after he signed, making Werblin's investment pay off. However, none of the flash would have mattered if Namath hadn't produced on the field.

Namath was old-school when it came to playing the game, which is why he was able to play for traditionalists like Bryant and Weeb Ewbank. He quickly replaced Mike Taliaferro as the Jets starter and became the AFL's Rookie of the Year in 1965.

His most famous moment came when he guaranteed a win over the favored Baltimore Colts in Super Bowl III, then delivered on the promise. Just as his signing had legitimized the AFL, so did the first victory over an established NFL team.

Knee injuries dogged Namath's career, which ended in 1977 with the Los Angeles Rams. He was voted into the Hall of Fame in 1985 and proved that underneath the "Broadway Joe" persona was a genuine person. His chosen presenter was Larry Bruno, his coach at Beaver Falls High School.

CAREER TOTALS

G	Att	Cmp	Pct.	Yds	TD	Y/A	Lg	Int
140	3762	1886	50.1	27663	173	7.35	91	220
Rush	Yds	Avg	TD	Lg	Total TD	Points	Rating	
71	140	2.0	7	16	8	48	65.5	

RAY NITSCHKE

Full name: **Raymond Ernest Nitschke**	Position: **Linebacker**
Date of Birth: **Dec. 29, 1936, Elmwood Park, IL**	Ht: **6-3**
Died: **March 8, 1998**	Wt: **235**
College: **Illinois**	
NFL Teams: **Green Bay Packers**	

"He had such a competitive personality and just got after it. But he was the exact opposite as a person."—Hall of Fame receiver Don Maynard

Ray Nitschke had a name that conveyed toughness.

But as Don Maynard pointed out, Nitschke led a double life. On the field, he was the fierce middle linebacker for the Green Bay Packers, a player who was seemingly always where the action was. Off the field, the prematurely bald Nitschke wore glasses and looked like an insurance agent, which he was in the off season.

Nitschke came from tough circumstances. His lost his father when he was three and his mother died when he was 13. He was adopted by a brother just eight years older than he was. That brother gave him some wise advice, though, convincing Ray to spurn the $3,000 bonus baseball's St. Louis Browns were offering. Instead, he accepted a football scholarship to the University of Illinois.

A high school quarterback, Nitschke played fullback and linebacker in college. The Packers drafted him in 1958 but it would take three seasons until he became a full-time starter. Part of the reason for his slow development was his off-the-field lifestyle. Nitschke was too rowdy away from the field to suit coach Vince Lombardi, who cautioned him he wasn't long for the Packers if he didn't change his ways.

It was then that Nitschke developed his two distinct personalities—angry and driven for the football field but gentle and kind for the real world. He would address this dichotomy by titling his autobiography, "Mean on Sunday."

Nitschke brought unique skills to the position of middle linebacker. He was a hard hitter but he also had the quickness and lateral speed to help with pass defense. He was a versatile player who could defend effectively against both the run and pass.

Nitschke retired after the 1972 season and appeared in the Burt Reynolds football movie "The Longest Yard" in 1974. He was voted into the Hall of Fame in 1978 and the Packers retired his No. 66. Nitschke died of a heart attack at age 61 in 1998.

CAREER TOTALS							
G	Sacks	FR	Int	Yds	Avg	Total TD	Points
190	0.0	23	25	385	15.4	2	12

JIM OTTO

Full name: **James Edwin Otto**
Date of Birth: **January 5, 1938, Wausau, WI**
College: **Miami**
NFL Teams: **Oakland Raiders**

Position: **Center**
Ht: **6-2**
Wt: **255**

"The greatest center to play the game."—Oakland Raiders coach John Madden

Nobody typifies the fighting spirit of the Oakland Raiders more than Jim Otto.

He anchored the offensive line for the Raiders for 15 seasons from the founding of the franchise in 1960.

His autobiography is titled "The Pain of Glory" and that sums up his career, which was built on dogged determination and an almost superhuman threshold for pain. Otto has had 38 major surgeries, 28 on his knees. He is currently sporting his sixth replacement right knee. His left knee has been replaced twice. He has two artificial shoulders.

Otto's nose was broken 10 times during his career. In 1972, he tore five ligaments in one of his knees during the preseason. But he not only continued to play that season, he made the Pro Bowl, too.

Despite the constant injuries, Otto played in 308 games and made 210 consecutive starts. He was an All Pro for 13 straight seasons. He didn't allow himself to be distracted by pain. He was responsible for calling the blocking signals at the line of scrimmage. One season he made more than 650 such calls. The Oakland staff determined he had been wrong fewer than five times. But even that low percentage of error bothered him.

"The plays I remember are the plays when I made a mistake," he said.

Otto was cut from his freshman team in high school because he was too small. By the time he was a senior he had scholarship offers from 48 schools. That would become a pattern for his career.

The NFL decided to skip on him in the 1959 draft because he was only 210 pounds, too small for the line. When the American Football League came into existence, the Raiders gave him a chance. Otto bulked up to 240 pounds in his rookie season and eventually settled in at nearly 260.

When he'd made himself into a player and the NFL came calling, Otto spurned them to stay with the Raiders. He later coached for the team and continues to assist owner Al Davis.

CAREER TOTALS

GP
210

ALAN PAGE

Full name: **Alan Cedric Page**

Date of Birth: **August 7, 1945, Canton, OH**

College: **Notre Dame**

NFL Teams: **Minnesota Vikings, Chicago Bears**

Position: **Defensive Line**

Ht: **6-5**

Wt: **244**

"Where the ball goes, Alan goes."—Former Vikings defensive line coach Jack Patera

Alan Page's career started in Canton, Ohio and wound up there, too.

Page was a native of the Ohio town that houses the Pro Football Hall of Fame, where he was enshrined in 1988.

Between his visits to Canton he spent 12 years with the Minnesota Vikings as a key component in one of the best defensive lines in NFL history. The "Purple People Eaters"—Page, Jim Marshall, Carl Eller and Gary Larsen—led an exceptional defense that helped the Vikings dominate in the 1970s.

Page broke into the starting lineup as a rookie, which was an unusual concession for conservative coach Bud Grant. Page, however, was so impressive in training camp that he debuted at right tackle when the Vikings opened the 1967 season. Page had been a standout at Notre Dame and was part of the Fighting Irish's 1966 national championship team.

His assets were speed, strength and especially quick reflexes. Page always seemed to be a split second faster off the ball and that gave him an edge in rushing the quarterback and getting after ball carriers. Page won the NFL's Most Valuable Player award in 1971, the first defensive player to recieve the honor.

"It was the kind of year you dream about as a player," Kansas City Chiefs lineman Buck Buchanan said.

Although he excelled on the field, Page was preparing for a career after football. He attended law school during his time with the Vikings and began practicing in 1979.

Weight issues have scuttled many careers but there was an unusual twist to Page's case. He was cut because his devotion to running had caused his weight to fall to 220 pounds. Grant didn't think he could make plays and cut him. It was a rare miscalculation by the Hall of Fame coach. The Chicago Bears spent $100 to claim Page on waivers and he played on for four more years.

After his playing career, Page spent six years as an assistant attorney general for the state of Minnesota. He then became the state's first African-American Supreme Court justice.

CAREER TOTALS							
G	Sacks	FR	Int	Yds	Avg	Total TD	Points
218	0.0	23	2	42	21.0	3	24

JIM PARKER

Full name: **James Thomas Parker**
Date of Birth: **April 3, 1934, Macon, GA**
College: **Ohio State**
NFL Teams: **Baltimore Colts**

Position: **Offensive Lineman**
Ht: **6-3**
Wt: **273**

"The best offensive lineman I have ever coached."

—Longtime Ohio State coach Woody Hayes.

Jim Parker was Johnny Unitas' insurance man.

He didn't get that title because he sold him a policy but rather because he was the lineman responsible for protecting Unitas' blind side. Parker did his job well, which is why he was voted to the Hall of Fame and and a big reason why the Baltimore Colts were so successful in the late 1950s and early '60s.

Parker was 6-foot-3 and 275 pounds, a veritable giant for the times. He won the Outland Award in 1956 as college football's standout lineman and was the Colts' first selection in that year's draft. It turned out to be one of the best choices the Colts ever made.

Parker started his career at left tackle and later shifted to guard on the same side of the line. His 11 NFL seasons were evenly split between the two positions and he was an All-NFL player in eight seasons—four at tackle and the other four at guard. Playing the left side, Parker's main responsibility was to protect his quarterback, who wouldn't be able to see the rush coming from that side.

"It didn't take me long to learn the one big thing," Parker once said of his role on the team. "Just keep them away from John."

That's what Parker did, although he was also an effective run blocker for Lenny Moore and Tom Matte. His size and technique let him neutralize some of the toughest defensive Lineman of the era. He made a smooth adjustment from tackle to guard, even though the responsibilities are different at each position.

Parker, who didn't miss a game for 10 seasons, retired in 1967 aged 33 because of a knee injury. He said he wanted to step aside so he didn't prevent another player from having a roster spot, a decision coach Don Shula called one of the most unselfish gestures he had ever seen.

Parker was voted to the Hall of Fame In 1973, becoming the first player inducted who had played exclusively on the offensive line.

CAREER TOTALS		
G		
135		

WALTER PAYTON

Full name: **Walter Jerry Payton**

Date of Birth: **July 25, 1954, Columbia, MS**

Died: **November 30, 1999**

College: **Jackson State**

NFL Teams: **Chicago Bears**

Position: **Running Back**

Ht: **5-10**

Wt: **202**

"Walter was a Chicago icon long before I arrived there."

—NBA legend Michael Jordan

If Walter Payton couldn't run past a tackler, he was more than willing to run over him.

Payton wasn't exceptionally big but he played like a big man. He had the moves to sidestep tacklers and the courage to confront them head-on. His powerful legs and tremendous balance helped him gain yards other backs couldn't get. The combination worked since Payton piled up 16,726 rushing yards, which was the NFL record at the time of his retirement in 1987. He had 10 seasons with at least 1,000 yards.

Payton was also dangerous as a pass catcher who could gain yards after the catch. He caught 492 passes for another 4,538 yards in his career, bringing his total career yardage to 21,803. He was also a dangerous blocker on plays when he didn't carry the ball.

"He was the most complete football player I ever saw," Bears coach Mike Ditka said.

Payton scored 464 points during his college career at Jackson State, which is a record for any NCAA division. He had 66 touchdowns, 53 extra points and five field goals. He once scored 46 points in a single game.

In 1984, Payton broke Jim Brown's career rushing record of 12,312 yards. In the same game he had his 59th game with at least 100 yards, which broke another of Brown's records.

Payton had 77 games with at least 100 yards and set an NFL record for yards in a single game when he gained 275 yards against Minnesota in 1977.

The Bears chose him on the first round of the 1975 draft. He was the fourth player chosen that year. Payton retired with plenty of records and no regrets. "When I left, I was ready," he said. "You don't miss the battering."

He was an automatic first-ballot Hall of Famer and chose his son Jarrett, then 12, to present him.

Payton died from a rare liver disease on Nov. 1, 1999. He was just 45.

CAREER TOTALS

G	Rush	Yds	Avg	TD	Lg	
190	3838	16726	4.4	110	76	
Rec	Yds	Avg	TD	Lg	Total TD	Points
492	4538	9.2	15	75t	125	750

JERRY RICE

Full name: **Jerry Lee Rice**

Date of Birth: **October 13, 1962, Crawford, MS**

College: **Mississippi Valley State**

NFL Teams: **San Francisco 49ers, Oakland Raiders**

Position: **Wide Receiver**

Ht: **6-2**

Wt: **200**

"I can't think of another player who more exemplifies the drive, work habits and commitment it takes to reach the top."—NFL Coach Mike Holmgren

Jerry Rice kills a lot of barroom arguments.

Start a debate about the greatest receiver in NFL history and the discussion usually ends as soon as Rice's name is mentioned.

He continues to play at a high level, even after some serious injuries, which is a testament to his dedication. Rice, of course, isn't as fast as he used to be. But he still has great hands, still runs precise routes and still has the dedication necessary to make the toughest catches.

The San Francisco 49ers knew how good he could be. In the 1985 draft, they traded away a bundle of draft choices to move up 12 spots and select Rice at the 16th position. At Mississippi Valley State, he'd set 18 NCAA Division II records and had 100 receptions in both his junior and senior years.

Rice was the NFL's Rookie of the Year in 1985, then started a streak of 11 consecutive years with at least 1,000 receiving yards. He won Most Valuable Player honors in Super Bowl XXIII with 11 catches for 215 yards.

He sustained a serious knee injury in 1997 and came back before the season ended, only to fracture his kneecap. By 1999, the 49ers fortunes had fallen. The team was 4-12 and Rice failed to collect 1,000 receiving yards for the first time since his rookie season. He spent one more season with San Francisco, then moved across the bay to Oakland in 2001.

The 2002 season saw him back on top of his game—92 catches for 1,211 yards and seven touchdowns. He passed 200 career touchdowns.

Although the Raiders lost the Super Bowl to Tampa Bay, Rice immediately said he would be back in 2003—at age 41.

"I'm not out to tell you I told you so," he said. "But if you challenge me, I'm going to do everything in my power to prove you wrong."

CAREER TOTALS							
G	Rec	Yds	Avg	TD	Lg		
286	1519	22466	14.8	194	96t		
Rush	Yds	Avg	TD	Lg	Total TD	Points	
87	645	7.4	10	43t	205	1238	

BARRY SANDERS

Full name: **Barry David Sanders**
Date of Birth: **July 16, 1968, Wichita, KS**
College: **Oklahoma State**
NFL Teams: **Detroit Lions**

Position: **Running Back**
Ht: **5-8**
Wt: **203**

"Anytime he touches the ball it's a highlight reel."
—Hall of Fame running back Marcus Allen

Elusiveness was always Barry Sanders' stock in trade as a running back so it was probably fitting that he chose to end his career by simply disappearing.

Sanders had put in 10 years with the Detroit Lions, rushing for at least 1,000 yards in all of them. He was just 1,457 yards short of breaking the existing record for career rushing yardage but Sanders opted not to come back. There were reports of friction with Coach Bobby Ross but Sanders didn't come back after the Lions made a coaching change. The closest Sanders came to offering a real explanation was three years later, when he told an interviewer matter-of-factly, "It got old."

That's the same feeling defensive players had when they were faced with the task of trying to stop Sanders. Just 5-foot-8 but a solid 200 pounds, he had powerful legs that helped him churn through would-be tacklers. Sanders also had great vision of the field.

Sanders fought the rap that he was too small throughout his football life. He ran for 1,417 yards as a high school senior but only two schools offered him a scholarship. He went to Oklahoma State and won the 1988 Heisman Trophy.

The Lions chose him in the first round and he was the third player taken in the 1989 draft. He ran for 1,470 yards as a rookie to set a team record. He rewarded his linemen with engraved watches worth more than $10,000 each.

He was the first player to run for at least 1,500 yards in four consecutive seasons. He tied the NFL record for most consecutive 100-yard seasons and went to the Pro Bowl every year he played. He had at least 100 yards in 76 of his 152 career games and led the NFC in rushing five times.

Sanders was elected to the Pro Football Hall of Fame on January 31, 2004.

CAREER TOTALS						
G	Rush	Yds	Avg	TD	Lg	
153	3062	15269	5.0	99	85	
Rec	Yds	Avg	TD	Lg	Total TD	Points
352	2921	8.3	10	66t	109	654

DEION SANDERS

Full name: **Deion Luwynn Sanders**	Position: **Defensive Back**
Date of Birth: **August 9, 1967, Fort Myers, FL**	Ht: **6-1**
College: **Florida State**	Wt: **198**
NFL Teams: **Atlanta Falcons, San Francisco 49ers,**	
Dallas Cowboys, Washington Redskins	

"I'm thinking about scoring any time I touch the ball,"—Deion Sanders

The case can be made that Deion Sanders was the most dangerous player in the NFL.

He played tight man-to-man coverage as a cornerback and was primed to get interceptions. He was a proficient return man who was a threat to go all the way with any kick he fielded. When he could talk his coaches into letting him play offense, he was a receiver who could turn defensive backs inside out.

Of course, he could only do those things when he wasn't playing baseball.

Sanders had dual careers that sometimes overlapped. He played baseball for four major league teams, fashioning a .263 average over nine years and 641 games. He hit 39 home runs, drove in 168 runs, scored 308 and stole 186 bases with the New York Yankees, Atlanta Braves, Cincinnati Reds and San Francisco Giants.

His 12-year football career was spread over four teams, which included stops in Atlanta and San Francisco. He was a better football player, earning his way to seven Pro Bowls. Sanders was the top pick of the Atlanta Falcons in 1989.

Sanders quickly established himself as one of the league's best cover cornerbacks. Critics complained that Sanders disliked contact but his ability to stay glued to a receiver opened up other coverage possibilities for a defense.

Teams had to work around Sanders' baseball schedule. There were times early in the football season when he wasn't available at all or was only available for games after missing a week of practice.

Baseball clearly challenged him more than football did. Sanders once said, "Baseball toys with your mind," an assessment of the built-in failure rate of baseball, where a 30 percent success rate makes a hitter a star.

Sanders is the only player to appear in a Super Bowl and the World Series.

After one unhappy year with the Washington Redskins, Sanders left football, saying the fire was no longer there. He almost came back with the Oakland Raiders for their 2002 playoff run but other teams blocked waivers.

CAREER TOTALS

G	Int	Yds	Avg	FR	Sacks	Total TD	Points
163	48	1187	24.7	13	1.0	21	126

GALE SAYERS

Full name: **Gale Eugene Sayers**	Position: **Running Back**
Date of Birth: **May 30, 1943, Wichita, KS**	Ht: **6-0**
College: **Kansas**	Wt: **200**
NFL Teams: **Chicago Bears**	

"Trying to bring Sayers down is like going rabbit hunting without a gun."
—Detroit Lions defensive tackle Roger Brown.

Gale Sayers' career was like a spectacular shooting star that burned brilliantly but briefly.

He had only four and a half healthy seasons with the Chicago Bears and had to retire at age 29 because of devastating injuries to both knees. At 34, he was voted into the Hall of Fame, the youngest person to be accorded that honor.

Sayers was one of two first-round picks in the 1965 draft for the Chicago Bears. Linebacker Dick Butkus was the other, which meant the Bears got Hall of Fame caliber players for offense and defense in the same round.

At 6-feet and 200 pounds, Sayers had an incredible ability to spot an opening and dart through it. His shifty moves made tacklers miss more often than not and he had the speed to then escape their pursuit.

"No one ever told me how to run like that," he said. "The moves I had were God-given."

Sayers scored 22 touchdowns with 2,272 all-purpose yards as a rookie—and he wasn't a starter until the third game of the season. On a cold December 1965 day, he wrapped up the season by scoring six touchdowns in a rout of the San Francisco 49ers played on a muddy Wrigley Field. Afterwards, teammate Mike Ditka said, "The mud affected the kid. If it had been dry, he would have scored 10 touchdowns."

Mud couldn't stop him and neither could defenses designed specifically to neutralize him. The knee injuries were another matter. He would eventually require four different surgeries. In the ninth game of the 1968 season Sayers sustained ligament damage in his right knee. His left knee was similarly injured on a kickoff return during the 1970 exhibition season.

Sayers played in only two games in 1971 and retired during the 1972 preseason.

Sayers' friendship with teammate Brian Piccolo became the basis for "Brian's Song," one of the most successful made-for-TV movies ever.

				CAREER TOTALS			
G	Rush	Yds	Avg	TD	Lg		
68	991	4956	5.0	39	70		
Rec	Yds	Avg	TD	Lg	Total TD	Points	
112	1307	11.7	9	80t	56	336	

ART SHELL

Full name: **Arthur Shell**
Date of Birth: **Nov. 26, 1946, Charleston, SC**
College: **Maryland-Eastern Shore**
NFL Teams: **Oakland Raiders, Los Angeles Raiders**

Position: **Offensive Line**
Ht: **6-5**
Wt: **265**

"He was one of those quiet leaders who commanded respect just by being a great player."—Oakland Raiders coach John Madden

The Oakland Raiders have long been one of the NFL's most intimidating teams.

It's a reputation the Raiders enjoy. They wear their black jerseys whenever possible and they seem to collect outsized personalities who don't mind being the center of attention.

In that regard, Shell, one of the greatest Raiders of all, was also one of the least typical members of the franchise.

Opponents report that Shell would greet them with a smile and a friendly word, usually, "Let's have a great game."

While the rest of the Raiders were snarling and cursing, the biggest player in an Oakland uniform was the quietest man on the field. Opponents learned quickly is was in their best interest to try to keep Shell in a placid frame of mind.

He was tough enough to beat under any circumstances. He was impossible when he was angry. Shell and Gene Upshaw ran the left side of the Raiders line, equally efficient at run blocking and pass protection. They played together so long that they functioned as a unit within a unit.

In Super Bowl XI, the Raiders ran for 266 yards against Minnesota's All Pro linemen Alan Page and Jim Marshall. Marshall, a formidable defensive player, didn't have a single tackle or assist that day, which showed how dominating Shell and Upshaw had been.

Shell was a self-made player from a small Division III college. He learned responsibility at home when his mother died and he had to help raise four younger siblings.

Shell played 207 games with the Raiders and made the Pro Bowl in eight of his 14 seasons. After serving Oakland as an assistant coach, he became head coach in 1989, the first African-American head coach of the modern era.

A plaque that he kept on his desk summed up his philosophy: "To achieve all that is possible, we must attempt the impossible. To be as much as we can be, we must dream of being more."

CAREER TOTALS		
GP		
207		

O.J. SIMPSON

Full name: **Orenthal James Simpson**
Date of Birth: **July 9, 1947, San Francisco, CA**
College: **Southern California**
NFL Teams: **Buffalo Bills, San Francisco 49ers**

Position: **Running Back**
Ht: **6-1**
Wt: **212**

"He was not just the greatest player I ever had. He was the greatest player anyone ever had."—Southern California coach John McKay

O.J. Simpson was such a sure-shot prospect that teams were hoping they'd lose games and get a chance to draft him.

The Buffalo Bills lost the most and won the right to select Simpson on the first round of the 1969 draft. They never regretted the choice. He set records, sold tickets and helped put the struggling Bills back on the map as a power in the NFL.

A San Francisco native, Simpson spent two years at the City College of San Francisco before he moved on to Southern California. He was the Heisman Trophy winner as a senior and was the consensus top pick in the draft.

Simpson had at least 1,000 yards in every season from 1972-76 after Lou Saban returned to coach the Bills and structured the offense around him. He won four rushing titles with the Bills and played in five Pro Bowls. He was also a formidable kick returner and gained 990 yards on kickoff returns during his 10 seasons with the Bills.

His greatest year was 1973, when he broke Jim Brown's single-season career rushing mark and wound up topping 2,000 yards for the season. Simpson headed into the Dec. 16 game against the New York Jets needing 61 yards to pass Brown's 1963 standard of 1,863 yards. He wound up rushing for 200 yards in the game to reach 2,003 yards on that snowy day at Shea Stadium.

Simpson left the Bills after 1977 and played two final seasons with his hometown San Francisco 49ers. He finished with 11,236 career rushing yards.

He had a high-profile career after football, working as a broadcaster, actor and commercial spokesman. In 1994, Simpson was charged with the murder of his ex-wife and her friend. He was acquitted in the infamous criminal trial that gripped the world but was forced to make reparations after a civil trial found him liable in the deaths.

CAREER TOTALS

G	Rush	Yds	Avg	TD	Lg	
135	2404	11236	4.7	61	94t	
Rec	Yds	Avg	TD	Lg	Total TD	Points
203	2142	10.6	14	64t	76	456

MIKE SINGLETARY

Full name: **Michael Singletary**
Date of Birth: **October 9, 1958, Houston, TX**
College: **Baylor**
NFL Teams: **Chicago Bears**

Position: **Linebacker**
Ht: **6-0**
Wt: **230**

"My favorite part of the game? The opportunity to play."—Mike Singletary.

Mike Singletary came from Houston but he was Chicago's kind of football player.

The Bears had a long history of dominating middle linebackers and Singletary quickly proved himself worthy of the Hall of Fame lineage established in Chicago by Bill George and Dick Butkus.

Scouts who dismissed him as too slow and too small underestimated his incredible passion for the game. Singletary studied his opponents, then went after them with a fervor that few players could match. TV networks quickly learned to keep an isolated camera on Singletary, whose eyes would widen with intensity as the signals were being called.

Anyone who followed his college career at Baylor should have known how seriously Singletary took the game. He broke 16 of his helmets in college and the Baylor equipment staff was instructed to have three helmets available on the sideline for every game. Those helmet-cracking collisions only intensified Singletary's desire to make plays.

He lasted until the second round of the 1981 draft and was the 38th player chosen overall. He became a starter midway through his rookie season and wound up starting 172 games, the second highest total in Bears history. His participation in 10 Pro Bowls remains a Bears record.

In Super Bowl XX, the Bears held the New England Patriots to just seven yards rushing and Singletary forced a pair of fumbles that helped Chicago to a lopsided win, the team's first championship since 1963.

Singletary was the Bears' first or second-leading tackler in each of his last 11 years with Chicago. He made 1,468 tackles in his career, including 885 solo efforts.

"He's one of the best football players I've ever seen," Bears Coach Mike Ditka said. "He's the leader of our defense, a coach on the field."

Singletary retired after the 1992 season and was elected to the Pro Football Hall of Fame in 1998. There was support for him to become the head coach at his alma mater Baylor, a possibility that Ditka endorsed publicly. Singletary returned to the NFL in 2003, signing on as linebackers coach with the Baltimore Ravens.

CAREER TOTALS							
G	Sacks	FR	Int	Yds	Avg	Total TD	Points
179	19.0	12	7	44	6.3	0	0

BRUCE SMITH

Full name: **Bruce Bernard Smith**

Date of Birth: **June 18, 1963, Norfolk, VA**

College: **Virginia Tech**

NFL Teams: **Buffalo Bills, Washington Redskins**

Position: **Defensive Line**

Ht: **6-4**

Wt: **261**

"Bruce has made a lot of real good football players look foolish."
—NFL coach Mike Holmgren

A lot of offensive linemen didn't sleep well the week before a game against the Buffalo Bills.

Those unsettled nights were caused by the knowledge of what Bruce Smith was capable of doing on Sunday afternoons. Smith was a force at defensive tackle for the Bills, the kind of dominant player who could make a team abandon its plan early in a game.

As teammate Thurman Thomas put it, "He can tear up an entire offense."

Smith grew up idolizing Joe Greene of the Pittsburgh Steelers and in some ways his career paralleled Greene's. They were both first-round draft picks and they both became the cornerstone of defenses for championship-caliber teams. But while Greene won four Super Bowls with the Steelers, Smith came up empty on four trips to the big game.

Smith built his reputation at Virginia Tech and won the Outland Trophy in 1984. The Bills made him the first choice in the draft. He was the defensive Rookie Of The Year and wound up playing in 11 Pro Bowls.

In one 13-year stretch, he had 12 years with double-digit sack totals. Before his career with the Bills ended in 2000, he was the franchise's all-time sack leader with 171.

Denver signed Smith to an offer sheet in 1989 but the Bills chose to match it. When they were faced with the same decision in 2000, the Bills opted to cut Smith, citing salary cap concerns.

"Never did I think I would play in a uniform other than that of the Buffalo Bills," Smith said. "But that's where the game is now."

Smith signed with Washington to continue his pursuit of the NFL career sack record at the age of 40. He tackled New York Giants quarterback Jesse Palmer for his record-setting 199th sack on December 7, 2003 and finished the season with an even 200.

CAREER TOTALS							
G	Sacks	FR	Int	Yds	Avg	Total TD	Points
279	200.0	15	2	0	0.0	1	10

EMMITT SMITH

Full name: **Emmett J. Smith III**	Position: **Running Back**
Date of Birth: **May 15, 1969, Pensacola, FL**	Ht: **5-9**
College: **Florida**	Wt: **212**
NFL Teams: **Dallas Cowboys, Arizona Cardinals**	

"People were saying he was too slow or too small. Every time I saw a film he was running 50 or 60 yards for a touchdown. That looked pretty good to me."
—Former Dallas Cowboys Coach Jimmy Johnson

Maybe Johnson was the only one who took the proper reading and saw how big Emmitt Smith's heart was.

The Dallas Cowboys' scouting department was one of the first to computerize and had a reputation for making sterile, detached judgments on players based strictly on raw, measurable data. Johnson broke that mold when he traded up to make Smith the 17th player taken overall in the 1990 draft.

The Cowboys reaped the benefits of that choice long after Johnson had moved on. Smith was a perfect fit in the Dallas system and his arrival coincided with a rapid rise in the Cowboys' fortunes. Smith handled the running game, aided by fullbacks who led the way behind a dominating line. Quarterback Troy Aikman and receiver Michael Irvin keyed a passing game that kept opponents from focusing solely on Smith and the Cowboys' offense roared.

At just 5-foot-9 and 212 pounds, Smith had been proving critics wrong for a long time. He was an all-state high school player in Florida, rushing for at least 100 yards in 45 of his 49 games. He maintained the consistency at the University of Florida, leading the Southeastern Conference in rushing as a freshman with 1,341 yards.

Smith was the NFL's Offensive Rookie of the Year in 1990 and the following season started an 11-year run of 1,000-yard seasons. He led the league in rushing four times and appeared in eight Pro Bowls. He participated in three Super Bowls and was the Most Valuable Player in Super Bowl XXVIII.

Midway through the 2002 season, Smith became the game's all-time leading rusher and finished the season, his last with the Cowboys, with a total of 17,162 yards. Smith signed with the Arizona Cardinals on March 26.

CAREER TOTALS

G	Rush	Yds	Avg	TD	Lg	
211	4142	17418	4.2	155	75t	
Rec	Yds	Avg	TD	Lg	Total TD	Points
500	3119	6.2	11	86	166	998

BART STARR

Full name: **Bryan Bartlett Starr**
Date of Birth: **January 9, 1934, Montgomery, AL**
College: **Alabama**
NFL Teams: **Green Bay Packers**

Position: **Quarterback**
Ht: **6-1**
Wt: **200**

"The will to win is meaningless without the will to prepare."—Bart Starr

Bart Starr performed well on Sunday because of what he did on all the other days of the week.

Starr wasn't the biggest quarterback, didn't have great mobility and didn't have the strongest arm. He compensated for any shortcomings with his intelligence and willingness to spend time preparing. Critics dismissed him as an extension of Coach Vince Lombardi. Starr took that as a supreme compliment.

Starr was barely invited into the world of professional football—he was a 17th round draft choice in 1956 and spent most of the first three years of his Green Bay career on the bench. He didn't start a game until 1959.

His run as a starter coincided with some glorious years for the Packers. Starr led the offense, executing Lombardi's game plans with calm precision. Starr studied opponents and thoroughly understood the Packers offense. He was an accurate passer who didn't make mistakes and he always played under complete control. The confidence was bred from his week-long classroom work.

"Bart was rarely the best quarterback in the league on a statistical basis," said Packers right guard Jerry Kramer. "But for three hours each Sunday, he was almost always the best quarterback in the game in which he was playing."

The Packers were the worst team in the NFL before Lombardi got there. After he installed Starr as the regular starter during the 1960 season, Green Bay went on a streak that included six divisional titles, five NFL championships and the first two Super Bowls. Starr was the Most Valuable Player in Super Bowls I and II.

Starr's specialty was error-free football. He once made 294 consecutive throws without an interception and was 9-1 in the postseason with a passer rating of 104.8.

Starr had a nine-year run as Packers head coach that started in 1974. He was elected to the Hall of Fame in 1977.

CAREER TOTALS								
G	Att	Cmp	Pct.	Yds	TD	Y/A	Lg	Int
196	3149	1808	57.4	24718	152	7.85	91t	138
Rush	Yds	Avg	TD	Lg	Total TD	Points	Rating	
247	1308	5.3	15	39	15	90	80.5	

ROGER STAUBACH

Full name: **Roger Thomas Staubach**
Date of Birth: **February 5, 1942, Cincinnati, OH**
College: **Navy**
NFL Teams: **Dallas Cowboys**

Position: **Quarterback**
Ht: **6-3**
Wt: **197**

"He always believed there was some way to come back and win."
—Dallas Cowboys defensive tackle Bob Lilly.

The Dallas Cowboys drafted Roger Staubach in 1964 and welcomed him to the team in 1969. He was well worth the wait.

Staubach attended the Naval Academy and had a four-year service obligation after his graduation. One of those years was spent in Vietnam.

He started his NFL career at age 27. Staubach had won the Heisman Trophy as a junior in 1963 and earned coach Wayne Hardin's praise as the greatest Navy quarterback ever. Perhaps it was the will of his personality, helped along by the military training, but Staubach was a natural leader.

"He can just get peoples' respect and following," Cowboys president Tex Schramm said.

The belief of his teammates helped Staubach engineer 23 fourth-quarter comebacks during his career. Fourteen of those came in the last two minutes of games or overtime and earned him the nickname "Captain Comeback."

"Every Cowboy player, offense and defense, felt that as long as he was in the game, they had a chance to win," former St. Louis Cardinals coach Jim Hanifan said. "To tell you the truth, his opponents felt the same way."

During his 11 seasons, the Cowboys won four NFC titles and two Super Bowls. He was the Most Valuable Player in Super Bowl VI. Staubach had the ability to avoid the pass rush and make accurate throws on the run. He could also carry the ball himself—he finished his career with 2,264 rushing yards and 20 touchdowns to go with 22,700 passing yards and 153 touchdown passes. His 83.4 passer rating was the best ever at the time of his retirement.

"He was the greatest competitor I've ever seen," Dallas coach Tom Landry said. Staubach was elected to the Hall of Fame in 1985. He started a real estate company while he was still playing and the multi-million dollar business has now grown international in scope.

CAREER TOTALS								
G	Att	Cmp	Pct.	Yds	TD	Y/A	Lg	Int
131	2958	1685	57.0	22700	153	7.67	91t	109
Rush	Yds	Avg	TD	Lg	Total TD	Points	Rating	
410	2264	5.5	20	33	20	120	83.4	

DWIGHT STEPHENSON

Full name: **Dwight Eugene Stephenson**	Position: **Offensive Line**
Date of Birth: **Nov. 20, 1957, Murfreesboro, NC**	Ht: **6-2**
College: **Alabama**	Wt: **255**
NFL Teams: **Miami Dolphins**	

"Dwight Stephenson was the best center I ever coached. He was a man among children."—Alabama coach Paul "Bear" Bryant

Dwight Stephenson was the best friend a Miami Dolphins quarterback could have.

He anchored a solid offensive line that consistently kept Miami at the top of the list in preventing quarterback sacks. For six straight seasons the Dolphins allowed the fewest sacks.

One of the stories frequently told about him is the time the New England Patriots sent two blitzers after the Dolphins quarterback. Stephenson took them both out of the play, using one forearm to fend off each and protect his quarterback.

Stephenson had good size but wasn't exceptionally big. He was quick to set up after the snap and was explosive off the ball. He worked hard in training and had a tremendous competitive fire as well.

"He makes it look so easy," said Dolphins running back Tony Nathan. "Sometimes you forget about Dwight during a game. Then on film day you remember. You watch him manhandle a player and you can't believe he's the same size as Dwight."

As New York Jets defensive lineman Joe Klecko said, "Dwight makes fools of people who make mistakes."

Stephenson was a second-round draft choice from Alabama, where he'd been a part of teams that won three Sugar Bowls. The Crimson Tide had a 21-game winning streak over his junior and senior years. Stephenson spent most of his rookie season playing on the Dolphins' special teams. He took over for the injured Mark Dennard in the 11th game of 1981 and stayed. He appeared in 107 consecutive games and started 80 in a row.

He spent his entire football career playing for legendary coaches—Bryant at Alabama and Don Shula at Miami. Stephenson appeared in two Super Bowls with the Dolphins and three conference championship games.

Severe knee injuries brought his career to a premature end. He spent eight seasons with the Dolphins and was forced to retire just short of his 30th birthday. He was voted into the Pro Football Hall of Fame in 1998.

CAREER TOTALS

G
114

LYNN SWANN

Full name: **Lynn Curtis Swann**	Position: **Wide Reciever**
Date of Birth: **March 7, 1952, Alcoa, TN**	Ht: **5-11**
College: **Southern California**	Wt: **180**
NFL Teams: **Pittsburgh Steelers**	

"Lynn Swann was an idol. It would amaze me how he could fly through the air and make the catches."—Jerry Rice

Lynn Swann lived up to his graceful surname.

He could leap to grab passes and he could dive for them, too. There were times when it seemed he should have gotten style points as well as yards.

His secret was an unconventional training regimen: Dance lessons. He was adept in ballet, tap and jazz. "It helped a great deal, with body control, balance, a sense of rhythm and timing," he said.

The Pittsburgh Steelers drafted him on the first round in 1974. He played only nine seasons and played on some teams that didn't throw the ball much. As a rookie, Swann saw only limited action, catching just 11 passes in 1974. His primary contribution came on special teams, where he averaged 14.1 yards per punt return. Swann did catch a touchdown pass in the AFC Championship game against Oakland.

He became a bigger part of the offense in his second season and the Steelers began to pass more as the game opened up in the late1970s. But they still didn't throw as often as some teams, preferring a run-first offense geared around their workhorse back Franco Harris.

Swann got his notice in the postseason. In Super Bowl X, he was the Most Valuable Player with four catches for 161 yards, which was then a record. In the Steelers' four Super Bowls, Swann had 364 receiving yards. In the regular season, though, he averaged just three catches per game and that was a factor in the annual debate about his candidacy for the Hall of Fame.

What was important—quality or quantity? Swann retired at 30 because he had an opportunity to join the staff of ABC-TV and wanted to get his post-football career underway.

"The mark of a good player is being able to play in big games and nobody played better in the big games than Lynn Swann," Steelers Coach Chuck Noll said.

Swann was voted into the Hall in 2001.

CAREER TOTALS							
G	Rec	Yds	Avg	TD	Lg		
115	336	5462	16.3	51	-		
Rush	Yds	Avg	TD	Lg	Total TD	Points	
11	72	6.5	1	-	52	-	

FRAN TARKENTON

Full name: **Francis Asbury Tarkenton**
Date of Birth: **February 3, 1940, Richmond, VA**
College: **Georgia**
NFL Teams: **Minnesota Vikings, New York Giants**

Position: **Quarterback**
Ht: **6-0**
Wt: **185**

"I never saw a quarterback who could get it done so many ways and who worked so hard at it."—Vikings coach Bud Grant

Fran Tarkenton was a hard man to pin down.

His scrambling style ran defenses ragged and entertained fans during an 18-year career that included two stints with the Minnesota Vikings wrapped around a five-year stay with the New York Giants.

Tarkenton earned headlines in his first game, throwing four touchdown passes against the Chicago Bears to lead the upstart Vikings to a 37-13 victory over one of the NFL's most established teams.

Quarterbacks didn't run much in those days and the ones who did couldn't move like Tarkenton. He could dart away from onrushing linemen and change direction, all the while studying the field to find an open receiver. Coaches didn't like quarterbacks who deviated from the play and old-school thinking held that abandoning the pocket showed a lack of courage.

One of the old-school types was Vikings coach Norm Van Brocklin, who had played quarterback in the NFL. He and Tarkenton clashed, which led the quarterback to request a trade. Shortly after he was dealt to the Giants, Van Brocklin resigned in Minnesota.

Bud Grant wanted Tarkenton and the trade brought him back to Minnesota. From 1973-78 Tarkenton led the Vikings to six consecutive NFC Central championships and three Super Bowls, all of which they lost. Tarkenton was in the Pro Bowl nine times. He passed for 47,003 yards and rushed for 3,674 yards.

The lack of postseason success didn't prevent his election to the Hall of Fame in 1986 and Tarkenton titled his autobiography, "What Losing Taught Me About Winning."

His post-football years have been busy. He spent four years in the Monday Night Football broadcast booth for ABC and co-hosted the series, "That's Incredible." Tarkenton became a successful businessman and is in demand as a motivational speaker.

CAREER TOTALS

G	Att	Cmp	Pct.	Yds	TD	Y/A	Lg	Int
246	6467	3686	57.0	47003	342	7.27	89t	266
Rush	Yds	Avg	TD	Lg	Total TD	Points	Rating	
675	3674	5.4	32	52t	32	192	80.4	

CHARLEY TAYLOR

Full name: **Charles Robert Taylor**	Position: **Wide Receiver**
Date of Birth: **Sept. 28, 1941, Grand Prairie, TX**	Ht: **6-3**
College: **Arizona State**	Wt: **210**
NFL Teams: **Washington Redskins**	

"He was a very complete receiver."

—Lem Barney, Detroit Lions Hall of Fame defensive back

The Washington Redskins drafted Charley Taylor in the first round in 1964 with the idea he'd be a big part of their offense for many years.

Their overview was right but the specifics of Taylor's contribution changed.

He was drafted as a running back and spent two seasons in the Redskins' backfield. Coach Otto Graham knew offense from his days of leading the Cleveland Browns to championships as their quarterback in the 1940s and '50s. He envisioned a different role for Taylor. Graham thought Taylor would be more valuable as a receiver.

His reasoning: Taylor had reliable hands, he was bigger than most of the defensive backs of the era and he wasn't afraid to go over the middle of the field. Taylor's willingness to confront contact spoke to his courage since he had fractured several vertebrae while playing in college for Arizona State.

The position switch was made by the ninth game of the 1966 season and it turned out to be the best thing for Taylor's career. He was a very good running back but he was a great receiver. In virtually no time, he gained quarterback Sonny Jurgensen's confidence and became one of his favorite targets.

Taylor had seven years in which he caught at least 50 passes. He played in eight Pro Bowls. He was a superb receiver long after Graham's coaching regime ended and long after Jurgensen left the quarterback position. Bill Kilmer found Taylor to be as reliable a receiver as Jurgensen had.

Despite being frequently double-teamed and getting a late start at the position, Taylor retired as Washington's all-time receiving leader. His marks of 649 catches, 9,110 yards and 79 touchdowns were later eclipsed by others.

Taylor was inducted into the Pro Football Hall of Fame in 1984.

CAREER TOTALS						
G	Rec	Yds	Avg	TD	Lg	
165	**649**	**9110**	**14.0**	**79**	**88t**	
Rush	Yds	Avg	TD	Lg	Total TD	Points
442	**1488**	**3.4**	**11**	**50**	**90**	**540**

JIM THORPE

Full name: **James Francis Thorpe**
Date of Birth: **May 28, 1888, Prague, OK**
Died: **March 28, 1953**
NFL Teams: **Canton Bulldogs, Cleveland Indians, Oorang Indians, Rock Island Independents, New York Giants, Chicago Cardinals**

Position: **Halfback**
Ht: **6-1**
Wt: **202**

"I was never content unless I was trying my skill in some game."—Jim Thorpe

Jim Thorpe helped create professional football.

He lent his fame and expertise to the American Professional Football Association in 1920 and that group would eventually evolve into the National Football League. Thorpe helped found the APFA and was the first president of the organization.

By the time he got around to professional football, Thorpe was already well known for his exploits in other sports. He had been the sensation of the 1912 Olympic games, winning Gold medals in the decathlon and pentathlon. From 1913-15 and again from 1917-19, he spent time as a professional baseball player, logging time with the New York Giants, Cincinnati Reds and Boston Braves.

His entry to football came in 1915 when he played two games for the legendary Canton Bulldogs. His fee was $250 per game, an enormous sum for the times.

Thorpe was born in Oklahoma and was of Sac and Fox heritage. His given name of Wa Tho Huck translated to "Bright Path." He played at Carlisle Indian School and there didn't seem to be an athletic challenge he couldn't meet. He could run, pass and kick proficiently.

Because of his national fame, he was an important gate attraction in the fledgling days of football as a professional sport. He helped get attention and draw fans who may not have been inclined to pay attention to football otherwise.

After playing for the Bulldogs from 1915-20, Thorpe spent a season with football's Cleveland Indians. He then went with the Oorang Indians for two years and spent a season with the Rock Island Independents. He logged a season with the New York football Giants before returning to the Bulldogs for one year. His last football season was 1928, when he spent the year with the Chicago Cardinals at the age of 40.

When the Pro Football Hall of Fame was created, Jim Thorpe was one of the charter members. Today, a life-sized statue of him stands at the entrance of the Hall of Fame in Canton, Ohio.

EMLEN TUNNELL

Full name: **Emlen Lewis Tunnell**	Position: **Defensive Back**
Date of Birth: **March 29, 1925, Bryn Mawr, PA**	Ht: **6-1**
Died: **July 22, 1975**	Wt: **187**
College: **Iowa**	
NFL Teams: **New York Giants, Green Bay Packers**	

"He could cover, tackle, do it all."—Hall of Fame receiver Raymond Berry

Emlen Tunnell had to talk his way into a tryout with the New York Giants.

The Giants were glad they took the time to listen to his pitch.

For all the science that goes into talent scouting, the Giants wound up with a Hall of Fame caliber player simply because he hitched a ride from Iowa and knocked on their door. Giants owner Tim Mara was so impressed with his effort that he granted Tunnell's request for a tryout.

Tunnell's college football career had been interrupted by a broken neck, which sent him to basketball. Despite the serious injury, he was a fearless tackler and an aggressive player. Tunnell is credited with developing many of the modern techniques for playing the safety position. He was an important part of the "umbrella defense" system which was unfolding at the time.

Tunnell broke in with the Giants in 1948, when it was still normal for players to play on both sides of the ball. Despite his desire to play on offense, he was one of the first defense-only specialists.

Tunnell had a knack for being where the ball was. That was no coincidence.

"At first I thought he was just lucky," teammate Frank Gifford said. "Then I realized he was great."

Tunnell was a dangerous kick returner. He had an unusual technique for catching punts. He'd let the ball come below his waist before he'd grab it, a style similar to the basket catch that baseball's Willie Mays used. Tunnell believed that it was a surer way to get the ball. In 1952, Tunnell gained 923 yards on interception and kickoff returns, which gave him more yards than the NFL rushing leader had that year.

Tunnell moved so stealthily that he seemed to come out of nowhere to make some interceptions. He earned the nickname "Emlen the Gremlin."

After 11 seasons with the Giants, Tunnell spent three years with Green Bay, then returned to New York as an assistant coach. He was the first black player elected to the Hall of Fame.

CAREER TOTALS							
G	Int	Yds	Avg	FR	Sacks	TotalTD	Points
167	79	1282	16.2	16	0.0	10	60

JOHNNY UNITAS

Full name: **John Constantine Unitas**	Position: **Quarterback**
Date of Birth: **May 7, 1933, Pittsburgh, PA**	Ht: **6-1**
Died: **September 11, 2002**	Wt: **194**
College: **Louisville**	
NFL Teams: **Baltimore Colts, San Diego Chargers**	

"He made the impossible possible."—Raymond Berry

Johnny Unitas was the NFL's first TV star. He helped put the game on the map with the legendary 1958 championship game, which happened to come right in the middle of his amazing run of success. America discovered professional football on TV and quickly learned that no one played the game better than Unitas did with the Baltimore Colts.

Unitas had a strong arm and decent speed. He had a great mind for the game and was able to store past experiences and apply them to fresh situations. The NFL was a much smaller league in Unitas' prime and remembering an opponent's tendencies was a valuable edge. Unitas called his own plays.

He was the leader, the man who had everyone's undivided attention. As Colts tight end John Mackey said, "It was like being in the huddle with God." Beyond that, there was the matter of Unitas' courage and toughness. He'd take hits and come back for more. "He was unshakable," said Packers defensive end Willie Davis.

Unitas' appearance typified his game. With his crew cut and black high top shoes, he was going to work. He had been a ninth round draft choice of the hometown Pittsburgh Steelers in 1955 but didn't survive training camp. He was cut without even taking a snap in a preseason game, not an unexpected fate for a fifth-string quarterback. Unitas, already a husband and father, worked construction and played semi-pro football for the Bloomfield Rams in Pittsburgh, earning $6 per game.

Coach Weeb Ewbank was sent a letter recommending that he give the sandlot quarterback a look. Ewbank used to jokingly accuse Unitas of writing the letter. Whoever sent it did the Colts a huge favor. From 1956-60, they won two NFL titles. Unitas had a streak in which he threw at least one touchdown pass in 47 consecutive games. When the NFL celebrated its first 50 years, Unitas was voted the league's all-time best with little dissent. "He was better than me," Sid Luckman said. "Better than Sammy Baugh. Better than anyone."

CAREER TOTALS

G	Att	Cmp	Pct.	Yds	TD	Y/A	Lg	Int
211	5186	2830	54.6	40239	290	7.8	-	253
Rush	Yds	Avg	TD	Lg	Total TD	Points	Rating	
450	1777	3.9	13	-	13	-	-	

STEVE VAN BUREN

Full name: **Stephen W. Van Buren**	Position: **Running Back**
Date of Birth: **December 28, 1920, Honduras**	Ht: **6-0**
College: **Louisiana State**	Wt: **200**
NFL Teams: **Philadelphia Eagles**	

"We had a good team but Van Buren made us great"
—Philadelphia Eagles Hall of Fame end Pete Pihos

Nearly 60 years after the Eagles balked at giving him a $200 signing bonus, many of Steve Van Buren's team records still stand.

The man they called the "Moving Van" was the NFL's best running back in the 1940s and was the career rushing leader at his retirement following the 1951 season.

Van Buren was solidly built with a strong upper body. Coach Earle (Greasy) Neale took a look at Van Buren's ability to shake tacklers and designed his offense around him. Van Buren led the NFL in rushing four times and also returned kickoffs and punts.

Said teammate Bucko Kilroy, "We used to say Steve was our paycheck. He could do everything."

Van Buren was often compared to Red Grange but Neale maintained he was even better, saying that Van Buren had the power to run through defenders that Grange lacked.

Van Buren had a pair of 1,000-yard seasons at a time when teams played only 12 games. He ran for 196 yards in a 1949 game, which was then a record. Today he's still in the Eagles record book for most rushing touchdowns (69), most rushing touchdowns in a season (15) and most yardage in a game (205 yards against Pittsburgh in 1949).

His most famous game was for the NFL title in 1948. He scored the game's only touchdown in a blizzard so furious that Van Buren said he couldn't even see the opposing safety from his fullback position.

Van Buren was born in Honduras, where his father worked for a fruit-packing company. The family moved to New Orleans and Van Buren wound up at Louisiana State. The Eagles made him their first-round choice in 1944. His 1,146 yards in 1949 were a team record until 1978 and stood as an NFL mark until Jim Brown topped it in 1958.

Van Buren was voted in the Hall of Fame in 1965.

CAREER TOTALS						
G	Rush	Yds	Avg	TD	Lg	
83	1320	5860	4.4	69	70t	
Rec	Yds	Avg	TD	Lg	Total TD	Points
45	523	11.6	3	50t	77	464

PAUL WARFIELD

Full name: **Paul Dryden Warfield**	Position: **Wide Receiver**
Date of Birth: **November 28, 1942, Warren, OH**	Ht: **6-0**
College: **Ohio State**	Wt: **188**
NFL Teams: **Cleveland Browns, Miami Dolphins,**	

"My recommendation is that the Browns draft Paul Warfield high up and draft him as a defensive back."
—Paul Brown's 1964 scouting report

The Cleveland Browns took most of the advice.

They used their first-round pick to choose Warfield from Ohio State. They knew they had an exceptional player; they just didn't know on which side of the ball he'd play.

They decided to keep him on offense and made the correct choice—although Warfield probably could have been an effective defensive back as well. His ability and dedication were likely to make him a success at any position.

Warfield was a rookie on a team of veterans that would win the NFL Championship. He took the place of Ray Renfro, who had retired but stayed around to tutor the rookie. Warfield enthusiastically credited Renfro with helping his development and that was typical Warfield, too. His character was impressive as his talent.

Warfield caught 427 passes for 8,565 yards and 85 touchdowns. His average per catch was 20.1 yards. He played in eight Pro Bowls. Warfield succeeded even though defenses keyed on him just about every week. He ran precise patterns, had sure hands and the ability to gain yards after the catch.

He arrived in Cleveland in time for the championship season and gave the Browns another significant weapon on offense. The team already had an All Pro receiver in Gary Collins and fullback Jim Brown, the game's best running back.

Still, the Browns traded him to Miami in 1970 because they wanted the draft rights to quarterback Mike Phipps. Browns fans remember it as one of the worst deals in franchise history. Warfield played in three Super Bowls with the Dolphins and collected two championship rings. He retired after the 1977 season and was elected to the Hall of Fame in 1983.

CAREER TOTALS

G	Rec	Yds	Avg	TD	Lg		
157	427	8565	20.1	85	86t		
Rush	Yds	Avg	TD	Lg	Total TD	Points	
22	204	9.3	0	39	86	516	

RANDY WHITE

Full name: **Randy Lee White**	Position: **Defensive Line**
Date of Birth: **January 15, 1953, Wilmington, DE**	Ht: **6-4**
College: **Maryland**	Wt: **272**
NFL Teams: **Dallas Cowboys**	

"Off the field, he's one of the nicest guys in the world. But he's mean otherwise."—Dallas Cowboys teammate Harvey Martin

They called Randy White "Manster"—half man, half monster.

It took a couple of years for him to live up to that billing, though. White was an accomplished college player at the University of Maryland, winning the Outland Trophy and Lombardi Award as a senior. The Cowboys believed in him so strongly that they manipulated the draft to get the second overall pick, trading quarterback Craig Morton to the New York Giants.

Two seasons in, though, some people were beginning to wonder if the legendary Dallas scouting computer had blown a circuit when it analyzed White. The problem was the Cowboys moved him to linebacker, a change that didn't go well.

"Those first two years I was fighting for my life out there," White said. "I never felt comfortable playing linebacker."

The coaching staff moved White back to the defensive line and he excelled. He was a weight room devotee, and his tremendous strength allowed him to power past blockers. Beyond that, he was gifted with quickness and balance that helped him get a fast first movement when the ball was snapped.

Playing the right position made the difference and White lived up to the potential he'd shown in college. "I was a lot more comfortable and my career took off," White said.

White missed just one game in his 14 years. He was in nine Pro Bowls and set a Cowboys record with eight consecutive selections. His career coincided with some golden years for the Cowboys. White played in six NFC Championship games and three Super Bowls. He and Martin shared Most Valuable Player honors in Super Bowl XII.

The Cowboys featured the "Doomsday Defense" in those days, with White at right tackle. "His performances range anywhere from spectacular to spectacular," Cowboys Coach Tom Landry said. White retired after the 1988 season was inducted into the Pro Football Hall of Fame in 1994.

CAREER TOTALS							
G	Sacks	FR	Int	Yds	Avg	Total TD	Points
209	52.0	12	1	0	0.0	0	0

LARRY WILSON

Full name: **Lawrence Frank Wilson**
Date of Birth: **March 24, 1938, Rigby, ID**
College: **Utah**
NFL Teams: **St. Louis Cardinals**

Position: **Defensive Back**
Ht: **6-0**
Wt: **190**

"He was, pound for pound, the toughest guy I ever saw in the NFL."
—Hall of Fame quarterback Bobby Layne

The St. Louis Cardinals were always a step or two behind the elite teams in the NFL, so Larry Wilson didn't get a lot of notice.

His peers recognized him, though, as a great player on a team that was often no better than average. New York Giants coach Allie Sherman called Wilson "the going-est player I ever saw," his way of paying tribute to Wilson's non-stop approach to the game. He was a relentless, hard-hitting defensive back who is credited with popularizing the safety blitz.

Wilson would rush the passer from his position in the defensive backfield in schemes designed by Chuck Drulis, the Cardinals' defensive coordinator. Good coaches maximize their players' abilities and Drules designed ways to make Wilson even more of a weapon.

Wilson had been a two-way star at Utah and the Cardinals drafted him on the seventh round, 74th overall, in 1960.

He quickly established himself a fearless player with boundless desire and worked his way into the starting lineup.

The Cardinals made the playoffs just three times in Wilson's 13-year career but he was all-NFL six times and played in eight consecutive Pro Bowls.

Stories of his toughness became legendary around the NFL. Layne recalled the time that Wilson was flattened by a John Henry Johnson block, then returned to the game after sitting out one play. Wilson not only played with two broken hands, he even managed to pick off a Bill Nelsen pass for one of his 52 career interceptions.

He punished quarterbacks with the blitzing techniques and never minded the contact.

"Contact is the most important part of football to me," he said.

Wilson served the Cardinals for a brief time as head coach. He took over the team on an interim basis in 1979 after Bud Wilkinson was fired. He later settled into a front office position with the Cardinals and stayed with the team when it moved to Arizona.

Wilson was elected to the Pro Football Hall of Fame in 1978.

CAREER TOTALS							
G	Int	Yds	Avg	FR	Sacks	Total TD	Points
169	52	800	15.4	14	0.0	8	50

KELLEN WINSLOW

Full name: **Kellen Boswell Winslow**	Position: **Tight End**
Date of Birth: **November 5, 1957, St. Louis, MO**	Ht: **6-5**
College: **Missouri**	Wt: **251**
NFL Teams: **San Diego Chargers**	

"You could put the ball anywhere and he'd come up with it,"
—San Diego Chargers quarterback Dan Fouts.

Kellen Winslow was a wide receiver hiding in a tight end's body.

At 6-foot-5 and 250 pounds, he was big enough to play the bruising game required of tight ends, who often serve as adjunct offensive lineman. But he had the speed, the moves and the hands necessary to get downfield and make plays.

The San Diego Chargers made a last-minute trade with Cleveland to improve their spot so they could draft Winslow on the first round from the University of Missouri.

It turned out he was in the right place at the right time. Head coach Don Coryell loved to throw the ball and was equally fond of devising new ways to attack with the pass. The Chargers' system became known as "Air Coryell" and Winslow was an integral part of plan.

A lot of teams used the tight end mostly as a blocker and an occasional last-resort passing option. With the Chargers, Winslow was often a primary receiver. Unlike other teams, who kept the tight end anchored to the tackle, Coryell came up with formations that were likely to have Winslow just about anywhere. He might go in motion, or line up in the slot and he was even in the backfield on occasion

The Chargers had a superb group of receivers and while opponents knew they planned to throw the ball, they didn't know where it was headed. Once Winslow was out on a pattern, Fouts had four viable options and defenses couldn't double-team all of them.

Over a five-year span from 1980-84, Winslow made 374 catches, the most by any NFL receiver in that timeframe.

Winslow's national reputation was made in the 1981 playoffs when he caught 13 passes and blocked a field goal against Miami. He had to be helped off the field three times in the sweltering conditions and Dolphins coach Don Shula referred to him as "Superman."

Winslow was inducted into the Pro Football Hall of Fame in 1995.

CAREER TOTALS						
G	Rec	Yds	Avg	TD	Lg	
109	541	6741	12.5	45	67t	
Rush	Yds	Avg	TD	Lg	Total TD	Points
0	0	-	0	-	45	270

WILLIE WOOD

Full name: **William Vernell Wood**
Date of Birth: **Dec. 23 1936, Washington DC**
College: **Southern California**
NFL Teams: **Green Bay Packers**

Position: **Defensive Back**
Ht: **5-10**
Wt: **190**

"I always thought that when it came to playing free safety, Willie Wood was the best." — Hall of Fame quarterback Fran Tarkenton

There were 30 rounds of the NFL draft in 1960 and Willie Wood's name was never called.

He was neglected even though he'd played in high profile program at Southern California. The problem was Wood had played quarterback at USC and no professional team projected him at that position because he was only 5-foot-10 and specialized in a running offense that didn't suit the pro style.

Wood sat down and wrote letters to a number of teams, asking for a chance to come to training camp and try out. The Green Bay Packers were one of the teams he contacted and a business manager named Jack Vainisi responded favorably to the request.

Their willingness to take that chance got them a player who would stay for 12 years, play in eight Pro Bowls and eventually earn election to the Pro Football Hall of Fame. He is one of six free agents to make the Hall of Fame.

"I was the only one who thought I had a chance," Wood would say later.

Going to Green Bay allowed him to meet Emlen Tunnell, a Hall of Fame defensive back who was at the end of his career. Wood roomed with Tunnell and the veteran served as his mentor.

"He taught me everything," Wood said.

Wood took Tunnell's place in the lineup in 1961 and settled in for a run that would extend through 1971. In that time, the Packers won six NFL championships and the first two Super Bowls.

Wood played a key role in Super Bowl I. He intercepted a Len Dawson pass intended for Otis Taylor and returned it 50 yards to the Kansas City 5. One play later, Elijah Pitts ran for a touchdown and the Packers changed the momentum in what had been a close game.

Wood later served as a head coach in the World Football League and Canadian Football League and was an assistant coach in the NFL.

CAREER TOTALS							
G	Int	Yds	TD	PR	Yds	TD	Points
166	48	699	2	187	1391	2	24

ROD WOODSON

Full name: **Roderick Kevin Woodson**
Date of Birth: **March 10, 1965, Fort Wayne, IN**
College: **Purdue**
NFL Teams: **Pittsburgh Steelers, San Francisco 49ers, Baltimore Ravens, Oakland Raiders**

Position: **Cornerback/Safety**
Ht: **6-0**
Wt: **205**

"So-called experts get too caught up in age. If you can still prepare and perform at a high level then your experience is a positive that young guys don't have."—Rod Woodson

The Pittsburgh Steelers had the salary cap to consider and they weren't sure how much Rod Woodson had left, so they let him leave as a free agent.

That kicked off his second career.

In 2002 the Steelers were dealing with secondary problems while Woodson, at 38, was helping the Oakland Raiders reach the Super Bowl. It was his third trip to the Super Bowl and second since leaving Pittsburgh. Woodson was a starter for the 2000 Baltimore Ravens, who won Super Bowl XXXV.

The Steelers should have known not to underestimate Woodson. They saw him become the only player in NFL history to suffer a torn anterior cruciate ligament and come back to play in the same season. Woodson injured his right knee in the 1995 season opener but was back when Pittsburgh reached the Super Bowl.

He was Pittsburgh's first-round pick in the 1987 draft, an accomplished multi-sport athlete from Purdue. After a contract holdout that lasted half of his rookie season, Woodson settled in as a starter at cornerback for the Steelers. He was also an explosive kick returner and still holds the team records for career yardage on punt and kickoff returns. Woodson was the NFL's Defensive Player of the Year in 1993. He was named to the NFL's 75th anniversary team and is the first player to appear in Pro Bowls at three different positions—cornerback, safety and kick returner.

Woodson left Pittsburgh for the San Francisco 49ers, then played in Baltimore and Oakland. In his second season with the Ravens, he switched to safety and established himself quickly at the new position. He's been to 10 Pro Bowls and was praised for his work in mentoring some younger defensive backs with the Raiders.

CAREER TOTALS							
G	Int	Yds	Avg	FR	Sacks	Total TD	Points
238	71	1483	20.9	32	13.5	17	102

STEVE YOUNG

Full name: **John Steven Young**

Date of Birth: **Oct. 11, 1961, Salt Lake City, UT**

College: **Brigham Young**

NFL Teams: **Tampa Bay Buccaneers, San Francisco 49ers**

Position: **Quarterback**

Ht: **6-2**

Wt: **215**

"He followed a legend and how do you that?"—Veteran NFL coach Paul Hackett

No matter how sunny it was in San Francisco, Steve Young was always in a shadow.

He was in the considerable shadow left by Joe Montana, the quarterback who led the 49ers to four Super Bowl championships and expertly ran what came to be known as the West Coast offense. Montana was the master of the last-minute comeback, so his style was as impressive as his substance.

Following Montana was going to be tough for anyone and the task fell to Young. He was a talented quarterback on his own but he had to compete against Montana's legend as well as the defenses he saw every week. Fans accustomed to excellence weren't about to settle for anything less than the standard Montana had established.

Young made two professional stops before he came to the 49ers. He signed with the Los Angeles Express of the United States Football League in 1984 after he left Brigham Young University. After two years in the USFL, he went to the Buccaneers and started 19 games over two unspectacular seasons. The 49ers acquired him for a couple of draft picks and some cash.

Upon arrival in San Francisco, Young backed up Montana for four years. When Montana was injured in 1991, Young became the starter. Montana eventually left for Kansas City in 1993.

In his first year as the starter, Young had a passer rating of 101.8. He would set a record with a 112.8 passer rating in the 1994 season. He was the first player in NFL history whose passer rating has been above 100 six times. He matched Sammy Baugh's record by winning six passing titles.

It wasn't until 1994 that Young became a Super Bowl quarterback. He threw six touchdown passes—breaking Montana's record of five—in the 49-26 rout of San Diego and earned Most Valuable Players honors for Super Bowl XXIX.

CAREER TOTALS								
G	Att	Cmp	Pct.	Yds	TD	Y/A	Lg	Int
169	4149	2667	64.3	33124	232	7.98	97t	107
Rush	Yds	Avg	TD	Lg	Total TD	Points	Rating	
722	4239	5.9	43	49t	43	260	96.8	

THE
COACHES

A–Z

GEORGE ALLEN

Full name: **George Allen**
Born: **April 29, 1922, Detroit, MI**
Died: **December 31, 1990**
Teams Coached: **Los Angeles Rams, Washington Redskins**

Record: **116-47-5**
Postseason Record: **2-7-0**
NFC Championship: **1972**

"Every time you win you're reborn. When you lose, you die a little."
—George Allen

Although George Allen never won a Super Bowl, he never had a losing season in 12 years as an NFL head coach. He completely transformed two bad franchises and was one of the league's unique characters.

The big break in his career was landing a job on George Halas' staff with the Chicago Bears. His defense was so dominating in the 1963 NFL Championship game—it produced five turnovers—that Allen was awarded the game ball.

The Los Angeles Rams had endured seven consecutive losing seasons when they hired Allen in 1966. When he left, he'd led the Rams to a 49-17-4 record for a .729 winning percentage. He had similar success when he moved to Washington, taking over a team that had managed just one winning season in 15 years. Allen's philosophy was "The future is now" and he lived it. He was always willing to trade a draft choice for immediate help. Players who hadn't succeeded elsewhere seemed to flourish in the environment Allen created.

His Redskins were known as "The Over The Hill Gang," a collection of veterans who had been discarded by other teams. Allen made 131 trades in his career, 81 of them while he led the Redskins.

In the rough and tumble world of the NFL, Allen was a milk drinker who loved the movie "The Sound of Music." After wins, he'd have an ice cream cart wheeled into the locker room to treat his players.

His pursuit of success knew few boundaries. He would interview people for jobs that didn't exist to hear their ideas. He twice was caught trading draft picks he didn't own. Redskins owner Edward Bennett Williams once said, "I gave him an unlimited budget and he exceeded it."

His legacy includes the nickel defense, the first special teams coach and the first office/training complex, Redskin Park.

Allen coached in the USFL and returned to the college ranks at Long Beach State. He died of pneumonia on Dec. 31, 1990 and was inducted into the Hall of Fame in 2002.

PAUL BROWN

Full name: **Paul Eugene Brown**

Born: **September 7, 1908, Norwalk, OH**

Died: **August 5, 1991**

Teams Coached: **Cleveland Browns, Cincinnati Bengals**

Record:**166-100-6**

Postseason Record: **4-8-0**

NFL Championships: **1950, 1954, 1955**

"No one—I mean no one—has ever had total respect and command like Paul Brown."

—Paul Wiggin

Calling Paul Brown a coach shortchanges his enormous contributions to the NFL.

After all, Brown founded two franchises, introduced the concept of playbooks, invented the facemask and was the first to have players sit in a classroom for film sessions to review their play. He came up with the concept of the taxi squad and was thought to be the first coach to regularly send in plays from the sideline. He broke sports' color line, using black players a year before Jackie Robinson debuted with baseball's Brooklyn Dodgers.

Brown's first experience came at Massillon High School in Ohio, where his record was 81-7-2. He was 18-8-1 as head coach at Ohio State. He assembled and coached the Cleveland franchise in the All-American Football Conference. He had an uncommon knack for recognizing talent and signed Otto Graham and Lou Groza to future contracts when they were still in the military.

Brown's teams were 47-4-3 in the AAFC and won four championships. The franchise was invited to join the NFL in 1950 and Brown's presence was so overwhelming that Cleveland fans suggested the team be named after him. The newly christened Browns were an instant success. They played for the NFL championship in each of their first six seasons. Combined with the AAFC, Cleveland won seven championships in 10 years with Graham at quarterback.

Each year Brown would administer IQ tests to his players. He had a fondness for intelligent players who could grasp and execute new concepts.

The Cleveland situation fell apart in the early 1960s when New York advertising executive Art Modell bought the franchise and a power struggle ensued. Brown was reminded that he was an employee and was fired on Jan. 9, 1963, replaced by his assistant Blanton Collier.

By 1965, Brown was working on acquiring an expansion franchise for Cincinnati. The Bengals were formed in 1967 and began play a year later. Brown retired as coach following the 1975 season and remained as General Manager until his death at age 82, on Aug. 5, 1991.

JOE GIBBS

Full name: **Joe Jackson Gibbs**
Born: **November 25, 1940, Mocksville, NC**
Teams Coached: **Washington Redskins**

Record: **124-60-0**
Postseason Record: **16-5-0**
NFL Championships: **1982, 1983, 1987, 1991**
Super Bowls: **1982, 1987, 1991**

"He was an innovative coach and he never stopped trying to improve on what he was doing."—Washington Redskins General Manager Charlie Casserly

The lights are burning late again at Washington Redskins headquarters.

Joe Gibbs, who led the Redskins to three Super Bowls with three different quarterbacks, shocked the NFL on January 7, 2004 by returning to coach the team. Gibbs had been out of football for 11 years and resisted many offers to return. His first stint with the Redskins ended after 12 seasons when he felt burned out after subjecting himself to long hours. There were times when Gibbs slept in the office after a long night in order to get an early start on the next workday.

While Gibbs was away from the game, he was elected to the Pro Football Hall of Fame, the Redskins foundered and the NFL changed. The salary cap system created a new way of doing business and Gibbs, typically, was on a fast learning curve when he came back to Washington.

"For coaching, for me, it was always a process of diving into it," Gibbs said. "I've always enjoyed that part of it. It stimulates me. I've generally found when you dive into it, that's the best way to learn things."

The Redskins haven't done much since Gibbs left in March of 1993. His immediate predecessor, Steve Spurrier, couldn't match the success he had in college. This time Gibbs takes the job as a proven Hall of Famer with a fistful of championship rings. The first time he was hired, the Redskins weren't sure he was a big enough name to excite their fan base.

Owner Jack Kent Cooke lobbied for someone more famous but General Manager Bobby Beathard wanted Gibbs, who had been the San Diego Chargers offensive coordinator.

The choice didn't look good when Gibbs started his first season 0-5. Yet when he left, the Redskins had won three Super Bowls in his 12 seasons, one more league title than the franchise had claimed in its first 50 seasons.

SID GILLMAN

Full name: **Sidney Gillman**

Born: **October 26, 1911, Minneapolis, MN**

Died: **January 3, 2003**

Teams Coached: **Los Angeles Rams, LA/San Diego Chargers, Houston Oilers**

Record: **123-104-7**

Postseason Record: **0-0-0**

Super Bowl winners:

"Listening to him is like going to graduate school"
—Dick Vermiel

Sid Gillman was a football lifer but movies were a big part of his life, too .

His father owned a movie theater and Gillman often played the piano to accompany the silent films. Once he moved into coaching, Gillman spent just as much time in a darkened room with a projector running. He was the man who pioneered the use of game films as a learning tool.

Gillman served three teams as head coach and his greatest success came in San Diego, where his Chargers won the West Division in five of the American Football League's first six years. Gillman was quick to recognize that the upstart league would need some flash to draw fans away from the established NFL and it happened that he believed in a passing offense.

His interest in game films went back to the 1930s when he was coaching at the college level. Once, he set up a system that allowed rush developing of films during a game so he and his staff could study the first quarter during halftime. The NCAA stepped in and disallowed the practice but it was clear Gillman was ahead of his time.

His career in football spanned seven decades. When the Philadelphia Eagles went to the Super Bowl in 1980, Gillman was on Vermeil's staff as a quality control specialist. That title meant—what else?—that Gillman studied game films, looking for things the coaching staff could exploit in games.

"He made all my coaches better," Vermeil said.

Even into the 1990s, Gillman served as a consultant to the University of Pittsburgh. They'd ship game films to him in California and he'd review them, offering suggestions based on what he'd seen.

After he'd retired from full-time work, Gillman maintained his interest in the game and what trends were developing. At age 79, he told an interviewer, "If there's something new in the game, I want to know about it."

Gillman was voted into the Pro Football Hall of Fame in 1983 and went into the College Hall six years later.

BUD GRANT

Full name: **Harold Peter Grant Jr.**
Born: **May 20, 1927, Superior, WI**
Teams Coached: **Minnesota Vikings**

Record: **158-96-5**
Postseason Record: **10-12-0**
NFL Championships: **1969**
NFC Championships: **1973, 1974, 1976**

"When he speaks he makes more sense than any human being I know."
—Fran Tarkenton

Despite his many accomplishments, Bud Grant is probably best remembered for what he didn't do—he didn't show emotion, he didn't allow heaters on his sideline and he didn't win the Super Bowl. Grant took the Minnesota Vikings to the Super Bowl four times and came away empty, losing to four different opponents. The stoic Grant didn't spend a lot of time second-guessing the results. "On those days, the victors were the better team," he said.

Grant's coaching career started when he was in seventh grade. His school didn't have organized teams so classmates turned to him to form teams and set up competitions with other schools. Grant was an outstanding athlete who played a season of professional basketball with the Minneapolis Lakers before turning to football with the Philadelphia Eagles. When he found he could make more money in Canada, he headed north and was a two-way standout for the Winnipeg Blue Bombers. He coached Winnipeg to a 105-53-2 record and the Vikings, whom he had spurned in 1961, came calling again in 1967.

The team went 3-8-3 in his first season but he had them in the playoffs the following year and the Vikings went to the Super Bowl in his third season. He established order and discipline and even had the team practice lining up respectfully for the national anthem. Playing in frigid Metropolitan Stadium, Grant banned sideline heaters so the players wouldn't fixate on the weather. Over three seasons from 1969-71, the Vikings were 35-7. In 1973, Minnesota brought Tarkenton back and together they won six division championships in six years.

Grant retired after the 1983 season and was replaced by Les Steckel. With the franchise in disarray, the Vikings asked him to return in 1985 and he did, spending just one season back on the job. He was then succeeded by longtime assistant Jerry Burns. Grant was voted into the Hall of Fame in 1994 and the man with the steely eyes who never showed emotion on the sidelines cried during his induction speech.

GEORGE HALAS

Full name: **George Stanley Halas**

Born: **February 2, 1895, Chicago, IL**

Died: **October 31, 1983**

Teams Coached: **Decatur Staleys, Chicago Staleys, Chicago Bears**

Record: **318-148-31**

Postseason Record: **6-3-0**

NFL Championships: **1921, 1933, 1940, 1941, 1946, 1963**

"Find out what the other team wants to do, then take it away from them."
—George Halas

He came to be known as "Papa Bear" but George Halas wasn't an especially cuddly figure.

He was a tough competitor who drove a notoriously hard bargain as the one-man front office of the Chicago Bears.

Once during a contract dispute, Mike Ditka complained that Halas, "tosses nickels around like they're manhole covers."

The Pro Football Hall of Fame calls Halas "Mr. Everything" in his official biography and that's a good way to sum up his contribution. Halas was among the founders of the NFL, who got together at a Canton, Ohio car dealership to outline plans for the league in 1920.

Halas played for the New York Yankees in the 1919 season. He batted just .091 in 12 games before his baseball career was derailed by a knee injury. Babe Ruth took over his spot the following season.

A Decatur, Illinois starch manufacturer hired Halas to organize a company football team that would help publicize the company and improve the morale of workers. The Decatur Staleys debuted wearing blue and orange uniforms, borrowing the colors from the University of Illinois.

After just one season, the Staley Starch Works gave Halas the franchise with the provision it carry the company name for one more season. He moved the team to Chicago and cut a deal to play at Wrigley Field, home of baseball's Cubs. When it came time to pick a new name, he chose bigger Cubs—Bears.

Halas coached the team for 40 years and was the only person associated with the NFL though its first 50 seasons. He won six NFL titles, the last in 1963. After he moved into the front office, he was a leader on league issues and often put the good of the NFL ahead of his own interests. A prime example is the NFL's revenue sharing system that is the envy of other sports.

Halas was a charter member of the Hall of Fame in 1963 and died in 1983 age 88.

EARL 'CURLY' LAMBEAU

Full name: **Earl Louis Lambeau**
Born: **April 9, 1898, Green Bay, WI**
Died: **June 1, 1965**
Teams Coached: **Green Bay Packers, Chicago Cardinals, Washington Redskins**

Record: **226-132-22**
Postseason Record: **3-2-0**
NFL Championships: **1936, 1939, 1944**

"If it hadn't been for Curly Lambeau, there would have been no Vince Lombardi. There would have been no Green Bay Packers."
—Packers historian Lee Remmel

Curly Lambeau was there before the National Football League even started.

Green Bay native Lambeau founded the Packers in 1919 and coached them through 1949. He won six championships and was one of the first advocates of the forward pass in a game dominated by running. Statistics from that era are spotty but Lambeau is believed to have been the first 1,000-yard passer.

Lambeau had played a season under Frank Leahy at Notre Dame before a severe case of tonsillitis interrupted his collegiate career. He got involved with professional football and never went back to school.

His systems were said to be fairly simple but Lambeau's calling card was not his tactical genius. His greatest skills were verbal. He could be a smooth salesman when circumstances dictated and he could motivate through fear.

How crude was the game in the early days? The Packers played at a field that had no fences, no bleachers and, therefore, no admission charge. It was a town team in the classic sense—the Packers got their name from their sponsor, the Indian Packing Company. That association almost led to the team being called the Indians.

The original owners of Packers were suspended from the league when they were found using college players. Lambeau got the franchise reinstated for the fee of $1,000 and also got control of the Packers.

Lambeau's training camp rules were simple: Players were expected at breakfast at 8 a.m. Curfew was 11 p.m. Players were prohibited from smoking while in uniform and weren't allowed to drink alcohol at any time. They were expected to wear football pants at every practice and were required to report any and all injuries to the team doctors. Lambeau believed in taking it easy on players during training camp so they'd stay fresh as the season wore on.

Lambeau, a charter member of the Hall of Fame in 1963, died in 1965.

TOM LANDRY

Full name: **Thomas Wade Landry**
Born: **September 11, 1924, Mission, TX**
Died: **February 12, 2000**
Teams Coached: **Dallas Cowboys**

Record: **250-162-6**
Postseason Record: **20-16-0**
NFC Championships: **1970, 1971, 1975, 1977, 1978**
Super Bowls: **1971, 1977**

"You always had to spend a lot of extra time preparing to play Tom Landry's teams"
— Chuck Noll

He was the man in the hat and the suit, long after other NFL coaches switched to more practical sideline attire.

Tom Landry's presence on the Dallas Cowboys' sideline was a constant and so, for a long time, was the Cowboys' presence in the NFL playoffs. He coached the team for 29 years and had a stretch of 20 consecutive winning seasons that included five National Conference titles and two Super Bowl victories.

Landry took over a ragtag collection of castoffs when the Cowboys joined the NFL as an expansion team in 1960. It took five years until the Cowboys could seriously compete. Landry's career record was 13-38-3 in 1964 when the team rewarded him with an unprecedented 10-year contract. It was the right move. In that time, the Cowboys developed into one of the NFL's premier franchises, one against which other teams would measure themselves.

"We based our whole program on beating Tom Landry," said Dick Vermeil, who was then coaching the division rival Philadelphia Eagles.

Landry was among the first coaches to use situational substitutions on obvious passing downs. He was the first to hire strength and speed coaches. The Cowboys took chances with superior athletes who hadn't played football, like basketball star Cornell Green and sprinter Bob Hayes. He hired an assistant for quality control whose duty it was to study game films and chart opponents' tendencies.

Landry is credited with inventing the Flex defense, which allowed the Cowboys to make up for personnel shortages with a different kind of gap control. He revived the shotgun offense in the mid-1970s, more than 10 years after anyone in the NFL had tried it.

Eventually, though, the success ended and Landry had to defend himself against charges that he'd stayed too long. The decision was made for him on Feb. 25, 1989 when new owner Jerry Jones fired Landry and replaced him with Jimmy Johnson.

Landry worked on behalf of the Fellowship of Christian Athletes until his death from leukemia in 2000.

MARV LEVY

Full name: **Marvin Daniel Levy**
Born: **August 3, 1928, Chicago, IL**
Teams Coached: **Kansas City Chiefs, Buffalo Bills**

Record: **143-112-0**
Postseason Record: **11-8-0**
AFC Championships: **1990, 1991, 1992, 1993**

"Marv knew exactly the right words to say at the right time,"
—Buffalo Bills Hall of Fame quarterback Jim Kelly

He was a Phi Beta Kappa, earned a Masters degree in English history from Harvard and was fond of quoting Sir Winston Churchill.

Yet Marv Levy was just as knowledgeable about the X's and O's of professional football and the psychology of handling a roster full of diverse personalities.

His locker room oratory was likely to make a player think and that's what Levy wanted. His teams were always well-prepared and he valued knowledge over the temporary rush of emotion.

"It's not that a player is fired up," Levy said. "It's that he knows what he's supposed to do. All that comes from being taught well. Teaching is the key."

Levy came to value education when he spent time in the hospital and picked up Charles Dickens' "A Tale of Two Cities," the only book available. His search for knowledge became voracious and he graduated from Coe College, then wrote his Masters thesis on the World War II lend-lease program. Churchill, he said, "provided inspiration against overwhelming odds."

Levy spent 46 years as a coach, starting his career at a prep school in St. Louis. He came to the NFL as a special teams coach for the Philadelphia Eagles in 1969, then filled that role for George Allen in Los Angeles and Washington. His opportunity to be a head coach came in the Canadian League, where he won two Grey Cups with Montreal.

The Kansas City Chiefs hired him in 1978 and he lasted there until 1982. After two years away from coaching and a stint in the United States Football League, the Buffalo Bills called in 1986 and he became the franchise's most successful coach with a 112-70 record over 11 1/2 seasons. He took the Bills to four consecutive Super Bowls, all of which they lost.

Disappointing as the results were, Levy always seemed to have the game in the proper perspective. When asked once if an upcoming game was a must-win, he replied, "No, World War II was a must-win."

VINCE LOMBARDI

Full name: **Vincent Thomas Lombardi**
Born: **June 11, 1913, Brooklyn, NY**
Died: **September 3, 1970**
Teams Coached: **Green Bay Packers, Washington Redskins**

Record: **96-34-6**
Postseason Record: **9-1-0**
NFL Championships: **1961, 1962, 1965, 1966, 1967**
Super Bowls: **1966, 1967**

"All he wanted from you was perfection."—Green Bay Packers running back Jim Taylor

Brooklyn born Vince Lombardi was 45 years old when he headed to Green Bay for a job that figured to challenge a much younger man.

He was charged with the task of turning around the NFL's worst team. He did it in a year, putting the Packers on a path of success that would last a decade.

The formula wasn't terribly complicated; get good people and put them in positions where they could succeed.

For all his legendary motivational skills, Lombardi's other great gift was his eye for talent. Quarterback Bart Starr was barely staying on the roster, but Lombardi saw the qualities that would make him a success as a starter. Willie Davis, a man without a position in Cleveland, became an anchor of the Packers' defensive line. Willie Wood, a college quarterback, was installed in the secondary. All three players wound up in the Hall of Fame.

Lombardi was an offensive lineman who was one of the legendary "Seven Blocks of Granite" at Fordham. After graduating from college, he juggled responsibilities: He worked in a foundry, went to law school at night and played semi-pro football. He scaled back to one job when he became a high school teacher, where his responsibilities included coaching the football, basketball and baseball teams.

He coached at Fordham and Army before entering the NFL as an offensive assistant to Jim Lee Howell with the New York Giants in 1954. Lombardi took a five-year contract with the Packers and beat the Giants for Green Bay's first title in his third season.

In nine seasons he never had a losing record, winning five NFL titles and the first two Super Bowls. Lombardi stepped down as coach in 1968 but stayed as general manager. He left a year later for a combined coach-GM role with the Washington Redskins. He led the team to its first winning record in 14 years but succumbed to intestinal cancer in September of 1970.

The Super Bowl trophy was named for Lombardi in 1971, the same year he entered the Hall of Fame.

CHUCK NOLL

Full name: **Charles Henry Noll**
Born: **January 5, 1932, Cleveland, OH**
Teams Coached: **Pittsburgh Steelers**

Record: **186-139-1**
Postseason Record: **16-8-0**
Super Bowl Winners: **1974, 1975, 1978, 1979**

"I don't motivate people. I direct motivated people."
—Chuck Noll

Chuck Noll wasn't much on Knute Rockne speeches and sideline histrionics. He was a teacher at heart and believed that preparation and execution were the keys to winning, not made-for-Hollywood oratory and displays of emotion. Who can argue with his success?

Noll took over the Pittsburgh Steelers in 1969 at the age of 37. He had never been a head coach but his credentials were impeccable. He had played for Paul Brown and served as an assistant to Sid Gillman and Don Shula. Noll was an especially bright pupil who went to school on his three Hall of Fame mentors.

He inherited a team that had gone 2-11-1 and had a long history of futility. He changed the attitude, the personnel got better and the Steelers finally made the playoffs in 1972, their 40th season. Two years later, in Noll's sixth season, Pittsburgh won the first of its four Super Bowls in six years. He became the first head coach to collect four Super Bowl rings.

Noll wasn't afraid to do things his way. The Steelers usually had fewer assistant coaches than most teams. They worked manageable hours at a time when more coaching staffs were bringing cots to the office. When the shotgun formation made a comeback, Noll's Steelers were one of the last holdouts.

But he was also willing to adapt. The Steelers' first two Super Bowl champions ran the ball. When rule changes loosened up the passing game and quarterback Terry Bradshaw had matured, the Steelers had as spectacular an air show as anyone in the NFL.

Away from work, Noll was something of a renaissance man who piloted his own plane and had avid interests in sailing, gourmet cooking and gardening.

The Steelers were unable to duplicate their 1970s success in the next decade. Noll announced his retirement days after the 1991 season ended, closing his career after 23 seasons. Although he was given an administrative title by the Steelers, he's devoted most of his time to helping charities in the Pittsburgh area.

STEVE OWEN

Full name: **Stephen Joseph Owen**
Born: **April 21, 1898, Cleo Springs, OK**
Died: **May 17, 1964**
Teams Coached: **New York Giants**

Record: **152-99-17**
Postseason Record: **2-8-0**
NFL Championships: **1934, 1938**

"Football is a game played down in the dirt and always will be. There's no use getting fancy about it."—Steve Owen

Owen's dismissal of sophisticated strategies belies his status as one of the game's innovators.

While the fundamentals of blocking and tackling have been constant, Owen is credited with dreaming up some ideas that changed the game.

He is acknowledged as the coach who popularized the A-formation offense, the umbrella defense and the two-platoon system.

Owen could also think on the fly. When his New York Giants found themselves playing the Chicago Bears on an icy field for the 1934 NFL title, he had the brainstorm to put the players in rubber-soled basketball shoes for better traction. The Giants used that superior footing to pull away from the Bears in the second half.

Owen came from Oklahoma, where he harbored the boyhood dream of being a jockey. That career possibility vanished as he grew into a 6-foot-2, 235-pound adult. Before he got into pro football, he worked in the oil fields and wrestled professionally under the name "Jack O'Brien."

He played football for three teams and settled in with the Giants. He was the defensive captain of the 1927 title team, which allowed only 20 points over the course of the season. He was the biggest defensive star of the 1920s. That experience convinced Owen that preventing points was the key to success in football.

"Steve was the first to stress the importance of defense and the advantage of settling for field goals instead (of trying) for touchdowns," Chicago Bears Hall of Famer George Halas said.

Owen wound up coaching the Giants from 1931-53. He never had a contract but kept the job on a handshake basis with ownership. In his later days, assistant Tom Landry helped him devise the umbrella formation, which was designed to combat the passing offense Paul Brown had developed with the Cleveland Browns.

Owen's teams won eight divisional titles and took two NFL championships.

His election to the Pro Football Hall of Fame came in 1966, two years after his death.

BILL PARCELLS

Full name: **Duane Charles Parcells**
Born: **August 22, 1941, Englewood, NJ**
Teams Coached: **New York Giants, New England Patriots, New York Jets, Dallas Cowboys**

Record: **148-106-1**
Postseason Record: **11-7-0**
AFC Championships: **1996**
NFC Championships: **1986, 1990**
Super Bowl Winners: **1986, 1990**

"He is one of those guys I'd come out of my grave to play for."
—running back Curtis Martin

Bill Parcells was a New York kind of coach. He was a no-nonsense, in-your-face autocrat who demanded excellence. Diplomacy wasn't part of his profile.

"He has one style—Do what he says," was the way quarterback Drew Bledsoe put it.

Parcells was equally tough on the people who worked for him and the people for whom he worked. When he was with the New York Giants, he almost completed a deal to move to Atlanta for more money and increased authority. He clashed with owner Robert Kraft in New England and went to the New York Jets, who had to compensate the Patriots in order to secure Parcells' services. The price was steep but the Jets believed he was worth it.

Parcells spent time at West Point, where he developed a lifelong friendship with basketball coach Bob Knight. The similarity in their styles is obvious and so are the results. Parcells was in the habit of dividing players into two camps—warriors and dogs. The warriors were to keep and the dogs were to unload on other teams so they'd become an opponent's problem.

"If you're sensitive, you'll have a hard time with me," Parcells said.

He was loud and his sense of humor could be cutting. Parcells rose through the college ranks and even spent a season as the head coach at Air Force in 1978. But it was no surprise that he hated recruiting and went to work as an NFL assistant, first in New England, then with the Giants. He became head coach of the Giants in 1983 and barely survived a debut season in which the team went 3-12-1. Parcells changed schemes and personnel and restored the Giants' winning tradition that had been missing for almost two decades.

After winning two Super Bowls with the Giants, he moved to New England in 1993 and led the Patriots to the Super Bowl in 1997. He bolted the Patriots for the Jets and turned a 1-15 team into a playoff qualifier. Parcells retired after the 2000 season and turned to broadcasting before returning to coaching in 2003 with the Dallas Cowboys.

DON SHULA

Full name: **Donald Francis Shula**
Born: **April 4, 1930, Painesville, OH**
Teams Coached: **Baltimore Colts, Miami Dolphins**

Record: **328-156-6** Postseason
Record: **19-17-0** NFL Champships:
1968 AFC Championships: **1971,
1972, 1973, 1982, 1984**
Super Bowls: **1972, 1973**

"I have no magic formula. The only way I know how to win is through hard work."—Don Shula

Don Shula became an NFL head coach at the tender age of 33 and stayed around long enough to compete against one his sons. That iron jaw and intense personality were sideline staples in the NFL from 1963 through 1995.

Shula began his career with the Baltimore Colts, then headed south to join the Miami Dolphins in 1970. He took 20 of his 33 teams to the playoffs and only had two losing seasons in his 26 years at Miami. Shula played at Cleveland under the legendary Paul Brown, then went to Baltimore as part of a 15-player trade.

His coaching career started early and he quickly ascended to the ranks of head coach. Shula had seven consecutive winning seasons in Baltimore, which made him attractive to a floundering Miami franchise. The Dolphins offered him a bigger say in personnel matters and a seat on the board of directors. It was an irresistible opportunity. Shula coached the Dolphins through their 17-0 season in 1972, the only perfect season in modern NFL history. They capped the year with a 14-7 win over Washington, one of two Super Bowl victories in Shula's six trips to the title game. Over two seasons in 1972-73, his Dolphins won 32 of 34 games. Only he and NFL pioneer George Halas recorded 300 career victories.

Shula had superb quarterbacks throughout his career—Johnny Unitas in Baltimore and Bob Griese and Dan Marino in Miami. He was known as a taskmaster who sometimes had an explosive temper. But there was another side to his personality, as his players saw when he would serve as an altar boy during the team's Sunday morning religious services.

Shula's son Mike played quarterback in the NFL and his son David spent time as head coach of the Cincinnati Bengals.

Shula retired after the 1995 season and his Hall of Fame induction was a mere formality. The stadium at his alma mater, John Carroll University near Cleveland, has been named in his honor.

BILL WALSH

Full name: **William Ernest Walsh**
Born: **November 30, 1931, Los Angeles, CA**
Teams Coached: **San Francisco 49ers**

Record: **92-59-1**
Postseason Record: **10-4-0**
NFC Champ'ships: **1981, 1984, 1988** Super Bowl Winners: **1981, 1984, 1988**

"They call it the West Coast offense but it's Bill Walsh's offense."
—George Seifert

Bill Walsh's San Francisco 49ers dominated the NFL in the 1980s and changed the way the game was played.

Walsh developed what came to be known as the West Coast offense and no one executed it better than the 49ers. The franchise had fallen on hard times before Walsh arrived in 1979. He took over a 2-14 team and made it a Super Bowl champion in just three seasons.

Blessed with an ability to understand and teach offensive strategies as well as a sharp eye for talent, Walsh quickly had the 49ers on the right track. His offense borrowed from principles he'd learned from Sid Gillman. The West Coast offense was a quick-strike attack. The quarterback generally released the ball three seconds after it was snapped. The system required running backs who could catch passes as well as carry the ball. It needed swift wide receivers who could get downfield quickly and gain yards after the catch. Tight ends had to do more than block. They had to be able to serve as receivers and run the occasional deep pattern. Linemen loved the plan because they didn't have to hold their blocks longer than a few seconds.

It was a good plan, even better when players as talented as quarterback Joe Montana, running back Roger Craig and receiver Jerry Rice executed it.

At Stanford, Walsh's teams went to three bowl games and won them all. He quickly established the same winning tradition in San Francisco and the 49ers dominated the decade.

Walsh stepped down after the 1988 season, ending a 10-year run that saw the 49ers win three Super Bowls and reach the playoffs seven times. After leaving the 49ers, he worked as a television analyst and served the NFL in a front office capacity. He came back to San Francisco as an assistant to George Seifert, his successor. When that proved awkward, Walsh left and went back to Stanford for a season as head coach. He then returned to the 49ers as General Manager and finally stepped down at age 69.

KEY
GAMES

GIANTS "SNEAKER" A VICTORY

New York Giants   **30**
Chicago Bears   **13**

December 9, 1934
NFL Championship game, Polo Grounds, New York

In the emotion that follows a big win, players sometimes make a point to thank everyone in the organization.

This was one time in pro football when the equipment managers actually had a direct bearing on a victory.

The New York Giants and unbeaten Chicago Bears were playing for the NFL Championship on an icy field at the Polo Grounds. The Bears were leading 13-3 when Coach Steve Owen and owner William Mara decided to follow through on their plan to have the Giants players switch from cleats to rubber-soled basketball shoes.

Some of the players already had sneakers. Equipment aide Abe Cohen was sent to Manhattan College to borrow more. The superior footing helped Ken Strong run for touchdowns of 42 and 11 yards. Tailback Ed Danowski ran nine yards for a score and threw a 28-yard touchdown pass to Malcolm (Ike) Frankian as the Giants scored 27 unanswered points to upset the Bears.

THE TELEVISION AGE BEGINS

Brooklyn Dodgers   23
Philadelphia Eagles   14

October 22, 1939
NFL regular season, Ebbets Field, New York

The game wasn't that special and neither was the attendance—just 13,050 people paid their way into Ebbets Field.

What made it noteworthy were the thousand or so people who saw the game without leaving home. NBC beamed the game to the approximately 1,000 television sets in New York City via its experimental station W2XBS. Two cameras were in place to cover the action and former New York University football player Allen (Skip) Walz called the play-by-play and also offered hand directions to the camera operators. The game was also seen at the RCA Pavilion at the World's Fair in New York.

Ralph Kerchener of the Dodgers kicked three long field goals.

There were no commercials but there were breaks. At times clouds would obscure the sun and interrupt transmission of the picture. In those cases, Walz would just provide extra description until the visual image returned.

BEARS' BLOWOUT

Chicago Bears   **73**
Washington Redskins   **0**

December 8, 1940
NFL Championship game, Griffith Stadium, Washington DC

The NFL championship game was expected to be a low-scoring struggle. After all, in a regular season meeting a month earlier, the Washington Redskins had managed to squeak out a 7-3 win over the Chicago Bears.

It was low-scoring only for the Redskins. Washington was helpless to stop the Bears' T-formation and came out on the wrong end of the most lopsided score in NFL history.

Just one minute into the game, Bill Osmanski ran 68 yards for a touchdown. Ten different players wound up scoring touchdowns as Chicago piled up 519 yards of total offense.

The Bears intercepted eight passes and returned three of them for scores. By the end of the game, the Bears were asked not to attempt any more kicks because the allotment of 12 game balls was almost exhausted by extra points that had gone into the stands and been claimed by fans.

GRITTY GRAHAM LEADS BROWNS

Cleveland Browns   **31**
San Francisco 49ers   **28**

November 28, 1948
AAFC regular season, Kezar Stadium, San Francisco

The Cleveland Browns' dream of an undefeated season in the All America Football Conference was in serious jeopardy.

Quarterback Otto Graham was functioning on one leg, the result of a knee injury he'd sustained a week earlier in Los Angeles. The Browns were losing 21-10 and Graham was limping.

But the future Hall of Famer came back to throw three touchdown passes and the Browns got by their toughest test to improve to 13-0. They won the regular season finale the following week against the Brooklyn Dodgers, finishing the season with four consecutive road wins.

The Browns pounded the Buffalo Bills 49-7 in the championship game to win their third consecutive title under Coach Paul Brown. It was the first time any team in the NFL or AAFC had gone through a season without a loss and Graham's performance at San Francisco was the season's turning point.

THE BLIZZARD BOWL

Philadelphia Eagles   7
Chicago Cardinals   0

December 19, 1948
NFL Championship game, Shibe Park, Philadelphia

Philadelphia Eagles running back Steve Van Buren woke the morning of the NFL championship game, looked out his window and promptly went back to bed. That's how certain he was the game would be postponed.

But the blizzard that hit Philadelphia didn't disrupt the game and Van Buren had to scramble to get to the stadium. Good thing, because he wound up scoring the only points and giving the Eagles their first title.

The teams were called upon to help remove the snow-covered tarps before the game. They couldn't budge them, nor could they do much else. The Cardinals had 35 passing yards while the Eagles managed seven.

The game turned on Frank Kilroy's recovery of a fumbled handoff at the Cardinals' 17. Four plays later, Van Buren ran five yards for the game's only score, part of his 98-yard day that almost didn't happen.

BROWNS' BIG BREAKOUT

Cleveland Browns   **35**
Philadelphia Eagles   **10**

September 15, 1950
NFL regular season, Shibe Park, Philadelphia

The Cleveland Browns dominated the All American Football Conference but didn't impress the old-guard NFL.

The feeling was that the Browns were a good team that had feasted against inferior competition in an upstart league. The real test for the Browns would come when the leagues merged for the 1950 season.

NFL commissioner Bert Bell matched the Browns against the defending NFL champion Eagles in Philadelphia for the season opener. He couldn't have been happy with the result.

Using their advanced passing game, the Browns routed the Eagles. Otto Graham threw touchdown passes to Dub Jones, Dante Lavelli and Mac Speedie. Then Graham and Jones scored on runs.

When some of the Eagles complained later that the Cleveland passing schemes weren't "real" football, Cleveland coach Paul Brown knew what he would do in the December rematch with the Eagles. The Browns won that game 13-7 without attempting a pass.

THE GREATEST GAME

Baltimore Colts   23
New York Giants   17

December 28, 1958
NFL Championship game, Yankee Stadium, New York

It can be argued whether the 1958 NFL Championship game really was the greatest or not, but there's no question it's the one that made pro football as a television attraction.

The Colts led 14-3 at halftime but were trailing 17-14 by the fourth quarter. With two minutes to go, they had the ball on their own 14. As Baltimore receiver Raymond Berry would say later, "The goalposts looked a million miles away."

Quarterback Johnny Unitas, the master of the two-minute drill, made up that yardage in a hurry. Four completions gained 73 yards, the last a pass to Berry that covered 22 yards. That got the Colts in position for Steve Myhra's game-tying 20-yard field goal with seven seconds on the clock.

In sudden death overtime, Alan Ameche scored on a 1-yard touchdown run to win the game and title for the Colts.

THE BROWNS BIG UPSET

Cleveland Browns	**27**
Baltimore Colts	**0**

December 27, 1964
NFL Championship game, Cleveland Stadium, Cleveland

Despite playing on their home field, the Cleveland Browns weren't given much of a chance against the Baltimore Colts in the NFL title game.

But a spirited week of practice helped the Browns' confidence. They passed at will against the NFL's best defense and completely shut down the league's top offense.

The Colts were unable to contain receiver Gary Collins and quarterback Frank Ryan exploited the mismatch in the second half. After a scoreless first half, Lou Groza's field goal gave the Browns the lead. Jim Brown's 47-yard run set up an 18-yard touchdown pass from Ryan to Collins. Then Collins caught a 42-yard scoring pass. Groza kicked another field goal and the Ryan-to-Collins connection closed the day with a 51-yard touchdown pass and the Browns' first title since 1955.

Collins caught five passes for 130 yards.

SAYERS' SIX TOUCHDOWNS

Chicago Bears   **61**
San Francisco 49ers   **20**

December 12, 1965
NFL regular season, Wrigley Field, Chicago

The Chicago Bears didn't have the best team in 1965 but they always had the best show.

Rookie running back Gale Sayers was capable of dominating games in spectacular fashion, as he did on this day in a 61-20 victory against the San Francisco 49ers.

Rain turned Wrigley Field sloppy and slippery but Sayers didn't seem to notice. He scored six touchdowns and gained 336 all-purpose yards. Sayers started by turning a routine screen pass into an 80-yard touchdown. He followed with TD runs of 21, 7, 50 and 1 yards. With the game well in hand, coach George Halas pulled Sayers in the third quarter. Fans were chanting for Sayers to get back in the game, knowing he was one short of the NFL record for touchdowns in a game.

His chance came on a punt. Sayers returned the kick 85 yards for his sixth touchdown.

THE PACKERS PREVAIL

Green Bay Packers   **34**
Dallas Cowboys   **27**

January 1, 1967
NFL Championship game, Cotton Bowl, Dallas

The Dallas Cowboys didn't look like a team playing its first postseason game.

Even after falling behind 14-0 to the Green Bay Packers, the Cowboys came back and tied the game before the first quarter ended. Green Bay's Bart Starr threw a 51-yard pass to Carroll Dale for a 21-14 lead but Dallas got within a point on two field goals.

Starr stretched the lead to 34-20 with touchdown passes to Boyd Dowler and Max McGee. The Cowboys answered quickly with Don Meredith's 68-yard touchdown pass to Frank Clarke. That left Dallas trailing by just seven points.

With momentum on their side, it looked as though the Cowboys were going to get the tying touchdown. Dallas had the ball at Green Bay's 1-yard line with less than two minutes left. Defensive back Tom Brown intercepted Meredith's pass in the end zone and the Packers won 34-27 to claim the NFL title and advance to the first Super Bowl.

THE FIRST SUPERMEN

Green Bay Packers   **35**
Kansas City Chiefs   **10**

January 15, 1967
Super Bowl I, Memorial Coliseum, Los Angeles

How good was the American Football League? That was the question the Super Bowl was supposed to answer.

Although a merger was looming, the AFL and the established NFL had distinct identities and were anxious for an interleague championship game. Green Bay and Kansas City were the first to compete for the combined title at a neutral site.

The Packers held a slim 14-10 lead at halftime but made an important adjustment. They blitzed quarterback Len Dawson in the second half and limited his effectiveness. Packers defensive back Willie Wood returned an interception 50 yards and Elijah Pitts then ran five yards for a touchdown that changed the momentum.

The unlikely Packers hero was receiver Max McGee, who was needed when Boyd Dowler was injured. McGee had seven catches after a celebrated night on the town that kept him out until 7:30 a.m. He had caught only four passes in the regular season.

THE ICE BOWL

Green Bay Packers   **21**
Dallas Cowboys   **17**

December 31, 1967
NFL championship game, Lambeau Field, Green Bay

The thermometer said minus-13 and the Dallas Cowboys were quickly down 14 points in the NFL Championship game against the Green Bay Packers.

Packers quarterback Bart Starr connected with Boyd Dowler on touchdown passes of 8 and 46 yards for a 14-0 lead.

George Andrie of the Cowboys returned a Starr fumble seven yards for a touchdown and a field goal made the score 14-10 at halftime.

The Cowboys went ahead 17-14 on the first play of the fourth quarter. On the halfback option, Dan Reeves threw a 50-yard touchdown pass to Lance Rentzel.

The Packers got the ball at their own 32 with just under five minutes remaining. Green Bay got to the Dallas 1 and and two runs were stuffed for no gain. With 16 seconds left, Green Bay eschewed a pass that could have stopped the clock and allowed for a field goal attempt. Starr followed right guard Jerry Kramer's block and scored the winning touchdown.

THE HEIDI GAME

Oakland Raiders   **43**
New York Jets   **32**

November 17, 1968
AFL regular season, Oakland-Alameda Coliseum, Oakland

It was the game everyone remembers not seeing.

The Oakland Raiders and New York Jets, both playoff contenders, met in Oakland, which meant kickoff was 4 p.m. on the east coast.

Games were slotted for three hours and could cause havoc with network schedules when they ran late. Jim Turner's field goal broke a tie with 1:05 left in the fourth quarter and gave the Jets a 32-29 lead. NBC-TV, satisfied that the game was effectively over, switched to the movie "Heidi."

While viewers were watching Heidi, the Raiders mounted a comeback. Daryle Lamonica engineered a touchdown drive that ended with a 43-yard touchdown pass to Charlie Smith. The Raiders led 36-32 with 42 seconds left.

The Jets fumbled the ensuing kickoff and Oakland's Preston Ridelhuber returned the ball two yards for a touchdown. Final score: Raiders 43, Jets 32. NBC missed Oakland's 14-point comeback and angry viewers swamped the network with calls.

NAMATH'S GUARANTEE

New York Jets   **16**
Baltimore Colts   **7**

January 12, 1969
Super Bowl III, Orange Bowl, Miami

The first two Super Bowls had hardly lived up to their name. They were dreary games that saw the NFL's powerful Green Bay Packers handle two challengers from the American Football League.

Super Bowl III looked like another easy win for the NFL, which sent the Baltimore Colts, a team which had lost only once during the season, against the New York Jets.

That didn't stop flamboyant Jets quarterback Joe Namath from guaranteeing victory in a poolside press conference on the Thursday before the game.

Namath was on the mark as a prognosticator and a quarterback. The Jets won behind Matt Snell's 121 yards, including a 4-yard touchdown. Namath got the Most Valuable Player award and the AFL got credibility.

Baltimore's Earl Morrall was intercepted three times in the first half. Johnny Unitas, who missed most of the season with an elbow injury, threw for the Colts' only touchdown.

THE CHIEFS' REVENGE

Kansas City Chiefs   **23**
Minnesota Vikings   **7**

January 11, 1970
Super Bowl IV, Tulane Stadium, New Orleans

The warring pro football leagues were to merge in 1970, which meant that Super Bowl IV would be the last between the NFL and American Football League.

The Kansas City Chiefs, losers in Super Bowl I, made sure the AFL finished even in the competition between the leagues by beating the Minnesota Vikings, first-time qualifiers from the NFL.

Kansas City jumped out to a 16-0 halftime lead on three Jan Stenerud field goals and Mike Garrett's 5-yard touchdown run, which followed the Vikings fumble of a kickoff.

Minnesota's Dave Osborn scored on the first possession of the second half but the Chiefs put the game away with a 46-yard touchdown pass from Len Dawson to Otis Taylor.

Dawson had endured a stressful week in which his name had been linked to a federal gambling investigation in news reports.

PRIME TIME FOR FOOTBALL

Cleveland Browns   31
New York Jets   21

September 21, 1970
NFL regular season, Municipal Stadium, Cleveland

Thanks to the vision of ABC-TV executive Roone Arledge, the NFL was no longer confined to Sunday afternoons.

Arledge convinced his network to commit the time and resources to a weekly Monday night game. The other networks had experimented with prime time football in the exhibition season but didn't want to disrupt their normal fall schedules to carry the regular season. CBS couldn't imagine Monday night without the "Doris Day Show" and NBC was riding high with a movie.

ABC didn't just carry a football game, it created a show. Arledge nearly doubled the number of cameras normally used for football and had hand-held cameras for sideline close-ups. He pioneered the three-man booth with the abrasive Howard Cosell as a key component. He hired colorful Don Meredith on the recommendation of Frank Gifford.

Cleveland's Homer Jones returned the second half kickoff 94 yards for a touchdown and the first prime time highlight.

CHRISTMAS BONUS

Miami Dolphins   **27**
Kansas City Chiefs   **24**

December 25, 1971
AFC Playoffs, Municipal Stadium, Kansas City

It was a playoff game that turned into an endurance contest.

The Miami Dolphins were in Kansas City for a rare Christmas Day game against the Chiefs. It looked like the Chiefs were poised to win when reliable kicker Jan Stenerud lined up for a 32-yard field goal in the final minutes of the fourth quarter. Stenerud barely missed to the right and the teams, tied at 24, went to sudden death overtime. It wound up lasting 22 minutes and 40 seconds, making it the longest game in NFL history.

Stenerud had a 42-yard attempt blocked in the first overtime and Miami's Garo Yepremian missed a 52-yard try. The Dolphins won in the second overtime when Yepremian connected from 37 yards. Miami recorded the first playoff win in team history. Meanwhile, it would be 15 years before the Chiefs appeared in another postseason game.

THE IMMACULATE RECEPTION

Pittsburgh Steelers   13
Oakland Raiders   7

December 23, 1972
AFC Playoffs, Three Rivers Stadium, Pittsburgh

Pittsburgh Steelers owner Art Rooney was so certain that his team had lost, he was on the elevator to console his team as the players entered the locker room.

He missed the most memorable play in the franchise's 40 seasons.

The Steelers were trailing the Oakland Raiders 7-6 and faced with fourth-and-10 from their 40. Quarterback Terry Bradshaw ducked the rush, scrambled and threw a pass to running back Frenchy Fuqua. Raiders defensive back Jack Tatum hit Fuqua and the ball caromed off one of them. Rookie running back Franco Harris scooped it before it hit the ground and raced down the sideline for an apparent touchdown. The call wasn't made instantly, though, because no one was quite sure how it unfolded. It was ruled a touchdown and the extra point gave the Steelers a 13-7 lead and a win in the playoff game.

The play was dubbed "The Immaculate Reception" by Steelers fans.

A PERFECT ENDING

Miami Dolphins   14
Washington Redskins   7

January 14, 1973
Super Bowl VII, Memorial Coliseum, Los Angeles

The Miami Dolphins headed into Super Bowl VII with a 16-0 record, unprecedented in NFL history.

Coach Don Shula, who had lost his two previous Super Bowl appearances with Baltimore and Miami, made a decision to start Bob Griese at quarterback over 38-year-old Earl Morrall, who had led the Dolphins to 11 consecutive wins when Griese was sidelined with an ankle injury.

Griese threw a 28-yard touchdown pass to Howard Twilley and led another drive that ended with Jim Kiick's 2-yard run for a 14-0 lead. Jake Scott helped preserve the margin with two of Miami's three interceptions.

Washington's only points came on special teams. Garo Yepremian's attempted 42-yard field goal was blocked. The panicky kicker tried to make a pass, which was partially blocked and then returned for a touchdown by Mike Bass. Miami had one last defensive stand to wrap up its perfect season.

THE JUICE POURS IT ON

Buffalo Bills   **34**
New York Jets   **14**

December 16, 1973
NFL regular season, Shea Stadium, New York

Buffalo Bills offensive lineman Reggie McKenzie spent part of a hot summer day setting a lofty goal for teammate O.J. Simpson: "I told O.J. let's shoot for two grand and set the world on fire."

On a cold day in December, Simpson reached that improbable goal, with the considerable help of McKenzie and the rest of the Buffalo line.

Simpson entered the Bills' season finale at New York needing 61 yards to break Jim Brown's single-season rushing record of 1,863 yards and 197 yards to become the first back to crack 2,000 yards in a season. Simpson broke Brown's record in the first quarter, following McKenzie and Joe DeLamielleure for a 6-yard gain.

With 5:56 remaining in the game, a 7-yard run put Simpson at 2,003 yards. He carried 34 times for 200 yards in the game as Buffalo attempted only five passes.

DOLPHINS DYNASTY DERAILED

Oakland Raiders   **28**
Miami Dolphins   **26**

December 21, 1974
AFC Playoffs, Oakland-Alameda County Coliseum, Oakland

The Oakland Raiders beat Miami just when the Dolphins appeared to be unbeatable.

Miami had won two consecutive Super Bowls and were favored to take a third. Beginning with their perfect season in 1972, the Dolphins went 43-5 over three seasons heading into their divisional playoff game against Oakland. Miami's Nat Moore returned the opening kickoff 89 yards for a touchdown.

Later in the game the Dolphins recovered from a mental mistake (no one touched Cliff Branch after a diving catch so he got up and ran 72 yards for a touchdown). The Dolphins' Benny Malone ended a 68-yard drive with a 23-yard touchdown run that gave the Dolphins a 26-21 lead with 2:08 remaining.

Oakland quarterback Ken Stabler threw into double coverage but Clarence Davis made the catch for an 8-yard touchdown with 26 seconds left. The Raiders' 28-26 win scuttled the Dolphins' burgeoning dynasty. Miami didn't win another playoff game until 1982.

PAYTON'S RECORD-BREAKING DAY

Chicago Bears   **10**
Minnesota Vikings   **7**

November 20, 1977
NFL regular season, Soldier Field, Chicago

Running back Walter Payton was a major part of the Chicago Bears' offense.

That was never more true on this day.

Despite fighting the effects of the flu, Payton carried the ball 40 times for 275 yards, breaking O.J. Simpson's record of 273 yards in a game.

Payton ran 13 times in the first quarter for 77 yards. At halftime, he already had 144 yards, a good day's work by anyone's standard.

He added 48 more yards in the third quarter, then finished with 83 yards on just six attempts in the fourth quarter. With about three minutes left in the game, Payton ran 58 yards to the Vikings' 9. That put him within five yards of Simpson's record. Payton carried two more times for seven yards and broke the record.

"I get stronger as the game goes on," was the way he explained his impressive finish.

Cincinnati's Corey Dillon would top Payton's record by three yards in 2000.

DALLAS DROPS CHANCE

Pittsburgh Steelers   **35**
Dallas Cowboys   **31**

January 21, 1979
Super Bowl XII, Orange Bowl, Miami

Super Bowl XIII was a rematch of the title game from three years earlier between the NFL's best-known teams.

The Pittsburgh Steelers, chasing their third title in five years, had zipped through the regular season with a franchise-record 14-2 mark. The Dallas Cowboys overcame a slow start and took an eight-game winning streak into the Super Bowl.

Pittsburgh led 21-14 at the half but the Cowboys had a golden opportunity for a tying touchdown. Veteran tight end Jackie Smith dropped an easy pass in the end zone and Dallas settled for a field goal and a four-point deficit. The Cowboys never caught up.

The Steelers stretched their lead to 35-17 with the aid of a controversial pass interference call and a fumbled kickoff. The Cowboys got two touchdowns in the last 2:30 but Dallas' attempt at an onside kick with 22 seconds left was unsuccessful.

FOUR FOR THE STEELERS

Pittsburgh Steelers   **31**
Los Angeles Rams   **19**

January 20, 1980
Super Bowl XIV, Rose Bowl, Pasadena

The Pittsburgh Steelers were still winning championships but their methods had changed.

Rules changes opened up the passing game, which took away from the Steelers' defense but gave quarterback Terry Bradshaw a chance to showcase his arm and receivers Lynn Swann and John Stallworth.

The Steelers wrapped up their fourth title in six years with a wild ride against the Los Angeles Rams. There were six lead changes before the Steelers finally pulled away in the fourth quarter.

Bradshaw was the game's Most Valuable Player but the unsung Steelers hero was Larry Anderson, who gained 162 yards on kickoff returns.

The turning point came when Stallworth caught a touchdown pass that put the Steelers ahead to stay at 24-19. Linebacker Jack Lambert's interception of a Vince Ferragamo pass snuffed a last Rams drive and led to a final Pittsburgh touchdown.

MIAMI STEAM BATH

San Diego Chargers   **41**
Miami Dolphins   **38**

January 2, 1982
AFC Playoffs, Orange Bowl, Miami

An American Conference playoff game between two warm-weather teams turned into an endurance contest in sweltering conditions in Miami.

The visiting San Diego Chargers prevailed but 13:52 of overtime had expired before Rolf Benirschke connected on the 29-yard field goal that allowed them to advance in the playoffs.

San Diego built a 24-0 lead only to see Miami roar back and tie the game. Each team scored one touchdown in the third quarter and another in the fourth to force overtime. The Dolphins had a chance to win the game as time expired but Kellen Winslow blocked Uwe von Schamann's field goal attempt.

Winslow was the hero of the emotional, exhausting afternoon, catching 13 passes for 166 yards and turning in a performance that led Dolphins' coach Don Shula to call him "Superman."

Benirschke missed in overtime before he won the game for the Chargers.

CLARK'S CLASSIC CATCH

San Francisco 49ers   **28**
Dallas Cowboys   **27**

January 10, 1982
NFC Championship game, Candlestick Park, San Francisco

A single reception helped put the San Francisco 49ers on the path to being the NFL's team of the 1980s.

"The Catch" came in the NFC Championship game against the Dallas Cowboys.

The 49ers trailed 27-21 with 4:54 left in the fourth quarter and the ball at their own 11. Quarterback Joe Montana drove the San Francisco offense to the Cowboys' 6 with 58 seconds remaining. The 49ers called a pass to Freddie Solomon on third-and-3. The same play had resulted in a touchdown earlier in the game.

This time, though, the Cowboys had Solomon covered. Montana avoided a hit and floated a high pass to the back of the end zone. Dwight Clark made a leaping catch just inside the end line for a touchdown with 51 seconds left.

The San Francisco defense held on the Cowboys' last possession and the 49ers won 28-27, advancing to their first Super Bowl.

IN THE DEEP FREEZE

Cincinnati Bengals   **27**
San Diego Chargers   **7**

January 10, 1982
AFC Championship game, Riverfront Stadium, Cincinnati

One week removed from the heat and humidity of Miami, the San Diego Chargers' next playoff stop was frostbitten Cincinnati for the AFC Championship game.

The Chargers actually lobbied the NFL to postpone the game when the kickoff temperature was minus-9 with a wind/chill factor of nearly 60 below zero. The Bengals linemen wore their usual short-sleeved jerseys and had a head start in the battle of wills.

Cincinnati forced four turnovers and advanced to the franchise's first Super Bowl with the victory. Ken Anderson threw for two touchdowns, Pete Johnson ran for a score and Jim Breech kicked a pair of field goals.

Bengals coach Forrest Gregg, who played in frigid weather during his career with Green Bay, told his team to approach the day like a trip to the dentist: "It's going to hurt, you're not going to like it but you have to do it."

NOT QUITE PERFECT

Miami Dolphins   **38**
Chicago Bears   **24**

December 2, 1985
NFL regular season, Orange Bowl, Miami

This Monday night showdown was made for prime time.

The Chicago Bears were 12-0 and trying for the first undefeated season since the 1972 Miami Dolphins went 17-0 (including three postseason victories). The current Dolphins were trying to protect that distinction against the Bears, with many of the 1972 alumni on hand.

Not only did the Dolphins beat the Bears, they did so handily.

The Dolphins were 8-4 and fighting for playoff position. Third-year quarterback Dan Marino picked apart a Bears defense that had held opponents to 10 or fewer points in nine of 12 games. Chicago had not allowed a touchdown in 13 quarters.

Miami led 31-10 at halftime, the first time the Bears had allowed that many points in a game since 1972.

It turned out to be the Bears' only loss. They outscored postseason opponents 91-10 en route to a Super Bowl victory.

DENVER'S DRIVE

Denver Broncos   **23**
Cleveland Browns   **20**

January 11, 1987
AFC Championship game, Cleveland Stadium, Cleveland

It was the day when quarterback John Elway proved nothing was impossible.

Elway's Denver Broncos were playing the Cleveland Browns in the AFC Championship game and facing dire circumstances—They were down by a touchdown on the road with 5:32 left and starting at their own 2-yard line.

It began as a possession and became "The Drive" in Broncos legend. Thanks to a 20-yard completion to Mark Jackson on third-and-18, the Broncos endured for a game-tying 5-yard touchdown pass to Jackson with 37 seconds left. Elway covered 98 yards in 15 plays in less than five minutes.

Rich Karlis kicked a 33-yard field goal in overtime to win the game and send Denver to the Super Bowl.

Elway would lead Denver to 46 fourth-quarter victories during his illustious career but this is the one that's best remembered.

"It definitely put me on the map," he said. "That was probably the highlight."

THE FOG BOWL

Chicago Bears   **20**
Philadelphia Eagles   **12**

December 31, 1988
NFC Playoffs, Soldier Field, Chicago

The stands were packed and a national television audience tuned in but no one saw much of the game.

Soldier Field's proximity to Lake Michigan became a major factor when the Philadelphia Eagles visited the Chicago Bears for a playoff game.

In the second half, a dense fog rolled in off the lake and severely compromised visibility. According to meteorologists, cold air blew in off the lake and merged with warm air on land. The result was the equivalent of a large cloud forming over the field.

The Bears were already ahead 17-6 before the fog arrived and made play extremely difficult. Mike Tomczak threw a 64-yard touchdown pass to Dennis McKinnon and Neal Anderson ran four yards for another score. The Eagles could only manage four field goals despite Randall Cunningham's 407 passing yards.

Said Eagles receiver Gregg Garrity, "I couldn't see into the backfield. It was eerie."

49ERS TIMES THREE

San Francisco 49ers   **20**
Cincinnati Bengals   **16**

January 22, 1989
Super Bowl XXIII, Joe Robbie Stadium, Miami

The Cincinnati Bengals had a 16-13 lead with 3:20 to play in Super Bowl XXIII. Unfortunately for them, the San Francisco 49ers had quarterback Joe Montana.

Montana was the master of the late comeback, even in the biggest games. Montana led an 11-play, 92-yard touchdown drive that ended with a 10-yard pass from Montana to John Taylor with just 34 seconds left. It was the first time a Super Bowl had been decided on a touchdown scored that late in the game.

The game see-sawed: Even when Cincinnati's Stanford Jennings returned a kickoff 93 yards for a touchdown, the 49ers came back with a four-play drive capped by Jerry Rice's 14-yard touchdown reception.

Jim Breech's field goal put the Bengals ahead for the third time before Montana got to work.

San Francisco became the first NFC team to win three Super Bowls.

WIDE RIGHT

New York Giants   **20**
Buffalo Bills   **19**

January 27, 1991
Super Bowl XXV, Tampa Stadium, Tampa

It is the Super Bowl remembered best for the points that weren't scored.

Scott Norwood lined up to attempt a 47-yard field goal that would give the Buffalo Bills a victory in their first Super Bowl appearance. The kick sailed wide right and the New York Giants had a one-point win for their second title in five years.

The Giants' ball control offense set a record for time of possession by holding the ball for 40:33. The Bills only had the ball for eight minutes in the second half. Despite that disadvantage, Buffalo's Thurman Thomas ran for 135 yards and caught passes for another 55 yards. He had a 31-yard touchdown run.

New York's Matt Bahr hit a 21-yard field goal in the fourth quarter to put the Giants ahead and set the stage for the kick that missed. Norwood's name became part of Super Bowl history for the wrong reason.

THE BILLS' BIG COMEBACK

Buffalo Bills   41
Houston Oilers   38

January 3, 1993
AFC Playoffs, Ralph Wilson Stadium, Buffalo

The Buffalo Bills were losing. Badly.

Less than two minutes into the second half of their wild card game against the Houston Oilers, they were trailing 35-3 and without quarterback Jim Kelly.

But backup Frank Reich was just getting started. He got a quick touchdown. After an onside kick, Reich threw a 38-yard touchdown pass to Don Beebe. Then it was a 26-yard pass to Andre Reed and the deficit was 35-24.

An interception led to another touchdown pass to Reed and a four-point deficit. Houston mishandled a field goal attempt and the Bills went ahead 38-35 on a pass to Reed. Al Del Greco's 26-yard field goal tied the score for Houston with 12 seconds left in the fourth quarter.

The Oilers won the coin toss in overtime but Nate Odomes picked off Warren Moon's pass to set up Steve Christie's 32-yard game-winning field goal.

DENVER'S FIRST WIN

Denver Broncos   **31**
Green Bay Packers   **24**

January 25, 1998
Super Bowl XXXII, Qualcomm Stadium, San Diego

The Denver Broncos had been to the Super Bowl four times without winning.

Super Bowl XXXII ended that streak and brought at least a measure of vindication for quarterback John Elway, who had been on the losing end three times.

Terrell Davis ran for 157 yards and a Super Bowl-record three touchdowns.

It wasn't easy—the Broncos didn't wrap up the game until John Mobley knocked away a pass intended for tight end Mark Chmura with 32 seconds left at the Denver 31-yard line.

Green Bay quarterback Brett Favre passed for 256 yards and three touchdowns. His only interception, by Tyrone Braxton, gave the Broncos the ball at the Packers 45 and led to a Denver touchdown. Neil Smith's recovery of a Favre fumble set up a field goal.

Elway completed 12 of 22 passes for 123 yards with an interception.

LATERAL MOVE ADVANCES TITANS

Tennessee Titans   22
Buffalo Bills   16

January 8, 2000
AFC Playoffs, Adelphia Coliseum, Nashville

It may have looked like an improvised sandlot play but it was actually in the Tennessee Titans' playbook.

Good thing, because it helped them win a game they appeared destined to lose.

Steve Christie had kicked a 41-yard field goal to put the Buffalo Bills ahead 16-15 in their wild card playoff game against the Titans.

Christie then squibbed a kick that Lorenzo Neal fielded around the 25-yard line. Neal handed off to tight end Frank Wycheck, who then advanced about five yards. The Bills converged on Wycheck, who threw a lateral to Kevin Dyson, part of a play the Titans called "Home Run Throwback."

Dyson turned the home run into a touchdown by running 75 yards to the end zone. Replays determined the play was legal and the Titans had the lead with just three seconds on the clock. It came to be known as the "Music City Miracle."

ONE YARD SHORT

St. Louis Rams	**23**
Tennessee Titans	**16**

January 30, 2000
Super Bowl XXXIV, Georgia Dome, Atlanta

It looked like a blowout in the making but turned out to be one of the best Super Bowls in the game's 34-year history.

The St. Louis Rams took a 16-0 lead with three first-half field goals by Jeff Wilkins and Kurt Warner's 9-yard touchdown pass to Torry Holt.

But Tennessee, which had shown a season-long ability to come back, put together a pair of drives that ended with short touchdown runs by Eddie George.

When Al Del Greco kicked a 43-yard field goal, the score was tied at 16.

Isaac Bruce got away from cornerback Denard Walker and ran 73 yards with a Warner pass for a go-ahead touchdown.

The Titans still weren't done, though. Quarterback Steve McNair took the team on one last drive and nearly tied the score. McNair completed a pass to Kevin Dyson, who was tackled at the 1-yard line by linebacker Mike Jones as time expired.

VINATIERI KICKS THE RAMS

New England Patriots   20
St. Louis Rams   17

February 3, 2002
Super Bowl XXXVI, Louisiana Superdome, New Orleans

The New England Patriots had gone 41 seasons without a title and were 50-1 shots to win one when the 2001 season opened.

It appeared the Patriots were doomed when quarterback Drew Bledsoe was sidelined.

But the Patriots endured, upset Pittsburgh in the AFC Championship game and were in the Super Bowl as 14-point underdogs to the St. Louis Rams.

The Patriots led 17-3 largely because of turnovers by Rams quarterback Kurt Warner. His fumble and two interceptions led to the Patriots' points.

The Rams came back to tie the score and it looked as though the Patriots would run out the clock and take their chances in overtime. Instead, rookie quarterback Tom Brady led a 53-yard, nine-play drive and Adam Vinatieri kicked a 48-yard field goal as time expired. The Patriots were champions on their third trip to the Super Bowl.

LEWIS PREDICTED BIG GAME

Baltimore Ravens 33
Cleveland Browns 13

September 14, 2003
NFL Regular Season, Ravens Stadium, Baltimore

A 100-yard game is a successful day for any running back. Jamal Lewis of the Baltimore Ravens had 100 yards by his second carry of the day, which meant he was on his way to an exceptional day.

When it was done, Lewis had 295 yards and the NFL record for rushing yards in a game. He topped the 278 yards Cincinnati's Corey Dillon had gained against Denver on October 22, 2000.

Lewis had an inkling a big game was due. In a phone conversation with Browns linebacker Andra Davis during the week, Lewis said that if he got the ball 30 times, he'd have a career day.

"I'm not going to say I predicted it," Lewis said. "It was lucky."

Lewis carried 30 times and averaged 9.8 yards per attempt. He had touchdown runs of 82 and 63 yards and had gained 180 yards by halftime.

In the second game against Cleveland in 2003, Lewis gained 205 yards and wound up with 2,066 yards for the year, the second-best rushing season in NFL history.

PANTHERS CLAW RAMS

Carolina Panthers 29
St. Louis Rams 23

January 10, 2004
NFL Playoffs, Edward Jones Dome, St. Louis

The Carolina Panthers had specialized in the fourth-quarter comeback all season. It looked like they were going to be victims of one this time.

The St. Louis Rams made up an 11-point deficit in the last 2:39 of their playoff game to force overtime. Carolina kicked an apparent game-winning field goal but the play was nullified by a delay of game penalty. Three plays later, John Kasay's second attempt, now five yards deeper, missed from 45 yards and the Rams survived.

St. Louis' Jeff Wilkins was inches short on a 53-yard field goal try. The Rams were driving again, reaching the Panthers' 38 when Ricky Manning Jr. of Carolina wrestled the ball from receiver Torry Holt for an interception.

The game ended on the first play of the second overtime period. On 3rd down and 14 from their own 31, quarterback Jake Delhomme hit Steve Smith on a slant pattern for a 69-yard game-winning touchdown.

VINATIERI'S SEQUEL

New England Patriots 32
Carolina Panthers 29

February 1, 2004
Super Bowl XXXVIII, Reliant Stadium, Houston

The game started slowly but what a finish.

After setting a Super Bowl record with 27 scoreless minutes, the Patriots and Panthers established another Super Bowl record by combining for 37 points in the fourth quarter.

Carolina tied the score at 29 with 1:08 left in the fourth quarter. The Panthers' third touchdown of the quarter was a 12-yard pass from Jake Delhomme to Ricky Proehl. The Patriots got the ball on the 40 after the kickoff went out of bounds and quarterback Tom Brady moved the team 37 yards on six plays to set up Adam Vinatieri for a 41-yard field goal attempt.

Vinatieri, who had earlier missed from 31 yards and had a 36-yard try blocked, made a Super Bowl-winning kick for the second time in three years.

Brady took Most Valuable Player honors with a 32-for-48 passing day that included 354 yards, three touchdowns and one interception.

THE FACTS

& STATS

CAREER REGULAR SEASON

CAREER GAMES

PLAYER	GAMES
George Blanda	340
Morten Andersen	338
Gary Anderson	338
Bruce Matthews	296
Darrell Green	295
Jerry Rice	286
Jim Marshall	282
Trey Junkin	281
Bruce Smith	279
Clay Matthews	278
Norm Johnson	273
Sean Landeta	269
Lomas Brown	263
Jan Stenerud	263
Nick Lowery	260
Lee Johnson	259
Jackie Slater	259
Jeff Feagles	256
Irving Fryar	255
Earl Morrall	255
Mike Kenn	251
Pat Leahy	250
Eddie Murray	250
Eugene Robinson	250
Al Del Greco	248
Blair Bush	246
Fran Tarkenton	246
Jeff Van Note	246
Mike Webster	245
Ray Donaldson	244

CAREER YEARS PLAYED

PLAYER	YEARS
George Blanda	26
Morten Andersen	22
Gary Anderson	22
Earl Morrall	21
Darrell Green	20
Jim Marshall	20
Jackie Slater	20
Len Dawson	19
Jim Hart	19
Trey Junkin	19
Dave Krieg	19
Sean Landeta	19
Bruce Matthews	19
Clay Matthews	19
Eddie Murray	19
Jerry Rice	19
Bruce Smith	19
Jan Stenerud	19
Lomas Brown	18
Lee Johnson	18
Norm Johnson	18
Charlie Joiner	18
Sonny Jurgensen	18
Pat Leahy	18
Nick Lowery	18
Ron McDole	18
Craig Morton	18
Fran Tarkenton	18
Johnny Unitas	18
Jeff Van Note	18

CAREER TOUCHDOWNS

PLAYER	RUN	REC	RET	TOT
Jerry Rice	10	194	1	205
Emmitt Smith	155	11	0	166
Marcus Allen	123	21	1	145
Cris Carter	0	130	1	131
Marshall Faulk	97	34	0	131
Jim Brown	106	20	0	126
Walter Payton	110	15	0	125
John Riggins	104	12	0	116
Lenny Moore	63	48	2	113
Barry Sanders	99	10	0	109
Don Hutson	3	99	3	105
Tim Brown	1	99	4	104
Steve Largent	1	100	0	101
Franco Harris	91	9	0	100
Eric Dickerson	90	6	0	96
Jim Taylor	83	10	0	93
Tony Dorsett	77	13	1	91
Bobby Mitchell	18	65	8	91
Ricky Watters	78	13	0	91
Leroy Kelly	74	13	3	90
Charley Taylor	11	79	0	90
Irving Fryar	1	84	3	88
Don Maynard	0	88	0	88
Andre Reed	1	87	0	88
Thurman Thomas	65	23	0	88
Lance Alworth	2	85	0	87
Ottis Anderson	81	5	0	86
Paul Warfield	0	85	1	86
Mark Clayton	0	84	1	85
Tommy McDonald	0	84	1	85

CAREER POINTS SCORED

PLAYER	POINTS SCORED
Gary Anderson	2346
Morten Andersen	2259
George Blanda	2002
Norm Johnson	1736
Nick Lowery	1711
Jan Stenerud	1699
Eddie Murray	1594
Al Del Greco	1584
Pat Leahy	1470
Jim Turner	1439
John Carney	1433
Matt Bahr	1422

CAREER POINTS SCORED cont.

PLAYER	POINTS SCORED
Mark Moseley	1382
Jim Bakken	1380
Steve Christie	1377
Fred Cox	1365
Matt Stover	1364
Lou Groza	1349
Jason Elam	1313
Jim Breech	1246
Jerry Rice	1238
Jason Hanson	1236
Pete Stoyanovich	1236
Chris Bahr	1213
Kevin Butler	1208
Gino Cappelletti	1130
Ray Wersching	1122
John Kasay	1100
Don Cockroft	1080
Garo Yepremian	1074

CAREER TOTAL YARDS GAINED

PLAYER	RUSH	REC	RET	TOT
Brian Mitchell	1967	2336	19027	23330
Jerry Rice	645	22466	6	23117
Walter Payton	16726	4538	539	21803
Emmitt Smith	17418	3119	-19	20518
Tim Brown	190	14734	4510	19434
Barry Sanders	15269	2921	118	18308
Herschel Walker	8225	4859	5084	18168
Marcus Allen	12243	5411	-6	17648
Marshall Faulk	11213	6274	36	17523
Eric Metcalf	2392	5572	9266	17230
Thurman Thomas	12074	4458	0	16532
Tony Dorsett	12739	3554	33	16326
Henry Ellard	50	13777	1891	15718
Irving Fryar	242	12785	2567	15594
Jim Brown	12312	2499	648	15459
Eric Dickerson	13259	2137	15	15411
Glyn Milburn	817	1322	12772	14911
James Brooks	7962	3621	3327	14910
Ricky Watters	10643	4248	0	14891
Curtis Martin	11669	2966	0	14635
Franco Harris	12120	2287	215	14622
O.J. Simpson	11236	2142	990	14368
James Lofton	246	14004	27	14277
Cris Carter	41	13899	244	14184
Bobby Mitchell	2735	7954	3389	14078
David Meggett	1684	3038	9274	13996
Jerome Bettis	12353	1363	2	13718
Andre Reed	500	13198	14	13712
Earnest Byner	8261	4605	631	13497
John Riggins	11352	2090	-7	13435

CAREER PASS ATTEMPTS

PLAYER	ATTEMPTS
Dan Marino	8358
John Elway	7250
Warren Moon	6823
Fran Tarkenton	6467
Brett Favre	6464
Vinny Testaverde	5925
Dan Fouts	5604
Drew Bledsoe	5599
Joe Montana	5391
Dave Krieg	5311
Boomer Esiason	5205
Johnny Unitas	5186
Jim Hart	5076
Steve DeBerg	5024
Jim Everett	4923
Jim Kelly	4779
Troy Aikman	4715
John Hadl	4688
Phil Simms	4647
Joe Ferguson	4519
Roman Gabriel	4498
John Brodie	4491
Ken Anderson	4475
Norm Snead	4353
Randall Cunningham	4289
Sonny Jurgensen	4262
Steve Young	4149
Rich Gannon	4138
Ron Jaworski	4117
George Blanda	4007

CAREER COMPLETIONS

PLAYER	COMPLETIONS
Dan Marino	4967
John Elway	4123
Warren Moon	3988
Brett Favre	3960
Fran Tarkenton	3686
Joe Montana	3409
Vinny Testaverde	3334
Dan Fouts	3297
Drew Bledsoe	3193
Dave Krieg	3105
Boomer Esiason	2969
Troy Aikman	2898
Steve DeBerg	2874
Jim Kelly	2874
Jim Everett	2841
Johnny Unitas	2830
Steve Young	2667
Ken Anderson	2654
Jim Hart	2593
Phil Simms	2576

CAREER REGULAR SEASON

Player	Completions
Rich Gannon	2492
John Brodie	2469
Sonny Jurgensen	2433
Randall Cunningham	2429
Joe Ferguson	2369
Roman Gabriel	2366
John Hadl	2363
Jim Harbaugh	2305
Jeff George	2290
Chris Chandler	2293

CAREER PASS COMPLETIONS %

PLAYER	COMPLETIONS (1500 ATTEMPTS)
Kurt Warner	66.4
Steve Young	64.3
Joe Montana	63.2
Daunte Culpepper	62.9
Peyton Manning	62.9
Tom Brady	61.9
Brian Griese	61.8
Brad Johnson	61.8
Troy Aikman	61.5
Jeff Garcia	61.4
Brett Favre	61.3
Mark Brunell	60.3
Rich Gannon	60.2
Jim Kelly	60.1
Ken Stabler	59.8
Tim Couch	59.8
Danny White	59.7
Dan Marino	59.4
Jay Fiedler	59.4
Ken Anderson	59.3
Bernie Kosar	59.3
Steve McNair	59.2
Elvis Grbac	59.1
Trent Green	59.0
Bobby Hebert	58.9
Dan Fouts	58.8
Jim Harbaugh	58.8
Jon Kitna	58.8
Ken O'Brien	58.6
Dave Krieg	58.5

CAREER PASSING YARDS

PLAYER	PASSING YARDS
Dan Marino	61361
John Elway	51475
Warren Moon	49325
Fran Tarkenton	47003
Brett Favre	45646
Dan Fouts	43040
Vinny Testaverde	40943
Joe Montana	40551
Johnny Unitas	40239
Dave Krieg	38147
Boomer Esiason	37920
Drew Bledsoe	36876
Jim Kelly	35467
Jim Everett	34837
Jim Hart	34665
Steve DeBerg	34241
John Hadl	33503
Phil Simms	33462
Steve Young	33124
Troy Aikman	32942
Ken Anderson	32838
Sonny Jurgensen	32224
John Brodie	31548
Norm Snead	30797
Randall Cunningham	29979
Joe Ferguson	29817
Roman Gabriel	29444
Len Dawson	28711
Y.A. Tittle	28339
Rich Gannon	28219

CAREER PASSING TOUCHDOWNS

PLAYER	PASSING TOUCHDOWNS
Dan Marino	420
Brett Favre	346
Fran Tarkenton	342
John Elway	300
Warren Moon	291
Johnny Unitas	290
Joe Montana	273
Dave Krieg	261
Sonny Jurgensen	255
Dan Fouts	254
Vinny Testaverde	251
Boomer Esiason	247
John Hadl	244
Len Dawson	239
Jim Kelly	237
George Blanda	236
Steve Young	232
John Brodie	214
Terry Bradshaw	212
Y.A. Tittle	212
Jim Hart	209
Randall Cunningham	207
Jim Everett	203
Drew Bledsoe	201
Roman Gabriel	201
Phil Simms	199
Ken Anderson	197
Steve DeBerg	196
Joe Ferguson	196
Bobby Layne	196
Norm Snead	196

CAREER YARDS PER PASS AVG.

PLAYER	YARDS/PASS AVG (1500 ATTEMPTS)
Otto Graham	8.63
Kurt Warner	8.56
Sid Luckman	8.42
Norm Van Brocklin	8.16
Steve Young	7.98
Ed Brown	7.85
Bart Starr	7.85
Johnny Unitas	7.76
Earl Morrall	7.74
Dan Fouts	7.68
Len Dawson	7.67
Roger Staubach	7.67
Sonny Jurgensen	7.56
Daunte Culpepper	7.53
Joe Montana	7.52
Frank Ryan	7.52
Trent Green	7.51
Steve Grogan	7.48
Lynn Dickey	7.46
Eddie LeBaron	7.46
Don Meredith	7.45
Danny White	7.44
Bill Nelsen	7.44
Y.A. Tittle	7.42
Jim Kelly	7.42
Craig Morton	7.37
Ken Stabler	7.37
Daryle Lamonica	7.36
Peyton Manning	7.36
Joe Namath	7.35

CAREER INTERCEPTED

PLAYER	INTERCEPTED
George Blanda	277
John Hadl	268
Fran Tarkenton	266
Norm Snead	257
Johnny Unitas	253
Dan Marino	252
Jim Hart	247
Bobby Layne	243
Dan Fouts	242
Vinny Testaverde	235
Warren Moon	233
John Elway	226
John Brodie	224
Ken Stabler	222
Y.A. Tittle	221
Joe Namath	220
Babe Parilli	220
Terry Bradshaw	210
Brett Favre	209
Joe Ferguson	209
Steve Grogan	208

Steve DeBerg	204
Sammy Baugh	203
Dave Krieg	199
Jim Plunkett	198
Tobin Rote	191
Sonny Jurgensen	189
Craig Morton	187
Boomer Esiason	184
Len Dawson	183
Jack Kemp	183

CAREER QB RATING

PLAYER	QB RATING (1500 ATTEMPTS)
Kurt Warner	97.2
Steve Young	96.8
Joe Montana	92.3
Jeff Garcia	88.3
Peyton Manning	88.1
Daunte Culpepper	88.0
Brett Favre	86.9
Dan Marino	86.4
Trent Green	86.1
Tom Brady	85.9
Mark Brunell	85.2
Rich Gannon	84.7
Jim Kelly	84.4
Brad Johnson	84.1
Steve McNair	84.1
Roger Staubach	83.4
Brian Griese	83.0
Neil Lomax	82.7
Sonny Jurgensen	82.6
Len Dawson	82.6
Aaron Brooks	82.1
Ken Anderson	81.9
Bernie Kosar	81.8
Neil O'Donnell	81.8
Danny White	81.7
Troy Aikman	81.6
Dave Krieg	81.5
Randall Cunningham	81.5
Boomer Esiason	81.1
Warren Moon	80.9

CAREER RUSHING YARDS

PLAYER	YARDS
Emmitt Smith	17418
Walter Payton	16726
Barry Sanders	15269
Eric Dickerson	13259
Tony Dorsett	12739
Jerome Bettis	12353
Jim Brown	12312
Marcus Allen	12243
Franco Harris	12120
Thurman Thomas	12074

CAREER REGULAR SEASON

CAREER RUSHING YARDS cont.

PLAYER	YARDS
Curtis Martin	11669
John Riggins	11352
O.J. Simpson	11236
Marshall Faulk	11213
Ricky Watters	10643
Ottis Anderson	10273
Eddie George	10009
Earl Campbell	9407
Terry Allen	8614
Jim Taylor	8597
Joe Perry	8378
Earnest Byner	8261
Herschel Walker	8225
Roger Craig	8189
Gerald Riggs	8188
Larry Csonka	8081
Freeman McNeil	8074
Corey Dillon	8061
James Brooks	7962
Garrison Hearst	7885

CAREER RUSHES

PLAYER	RUSHES
Emmitt Smith	4142
Walter Payton	3838
Jerome Bettis	3119
Barry Sanders	3062
Marcus Allen	3022
Eric Dickerson	2996
Franco Harris	2949
Tony Dorsett	2936
Curtis Martin	2927
John Riggins	2916
Thurman Thomas	2877
Eddie George	2733
Ricky Watters	2622
Marshall Faulk	2576
Ottis Anderson	2562
O.J. Simpson	2404
Jim Brown	2359
Earl Campbell	2187
Terry Allen	2152
Earnest Byner	2095
Roger Craig	1991
Gerald Riggs	1989
Herschel Walker	1954
Jim Taylor	1941
Larry Csonka	1891
Corey Dillon	1865
Mike Pruitt	1844
Rodney Hampton	1824
Garrison Hearst	1811
Freeman McNeil	1798

CAREER YARDS PER CARRY

PLAYER	YARDS (750 RUSHES)
Randall Cunningham	6.4
Jim Brown	5.2
Mercury Morris	5.1
Gale Sayers	5.0
Barry Sanders	5.0
Napoleon Kaufman	4.9
Paul Lowe	4.9
Lenny Moore	4.8
Robert Smith	4.8
Joe Perry	4.8
Marv Hubbard	4.8
Wendell Tyler	4.7
Greg Pruitt	4.7
Ahman Green	4.7
Jamal Lewis	4.7
Tank Younger	4.7
James Brooks	4.7
Priest Holmes	4.7
Stump Mitchell	4.7
Hugh McElhenny	4.7
O.J. Simpson	4.7
Charlie Garner	4.6
Fred Taylor	4.6
Terrell Davis	4.6
Gerry Ellis	4.6
Terry Metcalf	4.6
William Andrews	4.6
Hoyle Granger	4.5
Clarence Davis	4.5
Billy Sims	4.5

CAREER RUSHING TOUCHDOWNS

PLAYER	TOUCHDOWNS
Emmitt Smith	155
Marcus Allen	123
Walter Payton	110
Jim Brown	106
John Riggins	104
Barry Sanders	99
Marshall Faulk	97
Franco Harris	91
Eric Dickerson	90
Jim Taylor	83
Ottis Anderson	81
Ricky Watters	78
Tony Dorsett	77
Pete Johnson	76
Earl Campbell	74
Leroy Kelly	74
Terry Allen	73
Curtis Martin	73
Chuck Muncie	71
Jerome Bettis	69
Gerald Riggs	69
Steve Van Buren	69
Priest Holmes	66

RUSHING TOUCHDOWNS cont.

PLAYER	TOUCHDOWNS
Thurman Thomas	65
Larry Csonka	64
Eddie George	64
Lenny Moore	63
O.J. Simpson	61
Herschel Walker	61
Terrell Davis	60

CAREER RECEIVING YARDS BY RUNNING BACKS

PLAYER	YARDS
Larry Centers	6797
Marshall Faulk	6274
Ronnie Harmon	6065
Lenny Moore	6039
Keith Byars	5661
Frank Gifford	5434
Marcus Allen	5411
Joe Morrison	4993
Roger Craig	4911
Herschel Walker	4859
John L. Williams	4656
Earnest Byner	4605
Walter Payton	4538
Thurman Thomas	4458
Ricky Watters	4248
Tony Galbreath	4066
Ray Mathews	3963
John David Crow	3699
Billy Cannon	3656
Charlie Garner	3649
James Brooks	3621
Tiki Barber	3610
Tony Nathan	3592
Tony Dorsett	3554
Abner Haynes	3535
James Wilder	3500
Joe Washington	3413
Timmy Brown	3399
Clem Daniels	3314
Ollie Matson	3285
Rickey Young	3285

CAREER RECEIVING YARDS

PLAYER	YARDS
Jerry Rice	22466
Tim Brown	14734
James Lofton	14004
Cris Carter	13899
Henry Ellard	13777
Andre Reed	13198
Steve Largent	13089
Irving Fryar	12785
Art Monk	12721
Charlie Joiner	12146
Michael Irvin	11904
Don Maynard	11834
Gary Clark	10856
Stanley Morgan	10716
Isaac Bruce	10461
Harold Jackson	10372
Lance Alworth	10266
Andre Rison	10205
Jimmy Smith	10092
Marvin Harrison	10072
Shannon Sharpe	10060
Drew Hill	9831
Keenan McCardell	9370
Rob Moore	9368
Raymond Berry	9275
Herman Moore	9174
Anthony Miller	9148
Charley Taylor	9110
Tony Martin	9065
Harold Carmichael	8985

CAREER RECEPTIONS

PLAYER	RECEPTIONS
Jerry Rice	1519
Cris Carter	1101
Tim Brown	1070
Andre Reed	951
Art Monk	940
Irving Fryar	851
Larry Centers	827
Steve Largent	819
Shannon Sharpe	815
Henry Ellard	814
James Lofton	764
Marvin Harrison	759
Michael Irvin	750
Charlie Joiner	750
Andre Rison	743
Keenan McCardell	724
Jimmy Smith	718
Gary Clark	699
Terance Mathis	689
Isaac Bruce	688
Marshall Faulk	673
Herman Moore	670
Ozzie Newsome	662
Charley Taylor	649
Drew Hill	634
Don Maynard	633
Rod Smith	633
Raymond Berry	631
Rob Moore	628
Keith Byars	610

CAREER REGULAR SEASON

CAREER YARDS PER CATCH

PLAYER	YARDS/CATCH (200 RECEPTIONS)
Homer Jones	22.3
Buddy Dial	20.8
Harlon Hill	20.2
Flipper Anderson	20.1
Paul Warfield	20.1
Bob Hayes	20.0
Willie Gault	19.9
Jimmy Orr	19.8
Ray Renfro	19.6
Hugh Taylor	19.2
Stanley Morgan	19.2
Wesley Walker	19.0
Lance Alworth	18.9
Mel Gray	18.9
Carroll Dale	18.9
Roger Carr	18.7
Don Maynard	18.7
Frank Clarke	18.6
Gary Garrison	18.6
Del Shofner	18.5
John Gilliam	18.5
Max McGee	18.4
Elroy Hirsch	18.4
James Lofton	18.3
Ben Hawkins	18.3
Haven Moses	18.1
Carlos Carson	18.1
Mervyn Fernandez	18.0
Lance Rentzel	18.0
Elbert Dubenion	18.0

CAREER RECEIVING TOUCHDOWNS

PLAYER	TOUCHDOWNS
Jerry Rice	194
Cris Carter	130
Steve Largent	100
Tim Brown	99
Don Hutson	99
Don Maynard	88
Andre Reed	87
Lance Alworth	85
Paul Warfield	85
Mark Clayton	84
Irving Fryar	84
Tommy McDonald	84
Andre Rison	84
Marvin Harrison	83
Terrell Owens	81
Art Powell	81
Harold Carmichael	79
Charley Taylor	79
Randy Moss	77
Fred Biletnikoff	76
Harold Jackson	76
James Lofton	75
Nat Moore	74
Stanley Morgan	72
Bob Hayes	71
Wesley Walker	71
Gary Collins	70
Raymond Berry	00
Isaac Bruce	68
Art Monk	68

CAREER INTERCEPTIONS

PLAYER	INTERCEPTIONS
Paul Krause	81
Emlen Tunnell	79
Rod Woodson	71
Night Train Lane	68
Ken Riley	65
Ronnie Lott	63
Dave Brown	62
Dick LeBeau	62
Emmitt Thomas	58
Mel Blount	57
Bobby Boyd	57
Eugene Robinson	57
Johnny Robinson	57
Everson Walls	57
Lem Barney	56
Pat Fischer	56
Aeneas Williams	55
Eric Allen	54
Willie Brown	54
Darrell Green	54
Jack Butler	52
Bobby Dillon	52
Jimmy Patton	52
Mel Renfro	52
Larry Wilson	52
Bobby Bryant	51
Donnie Shell	51
Don Burroughs	50
Deron Cherry	50
John Harris	50
Yale Lary	50

CAREER FUMBLES RECOVERED

PLAYER	FUMBLES RECOVERED
Warren Moon	56
Dave Krieg	47
Boomer Esiason	45
Dan Marino	43
Fran Tarkenton	43
Dan Fouts	38
Randall Cunningham	37
Roman Gabriel	37
Chris Chandler	36
John Elway	35
Joe Ferguson	35
Ron Jaworski	35
Steve Grogan	34
Drew Bledsoe	33
Vinny Testaverde	33
Rod Woodson	32
Jim Marshall	30
Steve McNair	30
Brett Favre	29
Rickey Jackson	29
Jon Kitna	29
Johnny Unitas	29
Kermit Alexander	28
Phil Simms	28
Cornelius Bennett	27
Dick Butkus	27
Bobby Layne	27
Kerry Collins	26
Charlie Conerly	26
Lynn Dickey	26
Kevin Greene	26
Ken O'Brien	26
Dan Pastorini	26
Dewayne Washington	7
Larry Wilson	7
Dre' Bly	6
Derrick Brooks	6
Cris Dishman	6
Miller Farr	6
LeRoy Irvin	6
Tom Janik	6
Paul Krause	6
Night Train Lane	6
Ty Law	6
Darryll Lewis	6
Rod Martin	6
Jack Pardee	6
Jessie Tuggle	6

CAREER DEFENSIVE TDs

PLAYER	TOUCHDOWNS
Rod Woodson	13
Aeneas Williams	12
Ken Houston	10
Eric Allen	9
Deion Sanders	9
Erich Barnes	8
Bobby Bell	8
Darrell Green	8
Terry McDaniel	8
Herb Adderley	7
Lem Barney	7
Terrell Buckley	7
Erik McMillan	7
Anthony Parker	7
Lemar Parrish	7
Otis Smith	7
Billy Thompson	7

CAREER REGULAR SEASON

CAREER SACKS

PLAYER	SACKS
Bruce Smith	200.0
Reggie White	198.0
Kevin Greene	160.0
Chris Doleman	150.5
Richard Dent	137.5
John Randle	137.5
Leslie O'Neal	132.5
Lawrence Taylor	132.5
Rickey Jackson	128.0
Derrick Thomas	126.5
Clyde Simmons	121.5
Michael Strahan	114.0
Sean Jones	113.0
Greg Townsend	109.5
Pat Swilling	107.5
Trace Armstrong	106.0
Neil Smith	104.5
Jim Jeffcoat	102.5
William Fuller	100.5
Charles Haley	100.5
Andre Tippett	100.0
Simon Fletcher	97.5
Jacob Green	97.5
Dexter Manley	97.5
Robert Porcher	95.5
Steve McMichael	95.0
Henry Thomas	93.5
Simeon Rice	93.0
Ken Harvey	89.0
Howie Long	84.0

CAREER FIELD GOALS MADE

PLAYER	MADE
Gary Anderson	521
Morten Andersen	502
Nick Lowery	383
Jan Stenerud	373
Norm Johnson	366
Eddie Murray	352
Al Del Greco	347
John Carney	343
George Blanda	335
Matt Stover	321
Steve Christie	314
Pat Leahy	304
Jim Turner	304
Matt Bahr	300
Mark Moseley	300
Jason Elam	288
Jason Hanson	284
Jim Bakken	282
Fred Cox	282
Pete Stoyanovich	272

Kevin Butler	265
John Kasay	265
Jim Breech	243
Chris Bahr	241
Lou Groza	234
Jeff Jaeger	229
Greg Davis	224
Ray Wersching	222
Bruce Gossett	219
Don Cockroft	216

CAREER FIELD GOALS ATTEMPTED

PLAYER	ATTEMPTED
Gary Anderson	650
George Blanda	637
Morten Andersen	636
Jan Stenerud	558
Jim Turner	488
Nick Lowery	479
Norm Johnson	477
Eddie Murray	466
Mark Moseley	457
Fred Cox	455
Al Del Greco	449
Jim Bakken	447
Pat Leahy	426
John Carney	421
Matt Bahr	415
Lou Groza	405
Steve Christie	403
Matt Stover	391
Chris Bahr	381
Jason Elam	364
Kevin Butler	361
Bruce Gossett	360
Jason Hanson	352
Pete Stoyanovich	342
Lou Michaels	341
Jim Breech	340
Gino Cappelletti	333
John Kasay	331
Ray Wersching	329
Don Cockroft	328

CAREER EXTRA POINTS MADE

PLAYER	MADE
George Blanda	942
Gary Anderson	783
Morten Andersen	753
Lou Groza	641
Norm Johnson	638
Jan Stenerud	580
Nick Lowery	562

CAREER REGULAR SEASON

CAREER EXTRA POINTS MADE

PLAYER	MADE
Pat Leahy	558
Al Del Greco	543
Eddie Murray	538
Jim Bakken	534
Matt Bahr	522
Jim Turner	521
Fred Cox	519
Jim Breech	517
Chris Bahr	490
Mark Moseley	482
Ray Wersching	456
Jason Elam	449
Garo Yepremian	444
Steve Christie	435
Don Cockroft	432
Sam Baker	428
Rafael Septien	420
Pete Stoyanovich	420
Kevin Butler	413
John Carney	404
Matt Stover	401
Lou Michaels	385
Jason Hanson	384

CAREER EXTRA POINTS ATTEMPTED

PLAYER	ATTEMPTED
George Blanda	958
Gary Anderson	790
Morten Andersen	763
Lou Groza	657
Norm Johnson	644
Jan Stenerud	601
Pat Leahy	584
Nick Lowery	568
Jim Bakken	553
Al Del Greco	551
Eddie Murray	545
Jim Turner	543
Jim Breech	539
Fred Cox	539
Matt Bahr	534
Chris Bahr	519
Mark Moseley	512
Ray Wersching	477
Garo Yepremian	464
Don Cockroft	457
Jason Elam	451
Sam Baker	444
Steve Christie	440
Rafael Septien	433
Kevin Butler	426
Pete Stoyanovich	425

John Carney	410
Matt Stover	404
Lou Michaels	401
Jason Hanson	390

CAREER POINTS — KICKER

PLAYER	POINTS
Gary Anderson	2346
Morten Andersen	2259
Norm Johnson	1736
Nick Lowery	1711
Jan Stenerud	1699
Eddie Murray	1594
Al Del Greco	1584
Pat Leahy	1470
Jim Turner	1439
John Carney	1433
Matt Bahr	1422
Mark Moseley	1382
Jim Bakken	1380
Steve Christie	1377
Fred Cox	1365
Matt Stover	1364
Lou Groza	1349
Jason Elam	1313
Jim Breech	1246
Jason Hanson	1236
Pete Stoyanovich	1236
Chris Bahr	1213
Kevin Butler	1208
Ray Wersching	1122
John Kasay	1100
Don Cockroft	1080
Garo Yepremian	1074
Bruce Gossett	1031
Jeff Jaeger	1008
Jeff Wilkins	982

CAREER PUNTS

PLAYER	PUNTS
Sean Landeta	1327
Jeff Feagles	1290
Lee Johnson	1226
Dave Jennings	1154
Rohn Stark	1141
Mark Royals	1116
John James	1083
Chris Mohr	1076
Jerrel Wilson	1072
Brian Hansen	1057
Dan Stryzinski	1055
Ray Guy	1049
Rich Camarillo	1027
Bryan Barker	1016

CAREER PUNTS cont.

PLAYER	PUNTS
Mike Horan	1003
Reggie Roby	992
Jeff Gossett	982
Mike Bragg	978
Chris Gardocki	978
Bobby Walden	974
Bobby Joe Green	970
John Kidd	957
Tommy Barnhardt	890
Bob Parsons	884
Jim Arnold	866
David Lee	838
Greg Coleman	820
Tom Blanchard	819
Mike Saxon	813
Paul Maguire	795

CAREER PUNT YARDAGE

PLAYER	YARDAGE
Sean Landeta	57491
Jeff Feagles	53691
Lee Johnson	51979
Rohn Stark	49471
Dave Jennings	47567
Mark Royals	47021
Jerrel Wilson	46139
Brian Hansen	44700
Ray Guy	44493
John James	43992
Rich Camarillo	43895
Chris Mohr	43488
Reggie Roby	42951
Bryan Barker	42860
Mike Horan	42286
Dan Stryzinski	42072
Chris Gardocki	41967
Bobby Joe Green	41317
Jeff Gossett	40569
Bobby Walden	40529
John Kidd	39716
Mike Bragg	38949
Tommy Barnhardt	37469
Jim Arnold	36637
Bob Parsons	34180
David Lee	34019
Mike Saxon	33887
Tom Blanchard	33794
Darren Bennett	33776
Tom Tupa	33318

CAREER YARDS PER PUNT AVG

PLAYER	YARDS/PUNT AVG (250 PUNTS)
Shane Lechler	45.7
Sammy Baugh	45.1
Tommy Davis	44.7
Yale Lary	44.3
Todd Sauerbrun	44.0
Bob Scarpitto	43.8
Horace Gillom	43.8
Darren Bennett	43.8
Jerry Norton	43.8
Dave Lewis	43.7
Tom Rouen	43.6
Greg Montgomery	43.6
Don Chandler	43.5
Rick Tuten	43.4
Rohn Stark	43.4
Sean Landeta	43.3
Reggie Roby	43.3
Tom Tupa	43.3
Mitch Berger	43.2
Jerrel Wilson	43.0
Josh Miller	42.9
Chris Gardocki	42.9
Hunter Smith	42.9
Craig Hentrich	42.9
Norm Van Brocklin	42.9
Leo Araguz	42.8
Danny Villanueva	42.8
Rich Camarillo	42.7
Scott Player	42.7
Bobby Joe Green	42.6

CAREER KICKOFF RETURNS

PLAYER	RETURNS
Brian Mitchell	607
Mel Gray	421
Glyn Milburn	407
Michael Bates	373
Desmond Howard	359
Kevin Williams	322
Allen Rossum	286
Tyrone Hughes	283
Eric Metcalf	280
Ron Smith	275
David Meggett	252
Dexter Carter	250
Bruce Harper	243
Corey Harris	238
Clarence Verdin	237
Vai Sikahema	235
Tamarick Vanover	226
Rod Woodson	220
Charlie Rogers	217
Herschel Walker	215

CAREER KICKOFF RETURNS contd

PLAYER	RETURNS
Ron Brown	199
David Dunn	198
Steve Odom	194
Andre Coleman	193
Abe Woodson	193
Dennis Gentry	192
Al Carmichael	191
Jermaine Lewis	191
Ronney Jenkins	190
Larry Anderson	189
Qadry Ismail	189
Dick James	189

CAREER KICKOFF RETURN YARDS

PLAYER	YARDS
Brian Mitchell	14014
Mel Gray	10250
Glyn Milburn	9788
Michael Bates	9110
Desmond Howard	7959
Kevin Williams	7309
Tyrone Hughes	6999
Ron Smith	6922
Allen Rossum	6601
Eric Metcalf	5813
David Meggett	5566
Abe Woodson	5538
Corey Harris	5528
Tamarick Vanover	5422
Dexter Carter	5412
Bruce Harper	5407
Herschel Walker	5084
Vai Sikahema	4933
Clarence Verdin	4930
Rod Woodson	4894
Charlie Rogers	4877
Al Carmichael	4798
Timmy Brown	4781
Dick James	4676
David Dunn	4597
Ronney Jenkins	4550
Speedy Duncan	4539
Ron Brown	4493
Andre Coleman	4466
Steve Odom	4451

CAREER KICKOFF RETURN TDs

PLAYER	TOUCHDOWNS
Mel Gray	6
Ollie Matson	6
Gale Sayers	6
Travis Williams	6
Michael Bates	5
Timmy Brown	5
Bobby Mitchell	5
Abe Woodson	5
Ron Brown	4
Andre Coleman	4
Tony Horne	4
Brian Mitchell	4
Cecil Turner	4
Tamarick Vanover	4
Darrick Vaughn	4
Jon Vaughn	4
Cullen Bryant	3
Lynn Chandnois	3
Raymond Clayborn	3
Dennis Gentry	3
Dante Hall	3
Dave Hampton	3
Tyrone Hughes	3
Ronney Jenkins	3
Terry Kirby	3
Lenny Lyles	3
Mercury Morris	3
Chad Morton	3
Allen Rossum	3
Deion Sanders	3
Ron Smith	3
Vitamin Smith	3
Steve Van Buren	3
Charley Warner	3
Dave Williams	3
Derrick Witherspoon	3

CAREER PUNT RETURNS

PLAYER	RETURNS
Brian Mitchell	463
Eric Metcalf	351
David Meggett	349
Tim Brown	320
Darrien Gordon	314
Glyn Milburn	304
Vai Sikahema	292
Billy Johnson	282
Jermaine Lewis	272
J.T. Smith	267
Kelvin Martin	261
Rod Woodson	260
Emlen Tunnell	258
Alvin Haymond	253
Mike Fuller	252
Mel Gray	252
Rick Upchurch	248
Desmond Howard	244
Ron Smith	235
Kevin Williams	231

CAREER REGULAR SEASON

CAREER PUNT RETURNS contd.

PLAYER	RETURNS
Phil McConkey	228
Troy Brown	225
Danny Reece	222
Karl Williams	213
Mike Nelms	212
Deion Sanders	207
Irving Fryar	206
Speedy Duncan	202
Leo Lewis	201
Tamarick Vanover	197

CAREER PUNT RETURN YARDS

PLAYER	YARDS
Brian Mitchell	4999
David Meggett	3708
Darrien Gordon	3601
Eric Metcalf	3453
Billy Johnson	3317
Tim Brown	3272
Vai Sikahema	3169
Jermaine Lewis	3055
Rick Upchurch	3008
Glyn Milburn	2984
Desmond Howard	2895
J.T. Smith	2764
Mel Gray	2753
Mike Fuller	2660
Kelvin Martin	2567
Troy Brown	2441
Rod Woodson	2362
Kevin Williams	2295
Karl Williams	2279
Emlen Tunnell	2209
Speedy Duncan	2201
Deion Sanders	2158
Alvin Haymond	2148
Irving Fryar	2055
Tamarick Vanover	2016
Greg Pruitt	2007
Mike Nelms	1948
Leo Lewis	1868
Phil McConkey	1832
Billy Thompson	1814

CAREER PUNT RETURN TDs

PLAYER	TOUCHDOWNS
Eric Metcalf	10
Brian Mitchell	9
Jack Christiansen	8
Desmond Howard	8
Rick Upchurch	8

David Meggett	7
Darrien Gordon	6
Billy Johnson	6
Jermaine Lewis	6
Deion Sanders	6
Emlen Tunnell	5
Karl Williams	5
Dick Christy	4
Speedy Duncan	4
Henry Ellard	4
Joey Galloway	4
Dante Hall	4
LeRoy Irvin	4
Dana McLemore	4
Lemar Parrish	4
Vai Sikahema	4
J.T. Smith	4
Steve Smith	4
Freddie Solomon	4
Tamarick Vanover	4
Clarence Verdin	4
Butch Atkinson	3
Tim Brown	3
Troy Brown	3
Phillip Buchanon	3
Bill Dudley	3
Tim Dwight	3
Irving Fryar	3
Claude Gibson	3
Mel Gray	3
Az-Zahir Hakim	3
Rickie Harris	3
Bob Hayes	3
Leroy Kelly	3
Eddie Kennison	3
Yale Lary	3
Woodley Lewis	3
Louis Lipps	3
Kelvin Martin	3
Robbie Martin	3
Ray Mathews	3
Ollie Matson	3
Dennis McKinnon	3
Ray McLean	3
Bobby Mitchell	3
Keith Moody	3
Steve Schubert	3
Jon Staggers	3
Dick Todd	3
Amani Toomer	3
Tom Watkins	3
Kevin Williams	3
Bert Zagers	3

CAREER TOUCHDOWNS

PLAYER	RUN	REC	RET	TOT
Jerry Rice	0	22	0	22
Emmitt Smith	19	2	0	21
Thurman Thomas	16	5	0	21
Franco Harris	16	1	0	17
Marcus Allen	11	2	0	13
Terrell Davis	12	0	0	12
Antonio Freeman	0	10	2	12
John Riggins	12	0	0	12
John Stallworth	0	12	0	12
Ricky Watters	8	4	0	12
Larry Csonka	9	1	0	10
Tony Dorsett	9	1	0	10
Roger Craig	7	2	0	9
James Lofton	1	8	0	9
Andre Reed	0	9	0	9
Lynn Swann	0	9	0	9
Earnest Byner	5	3	0	8
Cris Carter	0	8	0	8
Ernest Givins	0	8	0	8
Michael Irvin	0	8	0	8
Curtis Martin	8	0	0	8
Drew Pearson	0	8	0	8
Steve Young	8	0	0	8
Mike Alstott	7	0	0	7
Dave Casper	0	7	0	7
Kenneth Davis	7	0	0	7
Marshall Faulk	5	2	0	7
Chuck Foreman	7	0	0	7
Art Monk	0	7	0	7
Randy Moss	0	7	0	7
Jimmy Smith	0	7	0	7

CAREER POINTS SCORED

PLAYER	POINTS
Gary Anderson	153
Jerry Rice	132
Emmitt Smith	126
Thurman Thomas	126
Matt Bahr	102
Franco Harris	102
Steve Christie	97
Norm Johnson	94
Chris Jacke	84
Adam Vinatieri	81
Marcus Allen	78
Chris Bahr	78
Mike Cofer	78
Tony Franklin	75
Kevin Butler	74
Terrell Davis	74
Mark Moseley	74
Rafael Septien	74
Antonio Freeman	72
John Riggins	72
John Stallworth	72
Ricky Watters	72
Jeff Wilkins	72
Mike Hollis	70
Eddie Murray	70
Ray Wersching	69
Morten Andersen	68
Scott Norwood	66
Jason Elam	64
Chris Boniol	63
Al Del Greco	63

CAREER PASS ATTEMPTS

PLAYER	ATTEMPTS
Joe Montana	734
Dan Marino	687
John Elway	651
Brett Favre	630
Jim Kelly	545
Troy Aikman	502
Steve Young	471
Terry Bradshaw	456
Roger Staubach	405
Warren Moon	403
Randall Cunningham	365
Danny White	359
Ken Stabler	351
Donovan McNabb	309
Fran Tarkenton	292
Dan Fouts	286
Dave Krieg	282
Steve McNair	282
Phil Simms	279
Neil O'Donnell	274
Jim Plunkett	272
Ron Jaworski	270
Bernie Kosar	270
Kurt Warner	268
Mark Brunell	255
Drew Bledsoe	252
Rich Gannon	240
Mark Rypien	234
Stan Humphries	228
Brad Johnson	224

CAREER PASS COMPLETIONS

PLAYER	COMPLETIONS
Joe Montana	460
Dan Marino	385
Brett Favre	379
John Elway	355
Jim Kelly	322
Troy Aikman	320
Steve Young	292
Terry Bradshaw	261
Warren Moon	259
Roger Staubach	219
Danny White	206
Ken Stabler	203
Randall Cunningham	192
Donovan McNabb	181
Kurt Warner	169
Steve McNair	166
Jim Plunkett	162
Dan Fouts	159
Neil O'Donnell	159
Phil Simms	157
Rich Gannon	154
Bernie Kosar	152
Fran Tarkenton	149
Dave Krieg	144
Tom Brady	135
Drew Bledsoe	129
Joe Theismann	128
Mark Brunell	127
Ron Jaworski	126
Mark Rypien	126

CAREER PASS COMPLETION % (150 ATTEMPTS)

PLAYER	COMPLETION %
Ken Anderson	66.3
Warren Moon	64.3
Rich Gannon	64.2
Troy Aikman	63.7
Kurt Warner	63.1
Joe Montana	62.7
Steve Young	62.0
Joe Theismann	60.7
Tom Brady	60.5
Vinny Testaverde	60.5
Brett Favre	60.2
Jim Plunkett	59.6
Jim Kelly	59.1
Steve McNair	58.9
Donovan McNabb	58.6
Neil O'Donnell	58.0
Ken Stabler	57.8
Kerry Collins	57.8
Danny White	57.4
Terry Bradshaw	57.2
Bernie Kosar	56.3
Phil Simms	56.3
Peyton Manning	56.3
Dan Marino	56.0
Brad Johnson	55.8
Dan Fouts	55.6
John Elway	54.5
Roger Staubach	54.1
Bob Griese	53.8
Mark Rypien	53.8

CAREER PASS YARDS

PLAYER	YARDS
Joe Montana	5772
John Elway	4964
Brett Favre	4686
Dan Marino	4510
Jim Kelly	3863
Troy Aikman	3849
Terry Bradshaw	3833
Steve Young	3326
Warren Moon	2870
Roger Staubach	2747
Ken Stabler	2641
Randall Cunningham	2426
Jim Plunkett	2293
Danny White	2284
Kurt Warner	2221
Dan Fouts	2126
Bernie Kosar	1953
Dave Krieg	1895
Donovan McNabb	1807
Fran Tarkenton	1803
Joe Theismann	1782
Mark Rypien	1776
Neil O'Donnell	1709
Rich Gannon	1691
Phil Simms	1679
Ron Jaworski	1669
Steve McNair	1591
Mark Brunell	1550
Peyton Manning	1476
Bob Griese	1467

CAREER PASSING TOUCHDOWNS

PLAYER	TOUCHDOWNS
Joe Montana	45
Brett Favre	33
Dan Marino	32
Terry Bradshaw	30
John Elway	27
Troy Aikman	23
Roger Staubach	23

CAREER POST SEASON

CAREER PASSING TDs cont.

PLAYER	TOUCHDOWNS
Jim Kelly	21
Steve Young	20
Ken Stabler	19
Warren Moon	17
Bernie Kosar	16
Kurt Warner	15
Danny White	14
Kerry Collins	12
Randall Cunningham	12
Dan Fouts	12
Rich Gannon	11
Dave Krieg	11
Donovan McNabb	11
Jim Plunkett	11
Fran Tarkenton	11
Joe Theismann	11
Mark Brunell	10
Bob Griese	10
Ron Jaworski	10
Peyton Manning	10
Phil Simms	10
Ken Anderson	9
Jeff George	9
Neil O'Donnell	9
Doug Williams	9

CAREER YARDS PER PASS AVG (150 ATTEMPTS)

PLAYER	YARDS PER PASS AVG
Joe Theismann	8.45
Jim Plunkett	8.43
Terry Bradshaw	8.41
Kurt Warner	8.29
Ken Anderson	7.96
Joe Montana	7.86
Troy Aikman	7.67
John Elway	7.63
Mark Rypien	7.59
Ken Stabler	7.52
Brett Favre	7.44
Dan Fouts	7.43
Bernie Kosar	7.23
Jim McMahon	7.17
Wade Wilson	7.15
Warren Moon	7.12
Peyton Manning	7.10
Jim Kelly	7.09
Steve Young	7.06
Bob Griese	7.05
Rich Gannon	7.05
Vinny Testaverde	6.99
Roger Staubach	6.78
Dave Krieg	6.72

Randall Cunningham	6.65
Doug Williams	6.57
Dan Marino	6.56
Vince Ferragamo	6.53
Kerry Collins	6.41
Jim Everett	6.36

CAREER INTERCEPTED

PLAYER	INTERCEPTED
Jim Kelly	28
Terry Bradshaw	26
Dan Marino	24
Brett Favre	22
John Elway	21
Joe Montana	21
Roger Staubach	19
Troy Aikman	17
Fran Tarkenton	17
Dan Fouts	16
Danny White	16
Warren Moon	14
Ken Stabler	14
Stan Humphries	13
Steve Young	13
Drew Bledsoe	12
Bob Griese	12
Pat Haden	12
Brad Johnson	12
Craig Morton	12
Jim Plunkett	12
Richard Todd	12
Jim Everett	11
Vince Ferragamo	11
Doug Williams	11
Mark Brunell	10
Kerry Collins	10
Ron Jaworski	10
Bernie Kosar	10
Mark Rypien	10
Kurt Warner	10

CAREER QB RATING (150 ATTEMPTS)

PLAYER	RATING
Joe Montana	95.6
Ken Anderson	93.5
Kurt Warner	92.3
Joe Theismann	91.4
Troy Aikman	88.3
Brett Favre	86.1
Steve Young	85.8
Warren Moon	84.9
Rich Gannon	84.6
Bernie Kosar	83.5

CAREER POST SEASON

Ken Stabler	83.1
Terry Bradshaw	83.0
Peyton Manning	82.5
Jim Plunkett	81.9
Tom Brady	81.4
Vinny Testaverde	81.2
John Elway	79.7
Dan Marino	77.1
Phil Simms	77.0
Kerry Collins	76.1
Jim McMahon	76.1
Wade Wilson	75.6
Neil O'Donnell	75.2
Donovan McNabb	75.0
Roger Staubach	74.8
Randall Cunningham	74.3
Dave Krieg	72.3
Jim Kelly	72.3
Mark Rypien	72.2
Danny White	70.8

CAREER RUSHING YARDS

PLAYER	YARDS
Emmitt Smith	1586
Franco Harris	1556
Thurman Thomas	1442
Tony Dorsett	1383
Marcus Allen	1347
Terrell Davis	1140
John Riggins	996
Larry Csonka	891
Chuck Foreman	860
Roger Craig	841
Earnest Byner	839
Eddie George	776
Eric Dickerson	724
Lawrence McCutcheon	687
Ricky Watters	666
Curtis Martin	652
Robert Newhouse	651
Natrone Means	650
Dorsey Levens	647
Freeman McNeil	633
Walter Payton	632
Mark van Eeghen	619
Robert Smith	590
Steve Young	585
Wendell Tyler	566
Edgar Bennett	561
Joe Morris	553
Antowain Smith	550
Kenneth Davis	549
Wilbert Montgomery	518
Duane Thomas	518

CAREER RUSHES

PLAYER	RUSHES
Franco Harris	400
Emmitt Smith	349
Thurman Thomas	339
Tony Dorsett	302
Marcus Allen	267
John Riggins	251
Chuck Foreman	229
Larry Csonka	225
Roger Craig	208
Eddie George	206
Terrell Davis	204
Earnest Byner	186
Walter Payton	180
Ricky Watters	175
Robert Newhouse	174
Lawrence McCutcheon	173
Mark van Eeghen	172
Edgar Bennett	163
Larry Brown	151
Freeman McNeil	149
Eric Dickerson	148
Dorsey Levens	148
Marshall Faulk	145
Curtis Martin	145
Robert Smith	145
Natrone Means	144
Sammy Winder	144
Rocky Bleier	141
Wilbert Montgomery	141
Joe Morris	140

CAREER YARDS PER CARRY (100 RUSHES)

PLAYER	YARDS PER CARRY
Terrell Davis	5.6
Marcus Allen	5.0
Eric Dickerson	4.9
Chuck Muncie	4.7
Tony Dorsett	4.6
Emmitt Smith	4.5
Natrone Means	4.5
Earnest Byner	4.5
Curtis Martin	4.5
Dorsey Levens	4.4
Kenneth Davis	4.3
Ottis Anderson	4.3
Thurman Thomas	4.3
Freeman McNeil	4.2
Wendell Tyler	4.1
Edgerrin James	4.1
Robert Smith	4.1
Roger Craig	4.0
Antowain Smith	4.0

CAREER YARDS PER CARRY (100 RUSHES) cont.

PLAYER	YARDS PER CARRY
Duane Thomas	4.0
Lawrence McCutcheon	4.0
John Riggins	4.0
Kevin Mack	4.0
Larry Csonka	4.0
Cullen Bryant	4.0
Clarence Davis	4.0
Joe Morris	4.0
Franco Harris	3.9
Tony Nathan	3.8
Ricky Watters	3.8

CAREER RUSHING TOUCHDOWNS

PLAYER	TOUCHDOWNS
Emmitt Smith	19
Franco Harris	16
Thurman Thomas	16
Terrell Davis	12
John Riggins	12
Marcus Allen	11
Larry Csonka	9
Tony Dorsett	9
Curtis Martin	8
Ricky Watters	8
Steve Young	8
Mike Alstott	7
Roger Craig	7
Kenneth Davis	7
Chuck Foreman	7
John Elway	6
Jim Kiick	6
Steve McNair	6
Wilbert Montgomery	6
Gerald Riggs	6
Edgar Bennett	5
Earnest Byner	5
Zack Crockett	5
Marshall Faulk	5
William Floyd	5
Eddie George	5
Leroy Hoard	5
Napoleon McCallum	5
Natrone Means	5
Pete Banaszak	4
Woody Bennett	4
Jerome Bettis	4
Rocky Bleier	4
Earl Campbell	4
Frank Hawkins	4
Dorsey Levens	4
Jamal Lewis	4
Derek Loville	4
Bam Morris	4
Joe Morris	4
Tom Rathman	4
Antowain Smith	4
Kordell Stewart	4
Duane Thomas	4
Mark van Eeghen	4
Ickey Woods	4
Amos Zereoue	4

CAREER RECEIVING YARDS BY RUNNING BACKS

PLAYER	YARDS
Thurman Thomas	672
Tony Nathan	649
Roger Craig	606
Marcus Allen	530
Preston Pearson	528
Franco Harris	504
Marshall Faulk	476
Ronnie Harmon	470
Ricky Watters	451
Chuck Foreman	447
Keith Byars	443
Dorsey Levens	404
Tony Dorsett	403
Earnest Byner	388
Steve Sewell	375
Emmitt Smith	342
Tom Rathman	327
Warrick Dunn	264
Duce Staley	263
Terry Kirby	255
Rob Carpenter	253
Daryl Johnston	247
John L. Williams	243
Amp Lee	233
Curtis Martin	229
Wendell Tyler	224
Kenny King	222
Rocky Bleier	202
Tim Wilson	202
Wilbert Montgomery	193
Sammy Winder	193

CAREER RECEIVING YARDS

PLAYER	YARDS
Jerry Rice	2245
Michael Irvin	1315
Cliff Branch	1289
Andre Reed	1229
Drew Pearson	1105
Art Monk	1062
John Stallworth	1054

CAREER POST SEASON

CAREER RECEIVING YARDS cont.

PLAYER	YARDS
Lynn Swann	907
Cris Carter	870
Keith Jackson	834
Gary Clark	826
Antonio Freeman	823
Shannon Sharpe	814
Ernest Givins	774
James Lofton	759
Brent Jones	740
John Taylor	734
Dwight Clark	726
Isaac Bruce	719
Vance Johnson	719
Paul Warfield	717
Fred Biletnikoff	698
Tony Martin	691
Thurman Thomas	672
Alvin Harper	655
Robert Brooks	651
Tony Nathan	649
Jay Novacek	645
Anthony Carter	644
Charlie Brown	643

Tony Dorsett	46
Marshall Faulk	46
Tony Hill	46
Emmitt Smith	46
John Taylor	46

CAREER YARDS PER CATCH (50 RECEPTIONS)

PLAYER	RECEPTIONS
John Stallworth	18.5
Cliff Branch	17.7
Drew Pearson	16.5
Keith Jackson	16.4
Antonio Freeman	15.5
Art Monk	15.4
Michael Irvin	15.1
Jerry Rice	14.9
Andre Reed	14.5
Gary Clark	14.2
Cris Carter	13.8
Shannon Sharpe	13.1
Ernest Givins	12.9
Brent Jones	12.3
O.J. McDuffie	12.1
Keenan McCardell	11.2
Jay Novacek	10.4
Marcus Allen	10.0
Tony Nathan	10.0
Franco Harris	9.9
Roger Craig	9.6
Ronnie Harmon	9.2
Thurman Thomas	8.8
Keith Byars	8.5

CAREER RECEPTIONS

PLAYER	RECEPTIONS
Jerry Rice	151
Michael Irvin	87
Andre Reed	85
Thurman Thomas	76
Cliff Branch	73
Art Monk	69
Drew Pearson	67
Tony Nathan	65
Cris Carter	63
Roger Craig	63
Jay Novacek	62
Shannon Sharpe	62
Ernest Givins	60
Brent Jones	60
Gary Clark	58
John Stallworth	57
Marcus Allen	53
Antonio Freeman	53
Keith Byars	52
Ronnie Harmon	51
Franco Harris	51
Keith Jackson	51
Keenan McCardell	51
O.J. McDuffie	50
Fred Biletnikoff	49
Dwight Clark	48
Lynn Swann	48

CAREER RECEIVING TOUCHDOWNS

PLAYER	TOUCHDOWNS
Jerry Rice	22
John Stallworth	12
Antonio Freeman	10
Andre Reed	9
Lynn Swann	9
Cris Carter	8
Ernest Givins	8
Michael Irvin	8
James Lofton	8
Drew Pearson	8
Dave Casper	7
Art Monk	7
Randy Moss	7
Jimmy Smith	7
Harold Carmichael	6
Gary Clark	6
Keith Jackson	6
Jay Novacek	6

CAREER RECEIVING TOUCHDOWNS cont.

PLAYER	TOUCHDOWNS
Webster Slaughter	6
Freddie Solomon	6
John Taylor	6
Cliff Branch	5
Mark Duper	5
Alvin Garrett	5
John Gilliam	5
Harold Jackson	5
Charlie Joiner	5
Brent Jones	5
Frank Lewis	5
Keenan McCardell	5
Thurman Thomas	5
Sammy White	5

CAREER POINTS — KICKER

PLAYER	POINTS
Gary Anderson	153
Matt Bahr	102
Steve Christie	97
Norm Johnson	94
Chris Jacke	84
Adam Vinatieri	81
Chris Bahr	78
Mike Cofer	78
Tony Franklin	75
Kevin Butler	74
Mark Moseley	74
Rafael Septien	74
Jeff Wilkins	72
Mike Hollis	70
Eddie Murray	70
Ray Wersching	69
Morten Andersen	68
Scott Norwood	66
Jason Elam	64
Chris Boniol	63
Al Del Greco	63
Rich Karlis	62
Ryan Longwell	60
Uwe von Schamann	59
David Akers	58
Sebastian Janikowski	57
Matt Stover	57
John Kasay	56
Chip Lohmiller	55
Jim Breech	52

HALL OF FAME

YEAR	INDUCTEE	YEAR	INDUCTEE
1963	Sammy Baugh	1969	Turk Edwards
1963	Bert Bell	1969	Greasy Neale
1963	Joe Carr	1969	Leo Nomellini
1963	Dutch Clark	1969	Joe Perry
1963	Red Grange	1969	Ernie Stautner
1963	George Halas	1970	Jack Christiansen
1963	Mel Hein	1970	Tom Fears
1963	Wilbur Henry	1970	Hugh McElhenny
1963	Cal Hubbard	1970	Pete Pihos
1963	Don Hutson	1971	Jim Brown
1963	Curly Lambeau	1971	Bill Hewitt
1963	Tim Mara	1971	Bruiser Kinard
1963	George Preston Marshall	1971	Vince Lombardi
1963	Johnny McNally	1971	Andy Robustelli
1963	Bronko Nagurski	1971	Y.A. Tittle
1963	Ernie Nevers	1971	Norm Van Brocklin
1963	Jim Thorpe	1972	Lamar Hunt
1964	Jimmy Conzelman	1972	Gino Marchetti
1964	Ed Healey	1972	Ollie Matson
1964	Clarke Hinkle	1972	Ace Parker
1964	Link Lyman	1973	Raymond Berry
1964	Mike Michalske	1973	Jim Parker
1964	Art Rooney	1973	Joe Schmidt
1964	George Trafton	1974	Tony Canadeo
1965	Guy Chamberlin	1974	Bill George
1965	Paddy Driscoll	1974	Lou Groza
1965	Danny Fortmann	1974	Night Train Lane
1965	Otto Graham	1975	Rosey Brown
1965	Sid Luckman	1975	George Connor
1965	Steve Van Buren	1975	Dante Lavelli
1965	Bob Waterfield	1975	Lenny Moore
1966	Bill Dudley	1976	Ray Flaherty
1966	Joe Guyon	1976	Len Ford
1966	Arnie Herber	1976	Jim Taylor
1966	Walt Kiesling	1977	Frank Gifford
1966	George McAfee	1977	Forrest Gregg
1966	Steve Owen	1977	Gale Sayers
1966	Hugh Ray	1977	Bart Starr
1966	Bulldog Turner	1977	Bill Willis
1967	Chuck Bednarik	1978	Lance Alworth
1967	Charles Bidwill	1978	Weeb Ewbank
1967	Paul Brown	1978	Tuffy Leemans
1967	Bobby Layne	1978	Ray Nitschke
1967	Dan Reeves	1978	Larry Wilson
1967	Ken Strong	1979	Dick Butkus
1967	Joe Stydahar	1979	Yale Lary
1967	Emlen Tunnell	1979	Ron Mix
1968	Cliff Battles	1979	Johnny Unitas
1968	Art Donovan	1980	Herb Adderley
1968	Elroy Hirsch	1980	Deacon Jones
1968	Wayne Millner	1980	Bob Lilly
1968	Marion Motley	1980	Jim Otto
1968	Charley Trippi		
1968	Alex Wojciechowicz		

HALL OF FAME

YEAR	INDUCTEE	YEAR	INDUCTEE
1981	Red Badgro	1992	Lem Barney
1981	George Blanda	1992	Al Davis
1981	Willie Davis	1992	John Mackey
1981	Jim Ringo	1992	John Riggins
1982	Doug Atkins	1993	Dan Fouts
1982	Sam Huff	1993	Larry Little
1982	George Musso	1993	Chuck Noll
1982	Merlin Olsen	1993	Walter Payton
1983	Bobby Bell	1993	Bill Walsh
1983	Sid Gillman	1994	Tony Dorsett
1983	Sonny Jurgensen	1994	Bud Grant
1983	Bobby Mitchell	1994	Jim Johnson
1983	Paul Warfield	1994	Leroy Kelly
1984	Willie Brown	1994	Jackie Smith
1984	Mike McCormack	1994	Randy White
1984	Charley Taylor	1995	Jim Finks
1984	Arnie Weinmeister	1995	Henry Jordan
1985	Frank Gatski	1995	Steve Largent
1985	Joe Namath	1995	Lee Roy Selmon
1985	Pete Rozelle	1995	Kellen Winslow
1985	O.J. Simpson	1996	Lou Creekmur
1985	Roger Staubach	1996	Dan Dierdorf
1986	Paul Hornung	1996	Joe Gibbs
1986	Ken Houston	1996	Charlie Joiner
1986	Willie Lanier	1996	Mel Renfro
1986	Fran Tarkenton	1997	Mike Haynes
1986	Doak Walker	1997	Wellington Mara
1987	Larry Csonka	1997	Don Shula
1987	Len Dawson	1997	Mike Webster
1987	Joe Greene	1998	Paul Krause
1987	John Henry Johnson	1998	Tommy McDonald
1987	Jim Langer	1998	Anthony Munoz
1987	Don Maynard	1998	Mike Singletary
1987	Gene Upshaw	1998	Dwight Stephenson
1988	Fred Biletnikoff	1999	Eric Dickerson
1988	Mike Ditka	1999	Tom Mack
1988	Jack Ham	1999	Ozzie Newsome
1988	Alan Page	1999	Billy Shaw
1989	Mel Blount	1999	Lawrence Taylor
1989	Terry Bradshaw	2000	Howie Long
1989	Art Shell	2000	Ronnie Lott
1989	Willie Wood	2000	Joe Montana
1990	Buck Buchanan	2000	Dan Rooney
1990	Bob Griese	2000	Dave Wilcox
1990	Franco Harris	2001	Nick Buoniconti
1990	Ted Hendricks	2001	Marv Levy
1990	Jack Lambert	2001	Mike Munchak
1990	Tom Landry	2001	Jackie Slater
1990	Bob St. Clair	2001	Lynn Swann
1991	Earl Campbell	2001	Ron Yary
1991	John Hannah	2001	Jack Youngblood
1991	Stan Jones		
1991	Tex Schramm		
1991	Jan Stenerud		

HALL OF FAME

YEAR	INDUCTEE
2002	George Allen
2002	Dave Casper
2002	Dan Hampton
2002	Jim Kelly
2002	John Stallworth
2003	Marcus Allen
2003	Elvin Bethea
2003	Joe Delamielleure
2003	James Lofton
2003	Hank Stram

AMERICAN FOOTBALL CONFERENCE

TEAM	RECORDS
Baltimore Ravens	Franchise Record: 63-64-1, .496 Franchise Postseason Record: 5-2-0, .714 AFC Championships: 2000 Super Bowl Winners: 2000
Buffalo Bills	Franchise Record: 313-339-8, .480 Franchise Postseason Record: 14-15-0, .483 AFL Championships: 1964, 1965 AFC Championships: 1990, 1991, 1992, 1993
Cincinnati Bengals	Franchise Record: 234-313-1, .428 Franchise Postseason Record: 5-7-0, .417 AFC Championships: 1981, 1988
Cleveland Browns	Franchise Record: 400-320-10, .555 Franchise Postseason Record: 11-20-0, .355 NFL Championships: 1950, 1954, 1955, 1964
Denver Broncos	Franchise Record: 339-311-10, .521 Franchise Postseason Record: 16-13-0, .552 AFC Championships: 1977, 1986, 1987, 1989, 1997, 1998 Super Bowl Winners: 1997, 1998
Houston Texans	Franchise Record: 9-23-0, .281 Franchise Postseason Record: 0-0-0, -
Indianapolis Colts Formerly: Baltimore Colts	Franchise Record: 364-371-7, .495 Franchise Postseason Record: 12-14-0, .462 NFL Championships: 1958, 1959, 1968 AFC Championships: 1970 Super Bowl Winners: 1970
Jacksonville Jaguars	Franchise Record: 73-71-0, .507 Franchise Postseason Record: 4-4-0, .500
Kansas City Chiefs Formerly: Dallas Texans	Franchise Record: 349-299-12, .538 Franchise Postseason Record: 8-12-0, .400 AFL Championships: 1962, 1966, 1969 Super Bowl Winners: 1969

AMERICAN FOOTBALL CONFERENCE

Miami Dolphins	Franchise Record: 349-223-4, .609
	Franchise Postseason Record: 20-19-0, .513
	AFC Championships: 1971, 1972, 1973, 1982, 1984
	Super Bowl Winners: 1972, 1973

New England Patriots	Franchise Record: 314-337-9, .483
Formerly:	Franchise Postseason Record: 13-10-0, .565
Boston Patriots	AFC Championships: 1985, 1996, 2001, 2003
	Super Bowl Winners: 2001, 2003

New York Jets	Franchise Record: 294-358-8, .452
Formerly:	Franchise Postseason Record: 7-9-0, .438
New York Titans	AFL Championships: 1968
	Super Bowl Winners: 1968

Oakland Raiders	Franchise Record: 385-264-11, .592
Formerly:	Franchise Postseason Record: 25-18-0, .581
Los Angeles Raiders	AFL Championships: 1967
	AFC Championships: 1976, 1980, 1983, 2002
	Super Bowl Winners: 1976, 1980, 1983

Pittsburgh Steelers	Franchise Record: 464-464-20, .500
Formerly:	Franchise Postseason Record: 23-17-0, .575
Pittsburgh Pirates	AFC Championships: 1974, 1975, 1978, 1979, 1995
	Super Bowl Winners: 1974, 1975, 1978, 1979

San Diego Chargers	Franchise Record: 308-341-11, .475
Formerly:	Franchise Postseason Record: 7-11-0, .389
Los Angeles Chargers	AFL Championships: 1963
	AFC Championships: 1994

Tennessee Titans	Franchise Record: 323-331-6, .494
Formerly:	Franchise Postseason Record: 14-17-0, .452
Houston Oilers,	AFL Championships: 1960, 1961
Tennessee Oilers	AFC Championships: 1999

Arizona Cardinals
Formerly:
Chicago Cardinals,
St. Louis Cardinals,
Phoenix Cardinals

Franchise Record: 440-617-39, .419
Franchise Postseason Record: 2-5-0, .286
NFL Championships: 1947

Atlanta Falcons

Franchise Record: 226-344-6, .398
Franchise Postseason Record: 5-7-0, .417
NFC Championships: 1998

Carolina Panthers

Franchise Record: 64-80-0, .444
Franchise Postseason Record: 4-2-0, .667
NFC Championships: 2003

Chicago Bears
Formerly:
Decatur Staleys,
Chicago Staleys

Franchise Record: 641-463-42, .578
Franchise Postseason Record: 14-15-0, .483
NFL Championships: 1933, 1940, 1941, 1943, 1946, 1963
NFC Championships: 1985
Super Bowl Winners: 1985

Dallas Cowboys

Franchise Record: 377-275-6, .578
Franchise Postseason Record: 32-22-0, .593
NFC Championships: 1970, 1971, 1975, 1977, 1978, 1992, 1993, 1995
Super Bowl Winners: 1971, 1977, 1992, 1993, 1995

Detroit Lions
Formerly:
Portsmouth Spartans

Franchise Record: 467-510-32, .479
Franchise Postseason Record: 7-10-0, .412
NFL Championships: 1935, 1952, 1953, 1957

Green Bay Packers

Franchise Record: 602-474-36, .558
Franchise Postseason Record: 24-13-0, .649
NFL Championships: 1936, 1939, 1944, 1961, 1962, 1965, 1966, 1967
NFC Championships: 1996, 1997
Super Bowl Winners: 1966, 1967, 1996

Minnesota Vikings

Franchise Record: 354-283-9, .555
Franchise Postseason Record: 17-23-0, .425
NFL Championships: 1969
NFC Championships: 1973, 1974, 1976

New Orleans Saints

Franchise Record: 226-331-5, .407
Franchise Postseason Record: 1-5-0, .167

NATIONAL FOOTBALL CONFERENCE

New York Giants   Franchise Record: 571-477-33, .543
Franchise Postseason Record: 16-21-0, .432
NFL Championships: 1934, 1938, 1956
NFC Championships: 1986, 1990, 2000
Super Bowl Winners: 1986, 1990

Philadelphia Eagles   Franchise Record: 437-493-24, .471
Franchise Postseason Record: 14-15-0, .483
NFL Championships: 1948, 1949, 1960
NFC Championships: 1980

St. Louis Rams
Formerly:
Cleveland Rams,
Los Angeles Rams
   Franchise Record: 476-415-20, .533
Franchise Postseason Record: 18-23-0, .439
NFL Championships: 1945, 1951
NFC Championships: 1979, 1999, 2001
Super Bowl Winners: 1999

San Francisco 49ers   Franchise Record: 432-333-13, .564
Franchise Postseason Record: 25-17-0, .595
NFC Championships: 1981, 1984, 1988, 1989, 1994
Super Bowl Winners: 1981, 1984, 1988, 1989, 1994

Seattle Seahawks   Franchise Record: 205-231-0, .470
Franchise Postseason Record: 3-6-0, .333

Tampa Bay
Buccaneers
   Franchise Record: 167-268-1, .384
Franchise Postseason Record: 6-7-0, .462
NFC Championships: 2002
Super Bowl Winners: 2002

Washington Redskins
Formerly:
Boston Braves,
Boston Redskins
   Franchise Record: 499-452-27, .524
Franchise Postseason Record: 22-15-0, .595
NFL Championships: 1937, 1942
NFC Championships: 1972, 1982, 1983, 1987, 1991
Super Bowl Winners: 1982, 1987, 1991

STANDINGS

1920 NFL FINAL STANDINGS

	W	L	T	PCT
Akron Pros	6	0	3	1.000
Buffalo All-Americans	3	0	2	1.000
Decatur Staleys	5	1	1	.833
Rock Island Independents	5	2	1	.714
Canton Bulldogs	3	2	1	.600
Dayton Triangles	3	3	2	.500
Chicago Tigers	2	4	1	.333
Chicago Cardinals	2	4	1	.333
Cleveland Tigers	1	3	2	.250
Hammond Pros	1	3	0	.250
Detroit Heralds	1	3	0	.250
Rochester Jeffersons	0	1	0	.000
Muncie Flyers	0	1	0	.000
Columbus Panhandles	0	4	0	.000

1921 NFL FINAL STANDINGS

	W	L	T	PCT
Chicago Staleys	9	1	1	.900
Buffalo All-Americans	9	1	2	.900
Akron Pros	8	3	1	.727
Canton Bulldogs	5	2	3	.714
Rock Island Independents	4	2	1	.667
Evansville Crimson Giants	3	2	0	.600
Green Bay Packers	3	2	1	.600
Dayton Triangles	4	4	1	.500
Chicago Cardinals	3	3	2	.500
Rochester Jeffersons	2	3	0	.400
Cleveland Indians	3	5	0	.375
Washington Senators	1	2	0	.333
Hammond Pros	1	3	1	.250
Minneapolis Marines	1	3	0	.250
Cincinnati Celts	1	3	0	.250
Detroit Heralds	1	5	1	.167
Columbus Panhandles	1	8	0	.111
Louisville Brecks	0	2	0	.000
Muncie Flyers	0	2	0	.000
Tonawanda Kardex	0	1	0	.000
New York Brickley Giants	0	2	0	.000

1922 NFL FINAL STANDINGS

	W	L	T	PCT
Canton Bulldogs	10	0	2	1.000
Chicago Bears	9	3	0	.750
Chicago Cardinals	8	3	0	.727
Toledo Maroons	5	2	2	.714
Rock Island Independents	4	2	1	.667
Racine Legion	6	4	1	.600
Dayton Triangles	4	3	1	.571
Green Bay Packers	4	3	3	.571
Buffalo All-Americans	5	4	1	.556
Akron Pros	3	5	2	.375
Milwaukee Badgers	2	4	3	.333
Oorang Indians	3	6	0	.333
Minneapolis Marines	1	3	0	.250
Louisville Brecks	1	3	0	.250
Rochester Jeffersons	0	4	1	.000
Hammond Pros	0	5	1	.000
Evansville Crimson Giants	0	3	0	.000
Columbus Panhandles	0	8	0	.000

1923 NFL FINAL STANDINGS

	W	L	T	PCT
Canton Bulldogs	11	0	1	1.000
Chicago Bears	9	2	1	.818
Green Bay Packers	7	2	1	.778
Milwaukee Badgers	7	2	3	.778
Cleveland Indians	3	1	3	.750
Chicago Cardinals	8	4	0	.667
Duluth Kelleys	4	3	0	.571
Columbus Tigers	5	4	1	.556
Buffalo All-Americans	5	4	3	.556
Racine Legion	4	4	2	.500
Toledo Maroons	3	3	2	.500
Rock Island Independents	2	3	3	.400
Minneapolis Marines	2	5	2	.286
St. Louis All-Stars	1	4	2	.200
Hammond Pros	1	5	1	.167
Dayton Triangles	1	6	1	.143
Akron Pros	1	6	0	.143
Oorang Indians	1	10	0	.091
Louisville Brecks	0	3	0	.000
Rochester Jeffersons	0	4	0	.000

STANDINGS

1924 NFL FINAL STANDINGS

	W	L	T	PCT
Cleveland Bulldogs	7	1	1	.875
Chicago Bears	6	1	4	.857
Frankford Yellow Jackets	11	2	1	.846
Duluth Kelleys	5	1	0	.833
Rock Island Independents	5	2	2	.714
Green Bay Packers	7	4	0	.636
Racine Legion	4	3	3	.571
Chicago Cardinals	5	4	1	.556
Buffalo Bisons	6	5	0	.545
Columbus Tigers	4	4	0	.500
Hammond Pros	2	2	1	.500
Milwaukee Badgers	5	8	0	.385
Dayton Triangles	2	6	0	.250
Akron Pros	2	6	0	.250
Kansas City Blues	2	7	0	.222
Kenosha Maroons	0	4	1	.000
Minneapolis Marines	0	6	0	.000
Rochester Jeffersons	0	7	0	.000

1925 NFL FINAL STANDINGS

	W	L	T	PCT
Chicago Cardinals	11	2	1	.846
Pottsville Maroons	10	2	0	.833
Detroit Panthers	8	2	2	.800
New York Giants	8	4	0	.667
Akron Pros	4	2	2	.667
Frankford Yellow Jackets	13	7	0	.650
Chicago Bears	9	5	3	.643
Rock Island Independents	5	3	3	.625
Green Bay Packers	8	5	0	.615
Providence Steam Roller	0	5	1	.545
Canton Bulldogs	4	4	0	.500
Cleveland Bulldogs	5	8	1	.385
Kansas City Cowboys	2	5	1	.286
Hammond Pros	1	4	0	.200
Buffalo Bisons	1	6	2	.143
Rochester Jeffersons	0	6	1	.000
Dayton Triangles	0	7	1	.000
Duluth Kelleys	0	3	0	.000
Columbus Tigers	0	9	0	.000
Milwaukee Badgers	0	6	0	.000

1926 NFL FINAL STANDINGS

	W	L	T	PCT
Frankford Yellow Jackets	14	1	2	.933
Chicago Bears	12	1	3	.923
Pottsville Maroons	10	2	2	.833
Kansas City Cowboys	8	3	0	.727
Green Bay Packers	7	3	3	.700
New York Giants	8	4	1	.667
Los Angeles Buccaneers	6	3	1	.667
Duluth Eskimoes	6	5	3	.545
Buffalo Rangers	4	4	2	.500
Chicago Cardinals	5	6	1	.455
Providence Steam Roller	5	7	1	.417
Detroit Panthers	4	6	2	.400
Hartford Blues	3	7	0	.300
Brooklyn Lions	3	8	0	.273
Milwaukee Badgers	2	7	0	.222
Akron Indians	1	4	3	.200
Dayton Triangles	1	4	1	.200
Racine Tornadoes	1	4	0	.200
Columbus Tigers	1	6	0	.143
Canton Bulldogs	1	9	3	.100
Hammond Pros	0	4	0	.000
Louisville Colonels	0	4	0	.000

1927 NFL FINAL STANDINGS

	W	L	T	PCT
New York Giants	11	1	1	.917
Green Bay Packers	7	2	1	.778
Chicago Bears	9	3	2	.750
Cleveland Bulldogs	8	4	1	.667
Providence Steam Roller	8	5	1	.615
New York Yankees	7	8	1	.467
Frankford Yellow Jackets	6	9	3	.400
Pottsville Maroons	5	8	0	.385
Chicago Cardinals	3	7	1	.300
Dayton Triangles	1	6	1	.143
Duluth Eskimoes	1	8	0	.111
Buffalo Bisons	0	5	0	.000

1928 NFL FINAL STANDINGS

	W	L	T	PCT
Providence Steam Roller	8	1	2	.889
Frankford Yellow Jackets	11	3	2	.786
Detroit Wolverines	7	2	1	.778
Green Bay Packers	6	4	3	.600
Chicago Bears	7	5	1	.583
New York Giants	4	7	2	.364
New York Yankees	4	8	1	.333
Pottsville Maroons	2	8	0	.200
Chicago Cardinals	1	5	0	.167
Dayton Triangles	0	7	0	.000

STANDINGS

1929 NFL FINAL STANDINGS

	W	L	T	PCT
Green Bay Packers	12	0	1	1.000
New York Giants	13	1	1	.929
Frankford Yellow Jackets	10	4	5	.714
Orange Tornadoes	3	3	3	.500
Chicago Cardinals	6	6	1	.500
Boston Bulldogs	4	4	0	.500
Staten Island Stapletons	3	4	3	.429
Providence Steam Roller	4	6	2	.400
Chicago Bears	4	9	2	.308
Buffalo Bisons	1	7	1	.125
Minneapolis Red Jackets	1	9	0	.100
Dayton Triangles	0	6	0	.000

1930 NFL FINAL STANDINGS

	W	L	T	PCT
Green Bay Packers	10	3	1	.769
New York Giants	13	4	0	.765
Chicago Bears	9	4	1	.692
Brooklyn Dodgers	7	4	1	.636
Providence Steam Roller	6	4	1	.600
Staten Island Stapletons	5	5	2	.500
Portsmouth Spartans	5	6	3	.455
Chicago Cardinals	5	6	2	.455
Frankford Yellow Jackets	4	13	1	.235
Minneapolis Red Jackets	1	7	1	.125
Newark Tornadoes	1	10	1	.091

1931 NFL FINAL STANDINGS

	W	L	T	PCT
Green Bay Packers	12	2	0	.857
Portsmouth Spartans	11	3	0	.786
Chicago Bears	8	5	0	.615
Chicago Cardinals	5	4	0	.556
New York Giants	7	6	1	.538
Providence Steam Roller	4	4	3	.500
Staten Island Stapletons	4	6	1	.400
Cleveland Indians	2	8	0	.200
Frankford Yellow Jackets	1	6	1	.143
Brooklyn Dodgers	2	12	0	.143

1932 NFL FINAL STANDINGS

	W	L	T	PCT
Portsmouth Spartans	6	1	4	.857
Chicago Bears	6	1	6	.857
Green Bay Packers	10	3	1	.769
Boston Braves	4	4	2	.500
New York Giants	4	6	2	.400
Chicago Cardinals	2	6	2	.250
Brooklyn Dodgers	3	9	0	.250
Staten Island Stapletons	2	7	3	.222

1933 NFL FINAL STANDINGS

EAST DIVISION	W	L	T	PCT
New York Giants	11	3	0	.786
Brooklyn Dodgers	5	4	1	.556
Boston Redskins	5	5	2	.500
Philadelphia Eagles	3	5	1	.375
Pittsburgh Pirates	3	6	2	.333

WEST DIVISION	W	L	T	PCT
Chicago Bears	10	2	1	.833
Portsmouth Spartans	6	5	0	.545
Green Bay Packers	5	7	1	.417
Cincinnati Reds	3	6	1	.333
Chicago Cardinals	1	9	1	.100

1934 NFL FINAL STANDINGS

EAST DIVISION	W	L	T	PCT
New York Giants	8	5	0	.615
Boston Redskins	6	6	0	.500
Brooklyn Dodgers	4	7	0	.364
Philadelphia Eagles	4	7	0	.364
Pittsburgh Pirates	2	10	0	.167

WEST DIVISION	W	L	T	PCT
Chicago Bears	13	0	0	1.000
Detroit Lions	10	3	0	.769
Green Bay Packers	7	6	0	.538
Chicago Cardinals	5	6	0	.455
Cincinnati Reds	1	10	0	.091

1935 NFL FINAL STANDINGS

EAST DIVISION	W	L	T	PCT
New York Giants	9	3	0	.750
Brooklyn Dodgers	5	6	1	.455
Pittsburgh Pirates	4	8	0	.333
Boston Redskins	2	8	1	.200
Philadelphia Eagles	2	9	0	.182

WEST DIVISION	W	L	T	PCT
Detroit Lions	7	3	2	.700
Green Bay Packers	8	4	0	.667
Chicago Bears	6	4	2	.600
Chicago Cardinals	6	4	2	.600

STANDINGS

1936 NFL FINAL STANDINGS

EAST DIVISION
	W	L	T	PCT
Boston Redskins	7	5	0	.583
Pittsburgh Pirates	6	6	0	.500
New York Giants	5	6	1	.455
Brooklyn Dodgers	3	8	1	.273
Philadelphia Eagles	1	11	0	.083

WEST DIVISION
	W	L	T	PCT
Green Bay Packers	10	1	1	.909
Chicago Bears	9	3	0	.750
Detroit Lions	8	4	0	.667
Chicago Cardinals	3	8	1	.273

1937 NFL FINAL STANDINGS

EAST DIVISION
	W	L	T	PCT
Washington Redskins	8	3	0	.727
New York Giants	6	3	2	.667
Pittsburgh Pirates	4	7	0	.364
Brooklyn Dodgers	3	7	1	.300
Philadelphia Eagles	2	8	1	.200

WEST DIVISION
	W	L	T	PCT
Chicago Bears	9	1	1	.900
Green Bay Packers	7	4	0	.636
Detroit Lions	7	4	0	.636
Chicago Cardinals	5	5	1	.500
Cleveland Rams	1	10	0	.091

1938 NFL FINAL STANDINGS

EAST DIVISION
	W	L	T	PCT
New York Giants	8	2	1	.800
Washington Redskins	6	3	2	.667
Brooklyn Dodgers	4	4	3	.500
Philadelphia Eagles	5	6	0	.455
Pittsburgh Pirates	2	9	0	.182

WEST DIVISION
	W	L	T	PCT
Green Bay Packers	8	3	0	.727
Detroit Lions	7	4	0	.636
Chicago Bears	6	5	0	.545
Cleveland Rams	4	7	0	.364
Chicago Cardinals	2	9	0	.182

1939 NFL FINAL STANDINGS

EAST DIVISION
	W	L	T	PCT
New York Giants	9	1	1	.900
Washington Redskins	8	2	1	.800
Brooklyn Dodgers	4	6	1	.400
Philadelphia Eagles	1	9	1	.100
Pittsburgh Pirates	1	9	1	.100

WEST DIVISION
	W	L	T	PCT
Green Bay Packers	9	2	0	.818
Chicago Bears	8	3	0	.727
Detroit Lions	6	5	0	.545
Cleveland Rams	5	5	1	.500
Chicago Cardinals	1	10	0	.091

1940 NFL FINAL STANDINGS

EAST DIVISION
	W	L	T	PCT
Washington Redskins	9	2	0	.818
Brooklyn Dodgers	8	3	0	.727
New York Giants	6	4	1	.600
Pittsburgh Steelers	2	7	2	.222
Philadelphia Eagles	1	10	0	.091

WEST DIVISION
	W	L	T	PCT
Chicago Bears	8	3	0	.727
Green Bay Packers	6	4	1	.600
Detroit Lions	5	5	1	.500
Cleveland Rams	4	6	1	.400
Chicago Cardinals	2	7	2	.222

1941 NFL FINAL STANDINGS

EAST DIVISION
	W	L	T	PCT
New York Giants	8	3	0	.727
Brooklyn Dodgers	7	4	0	.636
Washington Redskins	6	5	0	.545
Philadelphia Eagles	2	8	1	.200
Pittsburgh Steelers	1	9	1	.100

WEST DIVISION
	W	L	T	PCT
Chicago Bears	10	1	0	.909
Green Bay Packers	10	1	0	.909
Detroit Lions	4	6	1	.400
Chicago Cardinals	3	7	1	.300
Cleveland Rams	2	9	0	.182

STANDINGS

1942 NFL FINAL STANDINGS

EAST DIVISION	W	L	T	PCT
Washington Redskins	10	1	0	.909
Pittsburgh Steelers	7	4	0	.636
New York Giants	5	5	1	.500
Brooklyn Dodgers	3	8	0	.273
Philadelphia Eagles	2	9	0	.182

WEST DIVISION	W	L	T	PCT
Chicago Bears	11	0	0	1.000
Green Bay Packers	8	2	1	.800
Cleveland Rams	5	6	0	.455
Chicago Cardinals	3	8	0	.273
Detroit Lions	0	11	0	.000

1943 NFL FINAL STANDINGS

EAST DIVISION	W	L	T	PCT
New York Giants	6	3	1	.667
Washington Redskins	6	3	1	.667
Phil-Pitt Eagles-Steel	5	4	1	.556
Brooklyn Dodgers	2	8	0	.200

WEST DIVISION	W	L	T	PCT
Chicago Bears	8	1	1	.889
Green Bay Packers	7	2	1	.778
Detroit Lions	3	6	1	.333
Chicago Cardinals	0	10	0	.000

1944 NFL FINAL STANDINGS

EAST DIVISION	W	L	T	PCT
New York Giants	8	1	1	.889
Philadelphia Eagles	7	1	2	.875
Washington Redskins	6	3	1	.667
Boston Yanks	2	8	0	.200
Brooklyn Tigers	0	10	0	.000

WEST DIVISION	W	L	T	PCT
Green Bay Packers	8	2	0	.800
Detroit Lions	6	3	1	.667
Chicago Bears	6	3	1	.667
Cleveland Rams	4	6	0	.400
Chicago-Pitt Card-Pitt	0	10	0	.000

1945 NFL FINAL STANDINGS

EAST DIVISION	W	L	T	PCT
Washington Redskins	8	2	0	.800
Philadelphia Eagles	7	3	0	.700
Boston Yanks	3	6	1	.333
New York Giants	3	6	1	.333
Pittsburgh Steelers	2	8	0	.200

WEST DIVISION	W	L	T	PCT
Cleveland Rams	9	1	0	.900
Detroit Lions	7	3	0	.700
Green Bay Packers	6	4	0	.600
Chicago Bears	3	7	0	.300
Chicago Cardinals	1	9	0	.100

1946 NFL FINAL STANDINGS

EAST DIVISION	W	L	T	PCT
New York Giants	7	3	1	.700
Philadelphia Eagles	6	5	0	.545
Pittsburgh Steelers	5	5	1	.500
Washington Redskins	5	5	1	.500
Boston Yanks	2	8	1	.200

WEST DIVISION	W	L	T	PCT
Chicago Bears	8	2	1	.800
Los Angeles Rams	6	4	1	.600
Chicago Cardinals	6	5	0	.545
Green Bay Packers	6	5	0	.545
Detroit Lions	1	10	0	.091

1947 NFL FINAL STANDINGS

EAST DIVISION	W	L	T	PCT
Philadelphia Eagles	8	4	0	.667
Pittsburgh Steelers	8	4	0	.667
Boston Yanks	4	7	1	.364
Washington Redskins	4	8	0	.333
New York Giants	2	8	2	.200

WEST DIVISION	W	L	T	PCT
Chicago Cardinals	9	3	0	.750
Chicago Bears	8	4	0	.667
Green Bay Packers	6	5	1	.545
Los Angeles Rams	6	6	0	.500
Detroit Lions	3	9	0	.250

STANDINGS

1948 NFL FINAL STANDINGS

EAST DIVISION	W	L	T	PCT
Philadelphia Eagles	9	2	1	.818
Washington Redskins	7	5	0	.583
Pittsburgh Steelers	4	8	0	.333
New York Giants	4	8	0	.333
Boston Yanks	3	9	0	.250

WEST DIVISION	W	L	T	PCT
Chicago Cardinals	11	1	0	.917
Chicago Bears	10	2	0	.833
Los Angeles Rams	6	5	1	.545
Green Bay Packers	3	9	0	.250
Detroit Lions	2	10	0	.167

1949 NFL FINAL STANDINGS

EAST DIVISION	W	L	T	PCT
Philadelphia Eagles	11	1	0	.917
Pittsburgh Steelers	6	5	1	.545
New York Giants	6	6	0	.500
Washington Redskins	4	7	1	.364
New York Bulldogs	1	10	1	.091

WEST DIVISION	W	L	T	PCT
Los Angeles Rams	8	2	2	.800
Chicago Bears	9	3	0	.750
Chicago Cardinals	6	5	1	.545
Detroit Lions	4	8	0	.333
Green Bay Packers	2	10	0	.167

1950 NFL FINAL STANDINGS

AFC	W	L	T	PCT
New York Giants	10	2	0	.833
Cleveland Browns	10	2	0	.833
Pittsburgh Steelers	6	6	0	.500
Philadelphia Eagles	6	6	0	.500
Chicago Cardinals	5	7	0	.417
Washington Redskins	3	9	0	.250

NFC	W	L	T	PCT
Chicago Bears	9	3	0	.750
Los Angeles Rams	9	3	0	.750
New York Yanks	7	5	0	.583
Detroit Lions	6	6	0	.500
San Francisco 49ers	3	9	0	.250
Green Bay Packers	3	9	0	.250
Baltimore Colts	0	0	0	-

1951 NFL FINAL STANDINGS

AFC	W	L	T	PCT
Cleveland Browns	11	1	0	.917
New York Giants	9	2	1	.818
Washington Redskins	5	7	0	.417
Pittsburgh Steelers	4	7	1	.364
Philadelphia Eagles	4	8	0	.333
Chicago Cardinals	3	9	0	.250

NFC	W	L	T	PCT
Los Angeles Rams	8	4	0	.667
San Francisco 49ers	7	4	1	.636
Detroit Lions	7	4	1	.636
Chicago Bears	7	5	0	.583
Green Bay Packers	3	9	0	.250
New York Yanks	1	9	2	.100

1952 NFL FINAL STANDINGS

AFC	W	L	T	PCT
Cleveland Browns	8	4	0	.667
Philadelphia Eagles	7	5	0	.583
New York Giants	7	5	0	.583
Pittsburgh Steelers	5	7	0	.417
Washington Redskins	4	8	0	.333
Chicago Cardinals	4	8	0	.333

NFC	W	L	T	PCT
Detroit Lions	9	3	0	.750
Los Angeles Rams	9	3	0	.750
San Francisco 49ers	7	5	0	.583
Green Bay Packers	6	6	0	.500
Chicago Bears	5	7	0	.417
Dallas Texans	1	11	0	.083

1953 NFL FINAL STANDINGS

EASTERN CONFERENCE	W	L	T	PCT
Cleveland Browns	11	1	0	.917
Philadelphia Eagles	7	4	1	.636
Washington Redskins	6	5	1	.545
Pittsburgh Steelers	6	6	0	.500
New York Giants	3	9	0	.250
Chicago Cardinals	1	10	1	.091

WESTERN CONFERENCE	W	L	T	PCT
Detroit Lions	10	2	0	.833
San Francisco 49ers	9	3	0	.750
Los Angeles Rams	8	3	1	.727
Chicago Bears	3	8	1	.273
Baltimore Colts	3	9	0	.250
Green Bay Packers	2	9	1	.182

STANDINGS

1954 NFL FINAL STANDINGS

EASTERN CONFERENCE	W	L	T	PCT
Cleveland Browns	9	3	0	.750
Philadelphia Eagles	7	4	1	.636
New York Giants	7	5	0	.583
Pittsburgh Steelers	5	7	0	.417
Washington Redskins	3	9	0	.250
Chicago Cardinals	2	10	0	.167

WESTERN CONFERENCE	W	L	T	PCT
Detroit Lions	9	2	1	.818
Chicago Bears	8	4	0	.667
San Francisco 49ers	7	4	1	.636
Los Angeles Rams	6	5	1	.545
Green Bay Packers	4	8	0	.333
Baltimore Colts	3	9	0	.250

1955 NFL FINAL STANDINGS

EASTERN CONFERENCE	W	L	T	PCT
Cleveland Browns	9	2	1	.818
Washington Redskins	8	4	0	.667
New York Giants	6	5	1	.545
Philadelphia Eagles	4	7	1	.364
Chicago Cardinals	4	7	1	.364
Pittsburgh Steelers	4	8	0	.333

WESTERN CONFERENCE	W	L	T	PCT
Los Angeles Rams	8	3	1	.727
Chicago Bears	8	4	0	.667
Green Bay Packers	6	6	0	.500
Baltimore Colts	5	6	1	.455
San Francisco 49ers	4	8	0	.333
Detroit Lions	3	9	0	.250

1956 NFL FINAL STANDINGS

EASTERN CONFERENCE	W	L	T	PCT
New York Giants	8	3	1	.727
Chicago Cardinals	7	5	0	.583
Washington Redskins	6	6	0	.500
Pittsburgh Steelers	5	7	0	.417
Cleveland Browns	5	7	0	.417
Philadelphia Eagles	3	8	1	.273

WESTERN CONFERENCE	W	L	T	PCT
Chicago Bears	9	2	1	.818
Detroit Lions	9	3	0	.750
San Francisco 49ers	5	6	1	.455
Baltimore Colts	5	7	0	.417
Los Angeles Rams	4	8	0	.333
Green Bay Packers	4	8	0	.333

1957 NFL FINAL STANDINGS

EASTERN CONFERENCE	W	L	T	PCT
Cleveland Browns	9	2	1	.818
New York Giants	7	5	0	.583
Pittsburgh Steelers	6	6	0	.500
Washington Redskins	5	6	1	.455
Philadelphia Eagles	4	8	0	.333
Chicago Cardinals	3	9	0	.250

WESTERN CONFERENCE	W	L	T	PCT
San Francisco 49ers	8	4	0	.667
Detroit Lions	8	4	0	.667
Baltimore Colts	7	5	0	.583
Los Angeles Rams	6	6	0	.500
Chicago Bears	5	7	0	.417
Green Bay Packers	3	9	0	.250

1958 NFL FINAL STANDINGS

EASTERN CONFERENCE	W	L	T	PCT
New York Giants	9	3	0	.750
Cleveland Browns	9	3	0	.750
Pittsburgh Steelers	7	4	1	.636
Washington Redskins	4	7	1	.364
Philadelphia Eagles	2	9	1	.182
Chicago Cardinals	2	9	1	.182

WESTERN CONFERENCE	W	L	T	PCT
Baltimore Colts	9	3	0	.750
Chicago Bears	8	4	0	.667
Los Angeles Rams	8	4	0	.667
San Francisco 49ers	6	6	0	.500
Detroit Lions	4	7	1	.364
Green Bay Packers	1	10	1	.091

1959 NFL FINAL STANDINGS

EASTERN CONFERENCE	W	L	T	PCT
New York Giants	10	2	0	.833
Cleveland Browns	7	5	0	.583
Philadelphia Eagles	7	5	0	.583
Pittsburgh Steelers	6	5	1	.545
Washington Redskins	3	9	0	.250
Chicago Cardinals	2	10	0	.167

WESTERN CONFERENCE	W	L	T	PCT
Baltimore Colts	9	3	0	.750
Chicago Bears	8	4	0	.667
Green Bay Packers	7	5	0	.583
San Francisco 49ers	7	5	0	.583
Detroit Lions	3	8	1	.273
Los Angeles Rams	2	10	0	.167

STANDINGS

1960 NFL FINAL STANDINGS

EASTERN CONFERENCE	W	L	T	PCT
Philadelphia Eagles	10	2	0	.833
Cleveland Browns	8	3	1	.727
New York Giants	6	4	2	.600
St. Louis Cardinals	6	5	1	.545
Pittsburgh Steelers	5	6	1	.455
Washington Redskins	1	9	2	.100

WESTERN CONFERENCE	W	L	T	PCT
Green Bay Packers	8	4	0	.667
Detroit Lions	7	5	0	.583
San Francisco 49ers	7	5	0	.583
Baltimore Colts	6	6	0	.500
Chicago Bears	5	6	1	.455
Los Angeles Rams	4	7	1	.364
Dallas Cowboys	0	11	1	.000

1960 AFL FINAL STANDINGS

EAST DIVISION	W	L	T	PCT
Houston Oilers	10	4	0	.714
New York Titans	7	7	0	.500
Buffalo Bills	5	8	1	.385
Boston Patriots	5	9	0	.357

WEST DIVISION	W	L	T	PCT
Los Angeles Chargers	10	4	0	.714
Dallas Texans	8	6	0	.571
Oakland Raiders	6	8	0	.429
Denver Broncos	4	9	1	.308

1961 NFL FINAL STANDINGS

EASTERN CONFERENCE	W	L	T	PCT
New York Giants	10	3	1	.769
Philadelphia Eagles	10	4	0	.714
Cleveland Browns	8	5	1	.615
St. Louis Cardinals	7	7	0	.500
Pittsburgh Steelers	6	8	0	.429
Dallas Cowboys	4	9	1	.308
Washington Redskins	1	12	1	.077

WESTERN CONFERENCE	W	L	T	PCT
Green Bay Packers	11	3	0	.786
Detroit Lions	8	5	1	.615
Chicago Bears	8	6	0	.571
Baltimore Colts	8	6	0	.571
San Francisco 49ers	7	6	1	.538
Los Angeles Rams	4	10	0	.286
Minnesota Vikings	3	11	0	.214

1961 AFL FINAL STANDINGS

EAST DIVISION	W	L	T	PCT
Houston Oilers	10	3	1	.769
Boston Patriots	9	4	1	.692
New York Titans	7	7	0	.500
Buffalo Bills	6	8	0	.429

WEST DIVISION	W	L	T	PCT
San Diego Chargers	12	2	0	.857
Dallas Texans	6	8	0	.429
Denver Broncos	3	11	0	.214
Oakland Raiders	2	12	0	.143

1962 NFL FINAL STANDINGS

EASTERN CONFERENCE	W	L	T	PCT
New York Giants	12	2	0	.857
Pittsburgh Steelers	9	5	0	.643
Cleveland Browns	7	6	1	.538
Washington Redskins	5	7	2	.417
Dallas Cowboys	5	8	1	.385
St. Louis Cardinals	4	9	1	.308
Philadelphia Eagles	3	10	1	.231

WESTERN CONFERENCE	W	L	T	PCT
Green Bay Packers	13	1	0	.929
Detroit Lions	11	3	0	.786
Chicago Bears	9	5	0	.643
Baltimore Colts	7	7	0	.500
San Francisco 49ers	6	8	0	.429
Minnesota Vikings	2	11	1	.154
Los Angeles Rams	1	12	1	.077

1962 AFL FINAL STANDINGS

EAST DIVISION	W	L	T	PCT
Houston Oilers	11	3	0	.786
Boston Patriots	9	4	1	.692
Buffalo Bills	7	6	1	.538
New York Titans	5	9	0	.357

WEST DIVISION	W	L	T	PCT
Dallas Texans	11	3	0	.786
Denver Broncos	7	7	0	.500
San Diego Chargers	4	10	0	.286
Oakland Raiders	1	13	0	.071

STANDINGS

1963 NFL FINAL STANDINGS

EASTERN CONFERENCE	W	L	T	PCT
New York Giants	11	3	0	.786
Cleveland Browns	10	4	0	.714
St. Louis Cardinals	9	5	0	.643
Pittsburgh Steelers	7	4	3	.636
Dallas Cowboys	4	10	0	.286
Washington Redskins	3	11	0	.214
Philadelphia Eagles	2	10	2	.167

WESTERN CONFERENCE	W	L	T	PCT
Chicago Bears	11	1	2	.917
Green Bay Packers	11	2	1	.846
Baltimore Colts	8	6	0	.571
Detroit Lions	5	8	1	.385
Minnesota Vikings	5	8	1	.385
Los Angeles Rams	5	9	0	.357
San Francisco 49ers	2	12	0	.143

1963 AFL FINAL STANDINGS

EAST DIVISION	W	L	T	PCT
Boston Patriots	7	6	1	.538
Buffalo Bills	7	6	1	.538
Houston Oilers	6	8	0	.429
New York Jets	5	8	1	.385

WEST DIVISION	W	L	T	PCT
San Diego Chargers	11	3	0	.786
Oakland Raiders	10	4	0	.714
Kansas City Chiefs	5	7	2	.417
Denver Broncos	2	11	1	.154

1964 NFL FINAL STANDINGS

EASTERN CONFERENCE	W	L	T	PCT
Cleveland Browns	10	3	1	.769
St. Louis Cardinals	9	3	2	.750
Washington Redskins	6	8	0	.429
Philadelphia Eagles	6	8	0	.429
Dallas Cowboys	5	8	1	.385
Pittsburgh Steelers	5	9	0	.357
New York Giants	2	10	2	.167

WESTERN CONFERENCE	W	L	T	PCT
Baltimore Colts	12	2	0	.857
Green Bay Packers	8	5	1	.615
Minnesota Vikings	8	5	1	.615
Detroit Lions	7	5	2	.583
Los Angeles Rams	5	7	2	.417
Chicago Bears	5	9	0	.357
San Francisco 49ers	4	10	0	.286

1964 AFL FINAL STANDINGS

EAST DIVISION	W	L	T	PCT
Buffalo Bills	12	2	0	.857
Boston Patriots	10	3	1	.769
New York Jets	5	8	1	.385
Houston Oilers	4	10	0	.286

WEST DIVISION	W	L	T	PCT
San Diego Chargers	8	5	1	.615
Kansas City Chiefs	7	7	0	.500
Oakland Raiders	5	7	2	.417
Denver Broncos	2	11	1	.154

1965 NFL FINAL STANDINGS

EASTERN CONFERENCE	W	L	T	PCT
Cleveland Browns	11	3	0	.786
Dallas Cowboys	7	7	0	.500
New York Giants	7	7	0	.500
Washington Redskins	6	8	0	.429
Philadelphia Eagles	5	9	0	.357
St. Louis Cardinals	5	9	0	.357
Pittsburgh Steelers	2	12	0	.143

WESTERN CONFERENCE	W	L	T	PCT
Green Bay Packers	10	3	1	.769
Baltimore Colts	10	3	1	.769
Chicago Bears	9	5	0	.643
San Francisco 49ers	7	6	1	.538
Minnesota Vikings	7	7	0	.500
Detroit Lions	6	7	1	.462
Los Angeles Rams	4	10	0	.286

1965 AFL FINAL STANDINGS

EAST DIVISION	W	L	T	PCT
Buffalo Bills	10	3	1	.769
New York Jets	5	8	1	.385
Boston Patriots	4	8	2	.333
Houston Oilers	4	10	0	.286

WEST DIVISION	W	L	T	PCT
San Diego Chargers	9	2	3	.818
Oakland Raiders	8	5	1	.615
Kansas City Chiefs	7	5	2	.583
Denver Broncos	4	10	0	.286

STANDINGS

1966 NFL FINAL STANDINGS

EASTERN CONFERENCE	W	L	T	PCT
Dallas Cowboys	10	3	1	.769
Cleveland Browns	9	5	0	.643
Philadelphia Eagles	9	5	0	.643
St. Louis Cardinals	8	5	1	.615
Washington Redskins	7	7	0	.500
Pittsburgh Steelers	5	8	1	.385
Atlanta Falcons	3	11	0	.214
New York Giants	1	12	1	.077

WESTERN CONFERENCE	W	L	T	PCT
Green Bay Packers	12	2	0	.857
Baltimore Colts	9	5	0	.643
Los Angeles Rams	8	6	0	.571
San Francisco 49ers	6	6	2	.500
Chicago Bears	5	7	2	.417
Minnesota Vikings	4	9	1	.308
Detroit Lions	4	9	1	.308

1966 AFL FINAL STANDINGS

EAST DIVISION	W	L	T	PCT
Buffalo Bills	9	4	1	.692
Boston Patriots	8	4	2	.667
New York Jets	6	6	2	.500
Houston Oilers	3	11	0	.214
Miami Dolphins	3	11	0	.214

WEST DIVISION	W	L	T	PCT
Kansas City Chiefs	11	2	1	.846
Oakland Raiders	8	5	1	.615
San Diego Chargers	7	6	1	.538
Denver Broncos	4	10	0	.286

1967 NFL FINAL STANDINGS

EASTERN CONFERENCE

CAPITAL DIVISION	W	L	T	PCT
Dallas Cowboys	9	5	0	.643
Philadelphia Eagles	6	7	1	.462
Washington Redskins	5	6	3	.455
New Orleans Saints	3	11	0	.214

CENTURY DIVISION	W	L	T	PCT
Cleveland Browns	9	5	0	.643
New York Giants	7	7	0	.500
St. Louis Cardinals	6	7	1	.462
Pittsburgh Steelers	4	9	1	.308

WESTERN CONFERENCE

CENTRAL DIVISION	W	L	T	PCT
Green Bay Packers	9	4	1	.692
Chicago Bears	7	6	1	.538
Detroit Lions	5	7	2	.417
Minnesota Vikings	3	8	3	.273

COASTAL DIVISION	W	L	T	PCT
Los Angeles Rams	11	1	2	.917
Baltimore Colts	11	1	2	.917
San Francisco 49ers	7	7	0	.500
Atlanta Falcons	1	12	1	.077

1967 AFL FINAL STANDINGS

EAST DIVISION	W	L	T	PCT
Houston Oilers	9	4	1	.692
New York Jets	8	5	1	.615
Buffalo Bills	4	10	0	.286
Miami Dolphins	4	10	0	.200
Boston Patriots	3	10	1	.231

WEST DIVISION	W	L	T	PCT
Oakland Raiders	13	1	0	.929
Kansas City Chiefs	9	5	0	.643
San Diego Chargers	8	5	1	.615
Denver Broncos	3	11	0	.214

STANDINGS

1968 NFL FINAL STANDINGS
EASTERN CONFERENCE

CAPITAL DIVISION	W	L	T	PCT
Dallas Cowboys	12	2	0	.857
New York Giants	7	7	0	.500
Washington Redskins	5	9	0	.357
Philadelphia Eagles	2	12	0	.143

CENTURY DIVISION	W	L	T	PCT
Cleveland Browns	10	4	0	.714
St. Louis Cardinals	9	4	1	.692
New Orleans Saints	4	9	1	.308
Pittsburgh Steelers	2	11	1	.154

WESTERN CONFERENCE

CENTRAL DIVISION	W	L	T	PCT
Minnesota Vikings	8	6	0	.571
Chicago Bears	7	7	0	.500
Green Bay Packers	6	7	1	.462
Detroit Lions	4	8	2	.333

COASTAL DIVISION	W	L	T	PCT
Baltimore Colts	13	1	0	.929
Los Angeles Rams	10	3	1	.769
San Francisco 49ers	7	6	1	.538
Atlanta Falcons	2	12	0	.143

1968 AFL FINAL STANDINGS

EAST DIVISION	W	L	T	PCT
New York Jets	11	3	0	.786
Houston Oilers	7	7	0	.500
Miami Dolphins	5	8	1	.385
Boston Patriots	4	10	0	.286
Buffalo Bills	1	12	1	.077

WEST DIVISION	W	L	T	PCT
Oakland Raiders	12	2	0	.857
Kansas City Chiefs	12	2	0	.857
San Diego Chargers	9	5	0	.643
Denver Broncos	5	9	0	.357
Cincinnati Bengals	3	11	0	.214

1969 NFL FINAL STANDINGS
EASTERN CONFERENCE

CAPITAL DIVISION	W	L	T	PCT
Dallas Cowboys	11	2	1	.846
Washington Redskins	7	5	2	.583
New Orleans Saints	5	9	0	.357
Philadelphia Eagles	4	9	1	.308

CENTURY DIVISION	W	L	T	PCT
Cleveland Browns	10	3	1	.769
New York Giants	6	8	0	.429
St. Louis Cardinals	4	9	1	.308
Pittsburgh Steelers	1	13	0	.071

WESTERN CONFERENCE

CENTRAL DIVISION	W	L	T	PCT
Minnesota Vikings	12	2	0	.857
Detroit Lions	9	4	1	.692
Green Bay Packers	8	6	0	.571
Chicago Bears	1	13	0	.071

COASTAL DIVISION	W	L	T	PCT
Los Angeles Rams	11	3	0	.786
Baltimore Colts	8	5	1	.615
Atlanta Falcons	6	8	0	.429
San Francisco 49ers	4	8	2	.333

1969 AFL FINAL STANDINGS

EAST DIVISION	W	L	T	PCT
New York Jets	10	4	0	.714
Houston Oilers	6	6	2	.500
Boston Patriots	4	10	0	.286
Buffalo Bills	4	10	0	.286
Miami Dolphins	3	10	1	.231

WEST DIVISION	W	L	T	PCT
Oakland Raiders	12	1	1	.923
Kansas City Chiefs	11	3	0	.786
San Diego Chargers	8	6	0	.571
Denver Broncos	5	8	1	.385
Cincinnati Bengals	4	9	1	.308

STANDINGS

1970 NFL FINAL STANDINGS

AFC

EAST DIVISION	W	L	T	PCT
Baltimore Colts	11	2	1	.846
Miami Dolphins	10	4	0	.714
New York Jets	4	10	0	.286
Buffalo Bills	3	10	1	.231
Boston Patriots	2	12	0	.143

CENTRAL DIVISION	W	L	T	PCT
Cincinnati Bengals	8	6	0	.571
Cleveland Browns	7	7	0	.500
Pittsburgh Steelers	5	9	0	.357
Houston Oilers	3	10	1	.231

WEST DIVISION	W	L	T	PCT
Oakland Raiders	8	4	2	.667
Kansas City Chiefs	7	5	2	.583
San Diego Chargers	5	6	3	.455
Denver Broncos	5	8	1	.385

NFC

EAST DIVISION	W	L	T	PCT
Dallas Cowboys	10	4	0	.714
New York Giants	9	5	0	.643
St. Louis Cardinals	8	5	1	.615
Washington Redskins	6	8	0	.429
Philadelphia Eagles	3	10	1	.231

CENTRAL DIVISION	W	L	T	PCT
Minnesota Vikings	12	2	0	.857
Detroit Lions	10	4	0	.714
Green Bay Packers	6	8	0	.429
Chicago Bears	6	8	0	.429

WEST DIVISION	W	L	T	PCT
San Francisco 49ers	10	3	1	.769
Los Angeles Rams	9	4	1	.692
Atlanta Falcons	4	8	2	.333
New Orleans Saints	2	11	1	.154

1971 NFL FINAL STANDINGS

AFC

EAST DIVISION	W	L	T	PCT
Miami Dolphins	10	3	1	.769
Baltimore Colts	10	4	0	.714
New England Patriots	6	8	0	.429
New York Jets	6	8	0	.429
Buffalo Bills	1	13	0	.071

CENTRAL DIVISION	W	L	T	PCT
Cleveland Browns	9	5	0	.643
Pittsburgh Steelers	6	8	0	.429
Houston Oilers	4	9	1	.308
Cincinnati Bengals	4	10	0	.286

WEST DIVISION	W	L	T	PCT
Kansas City Chiefs	10	3	1	.769
Oakland Raiders	8	4	2	.667
San Diego Chargers	6	8	0	.429
Denver Broncos	4	9	1	.308

NFC

EAST DIVISION	W	L	T	PCT
Dallas Cowboys	11	3	0	.786
Washington Redskins	9	4	1	.692
Philadelphia Eagles	6	7	1	.462
St. Louis Cardinals	4	9	1	.308
New York Giants	4	10	0	.286

CENTRAL DIVISION	W	L	T	PCT
Minnesota Vikings	11	3	0	.786
Detroit Lions	7	6	1	.538
Chicago Bears	6	8	0	.429
Green Bay Packers	4	8	2	.333

WEST DIVISION	W	L	T	PCT
San Francisco 49ers	9	5	0	.643
Los Angeles Rams	8	5	1	.615
Atlanta Falcons	7	6	1	.538
New Orleans Saints	4	8	2	.333

STANDINGS

1972 NFL FINAL STANDINGS
AFC

EAST DIVISION	W	L	T	PCT
Miami Dolphins	14	0	0	1.000
New York Jets	7	7	0	.500
Baltimore Colts	5	9	0	.357
Buffalo Bills	4	9	1	.321
New England Patriots	3	11	0	.214

CENTRAL DIVISION	W	L	T	PCT
Pittsburgh Steelers	11	3	0	.786
Cleveland Browns	10	4	0	.714
Cincinnati Bengals	8	6	0	.571
Houston Oilers	1	13	0	.071

WEST DIVISION	W	L	T	PCT
Oakland Raiders	10	3	1	.750
Kansas City Chiefs	8	6	0	.571
Denver Broncos	5	9	0	.357
San Diego Chargers	4	9	1	.321

NFC

EAST DIVISION	W	L	T	PCT
Washington Redskins	11	3	0	.786
Dallas Cowboys	10	4	0	.714
New York Giants	8	6	0	.571
St. Louis Cardinals	4	9	1	.321
Philadelphia Eagles	2	11	1	.179

CENTRAL DIVISION	W	L	T	PCT
Green Bay Packers	10	4	0	.714
Detroit Lions	8	5	1	.607
Minnesota Vikings	7	7	0	.500
Chicago Bears	4	9	1	.321

WEST DIVISION	W	L	T	PCT
San Francisco 49ers	8	5	1	.607
Atlanta Falcons	7	7	0	.500
Los Angeles Rams	6	7	1	.464
New Orleans Saints	2	11	1	.179

1973 NFL FINAL STANDINGS
AFC

EAST DIVISION	W	L	T	PCT
Miami Dolphins	12	2	0	.857
Buffalo Bills	9	5	0	.643
New England Patriots	5	9	0	.357
New York Jets	4	10	0	.286
Baltimore Colts	4	10	0	.286

CENTRAL DIVISION	W	L	T	PCT
Cincinnati Bengals	10	4	0	.714
Pittsburgh Steelers	10	4	0	.714
Cleveland Browns	7	5	2	.571
Houston Oilers	1	13	0	.071

WEST DIVISION	W	L	T	PCT
Oakland Raiders	9	4	1	.679
Kansas City Chiefs	7	5	2	.571
Denver Broncos	7	5	2	.571
San Diego Chargers	2	11	1	.179

NFC

EAST DIVISION	W	L	T	PCT
Dallas Cowboys	10	4	0	.714
Washington Redskins	10	4	0	.714
Philadelphia Eagles	5	8	1	.393
St. Louis Cardinals	4	9	1	.321
New York Giants	2	11	1	.179

CENTRAL DIVISION	W	L	T	PCT
Minnesota Vikings	12	2	0	.857
Detroit Lions	6	7	1	.464
Green Bay Packers	5	7	2	.429
Chicago Bears	3	11	0	.214

WEST DIVISION	W	L	T	PCT
Los Angeles Rams	12	2	0	.857
Atlanta Falcons	9	5	0	.643
San Francisco 49ers	5	9	0	.357
New Orleans Saints	5	9	0	.357

STANDINGS

1974 NFL FINAL STANDINGS

AFC

EAST DIVISION	W	L	T	PCT
Miami Dolphins	11	3	0	.786
Buffalo Bills	9	5	0	.643
New York Jets	7	7	0	.500
New England Patriots	7	7	0	.500
Baltimore Colts	2	12	0	.143

CENTRAL DIVISION	W	L	T	PCT
Pittsburgh Steelers	10	3	1	.750
Houston Oilers	7	7	0	.500
Cincinnati Bengals	7	7	0	.500
Cleveland Browns	4	10	0	.286

WEST DIVISION	W	L	T	PCT
Oakland Raiders	12	2	0	.857
Denver Broncos	7	6	1	.536
Kansas City Chiefs	5	9	0	.357
San Diego Chargers	5	9	0	.357

NFC

EAST DIVISION	W	L	T	PCT
St. Louis Cardinals	10	4	0	.714
Washington Redskins	10	4	0	.714
Dallas Cowboys	8	6	0	.571
Philadelphia Eagles	7	7	0	.500
New York Giants	2	12	0	.143

CENTRAL DIVISION	W	L	T	PCT
Minnesota Vikings	10	4	0	.714
Detroit Lions	7	7	0	.500
Green Bay Packers	6	8	0	.429
Chicago Bears	4	10	0	.286

WEST DIVISION	W	L	T	PCT
Los Angeles Rams	10	4	0	.714
San Francisco 49ers	6	8	0	.429
New Orleans Saints	5	9	0	.357
Atlanta Falcons	3	11	0	.214

1975 NFL FINAL STANDINGS

AFC

EAST DIVISION	W	L	T	PCT
Baltimore Colts	10	4	0	.714
Miami Dolphins	10	4	0	.714
Buffalo Bills	8	6	0	.571
New York Jets	3	11	0	.214
New England Patriots	3	11	0	.214

CENTRAL DIVISION	W	L	T	PCT
Pittsburgh Steelers	12	2	0	.857
Cincinnati Bengals	11	3	0	.786
Houston Oilers	10	4	0	.714
Cleveland Browns	3	11	0	.214

WEST DIVISION	W	L	T	PCT
Oakland Raiders	11	3	0	.786
Denver Broncos	6	8	0	.429
Kansas City Chiefs	5	9	0	.357
San Diego Chargers	2	12	0	.143

NFC

EAST DIVISION	W	L	T	PCT
St. Louis Cardinals	11	3	0	.786
Dallas Cowboys	10	4	0	.714
Washington Redskins	8	6	0	.571
New York Giants	5	9	0	.357
Philadelphia Eagles	4	10	0	.206

CENTRAL DIVISION	W	L	T	PCT
Minnesota Vikings	12	2	0	.857
Detroit Lions	7	7	0	.500
Chicago Bears	4	10	0	.206
Green Bay Packers	4	10	0	.206

WEST DIVISION	W	L	T	PCT
Los Angeles Rams	12	2	0	.857
San Francisco 49ers	5	9	0	.357
Atlanta Falcons	4	10	0	.286
New Orleans Saints	2	12	0	.143

STANDINGS

1976 NFL FINAL STANDINGS

AFC

EAST DIVISION

	W	L	T	PCT
Baltimore Colts	11	3	0	.786
New England Patriots	11	3	0	.786
Miami Dolphins	6	8	0	.429
New York Jets	3	11	0	.214
Buffalo Bills	2	12	0	.143

CENTRAL DIVISION

	W	L	T	PCT
Pittsburgh Steelers	10	4	0	.714
Cincinnati Bengals	10	4	0	.714
Cleveland Browns	9	5	0	.643
Houston Oilers	5	9	0	.357

WEST DIVISION

	W	L	T	PCT
Oakland Raiders	13	1	0	.929
Denver Broncos	9	5	0	.643
San Diego Chargers	6	8	0	.429
Kansas City Chiefs	5	9	0	.357
Tampa Bay Buccaneers	0	14	0	.000

NFC

EAST DIVISION

	W	L	T	PCT
Dallas Cowboys	11	3	0	.786
Washington Redskins	10	4	0	.714
St. Louis Cardinals	10	4	0	.714
Philadelphia Eagles	4	10	0	.286
New York Giants	3	11	0	.214

CENTRAL DIVISION

	W	L	T	PCT
Minnesota Vikings	11	2	1	.821
Chicago Bears	7	7	0	.500
Detroit Lions	6	8	0	.429
Green Bay Packers	5	9	0	.357

WEST DIVISION

	W	L	T	PCT
Los Angeles Rams	10	3	1	.750
San Francisco 49ers	8	6	0	.571
Atlanta Falcons	4	10	0	.286
New Orleans Saints	4	10	0	.286
Seattle Seahawks	2	12	0	.143

1977 NFL FINAL STANDINGS

AFC

EAST DIVISION

	W	L	T	PCT
Baltimore Colts	10	4	0	.714
Miami Dolphins	10	4	0	.714
New England Patriots	9	5	0	.643
New York Jets	3	11	0	.214
Buffalo Bills	3	11	0	.214

CENTRAL DIVISION

	W	L	T	PCT
Pittsburgh Steelers	9	5	0	.643
Cincinnati Bengals	8	6	0	.571
Houston Oilers	8	6	0	.571
Cleveland Browns	6	8	0	.429

WEST DIVISION

	W	L	T	PCT
Denver Broncos	12	2	0	.857
Oakland Raiders	11	3	0	.786
San Diego Chargers	7	7	0	.500
Seattle Seahawks	5	9	0	.357
Kansas City Chiefs	2	12	0	.143

NFC

EAST DIVISION

	W	L	T	PCT
Dallas Cowboys	12	2	0	.857
Washington Redskins	9	5	0	.643
St. Louis Cardinals	7	7	0	.500
Philadelphia Eagles	5	9	0	.357
New York Giants	5	9	0	.357

CENTRAL DIVISION

	W	L	T	PCT
Chicago Bears	9	5	0	.643
Minnesota Vikings	9	5	0	.643
Detroit Lions	6	8	0	.429
Green Bay Packers	4	10	0	.286
Tampa Bay Buccaneers	2	12	0	.143

WEST DIVISION

	W	L	T	PCT
Los Angeles Rams	10	4	0	.714
Atlanta Falcons	7	7	0	.500
San Francisco 49ers	5	9	0	.357
New Orleans Saints	3	11	0	.214

STANDINGS

1978 NFL FINAL STANDINGS

AFC

EAST DIVISION	W	L	T	PCT
New England Patriots	11	5	0	.688
Miami Dolphins	11	5	0	.688
New York Jets	8	8	0	.500
Buffalo Bills	5	11	0	.313
Baltimore Colts	5	11	0	.313

CENTRAL DIVISION	W	L	T	PCT
Pittsburgh Steelers	14	2	0	.875
Houston Oilers	10	6	0	.625
Cleveland Browns	8	8	0	.500
Cincinnati Bengals	4	12	0	.250

WEST DIVISION	W	L	T	PCT
Denver Broncos	10	6	0	.625
San Diego Chargers	9	7	0	.563
Seattle Seahawks	9	7	0	.563
Oakland Raiders	9	7	0	.563
Kansas City Chiefs	4	12	0	.250

NFC

EAST DIVISION	W	L	T	PCT
Dallas Cowboys	12	4	0	.750
Philadelphia Eagles	9	7	0	.563
Washington Redskins	8	8	0	.500
St. Louis Cardinals	6	10	0	.375
New York Giants	6	10	0	.375

CENTRAL DIVISION	W	L	T	PCT
Minnesota Vikings	8	7	1	.531
Green Bay Packers	8	7	1	.531
Detroit Lions	7	9	0	.438
Chicago Bears	7	9	0	.438
Tampa Bay Buccaneers	5	11	0	.313

WEST DIVISION	W	L	T	PCT
Los Angeles Rams	12	1	0	.750
Atlanta Falcons	9	7	0	.563
New Orleans Saints	7	9	0	.438
San Francisco 49ers	2	14	0	.125

1979 NFL FINAL STANDINGS

AFC

EAST DIVISION	W	L	T	PCT
Miami Dolphins	10	6	0	.625
New England Patriots	9	7	0	.563
New York Jets	8	8	0	.500
Buffalo Bills	7	9	0	.438
Baltimore Colts	5	11	0	.313

CENTRAL DIVISION	W	L	T	PCT
Pittsburgh Steelers	12	4	0	.750
Houston Oilers	11	5	0	.688
Cleveland Browns	9	7	0	.563
Cincinnati Bengals	4	12	0	.250

WEST DIVISION	W	L	T	PCT
San Diego Chargers	12	4	0	.750
Denver Broncos	10	6	0	.625
Seattle Seahawks	9	7	0	.563
Oakland Raiders	9	7	0	.563
Kansas City Chiefs	7	9	0	.438

NFC

EAST DIVISION	W	L	T	PCT
Dallas Cowboys	11	5	0	.688
Philadelphia Eagles	11	5	0	.688
Washington Redskins	10	6	0	.625
New York Giants	6	10	0	.375
St. Louis Cardinals	5	11	0	.313

CENTRAL DIVISION	W	L	T	PCT
Tampa Bay Buccaneers	10	6	0	.625
Chicago Bears	10	6	0	.625
Minnesota Vikings	7	9	0	.438
Green Bay Packers	5	11	0	.313
Detroit Lions	2	14	0	.125

WEST DIVISION	W	L	T	PCT
Los Angeles Rams	9	7	0	.563
New Orleans Saints	8	8	0	.500
Atlanta Falcons	6	10	0	.375
San Francisco 49ers	2	14	0	.125

STANDINGS

1980 NFL FINAL STANDINGS

AFC

EAST DIVISION	W	L	T	PCT
Buffalo Bills	11	5	0	.688
New England Patriots	10	6	0	.625
Miami Dolphins	8	8	0	.500
Baltimore Colts	7	9	0	.438
New York Jets	4	12	0	.250

CENTRAL DIVISION	W	L	T	PCT
Cleveland Browns	11	5	0	.688
Houston Oilers	11	5	0	.688
Pittsburgh Steelers	9	7	0	.563
Cincinnati Bengals	6	10	0	.375

WEST DIVISION	W	L	T	PCT
San Diego Chargers	11	5	0	.688
Oakland Raiders	11	5	0	.688
Kansas City Chiefs	8	8	0	.500
Denver Broncos	8	8	0	.500
Seattle Seahawks	4	12	0	.250

NFC

EAST DIVISION	W	L	T	PCT
Philadelphia Eagles	12	4	0	.750
Dallas Cowboys	12	4	0	.750
Washington Redskins	6	10	0	.375
St. Louis Cardinals	5	11	0	.313
New York Giants	4	12	0	.250

CENTRAL DIVISION	W	L	T	PCT
Minnesota Vikings	9	7	0	.563
Detroit Lions	9	7	0	.563
Chicago Bears	7	9	0	.438
Tampa Bay Buccaneers	5	10	1	.344
Green Bay Packers	5	10	1	.344

WEST DIVISION	W	L	T	PCT
Atlanta Falcons	12	4	0	.750
Los Angeles Rams	11	5	0	.688
San Francisco 49ers	6	10	0	.375
New Orleans Saints	1	15	0	.063

1981 NFL FINAL STANDINGS

AFC

EAST DIVISION	W	L	T	PCT
Miami Dolphins	11	4	1	.719
New York Jets	10	5	1	.656
Buffalo Bills	10	6	0	.625
Baltimore Colts	2	14	0	.125
New England Patriots	2	14	0	.125

CENTRAL DIVISION	W	L	T	PCT
Cincinnati Bengals	12	4	0	.750
Pittsburgh Steelers	8	8	0	.500
Houston Oilers	7	9	0	.438
Cleveland Browns	5	11	0	.313

WEST DIVISION	W	L	T	PCT
San Diego Chargers	10	6	0	.625
Denver Broncos	10	6	0	.625
Kansas City Chiefs	9	7	0	.563
Oakland Raiders	7	9	0	.438
Seattle Seahawks	6	10	0	.375

NFC

EAST DIVISION	W	L	T	PCT
Dallas Cowboys	12	4	0	.750
Philadelphia Eagles	10	6	0	.625
New York Giants	9	7	0	.563
Washington Redskins	8	8	0	.500
St. Louis Cardinals	7	9	0	.438

CENTRAL DIVISION	W	L	T	PCT
Tampa Bay Buccaneers	9	7	0	.563
Detroit Lions	8	8	0	.500
Green Bay Packers	8	8	0	.500
Minnesota Vikings	7	9	0	.438
Chicago Bears	6	10	0	.375

WEST DIVISION	W	L	T	PCT
San Francisco 49ers	13	3	0	.813
Atlanta Falcons	7	9	0	.438
Los Angeles Rams	6	10	0	.375
New Orleans Saints	4	12	0	.250

STANDINGS

1982 NFL FINAL STANDINGS

AFC

EAST DIVISION	W	L	T	PCT
Miami Dolphins	7	2	0	.778
New York Jets	6	3	0	.667
New England Patriots	5	4	0	.556
Buffalo Bills	4	5	0	.444
Baltimore Colts	0	8	1	.056

CENTRAL DIVISION	W	L	T	PCT
Cincinnati Bengals	7	2	0	.778
Pittsburgh Steelers	6	3	0	.667
Cleveland Browns	4	5	0	.444
Houston Oilers	1	8	0	.111

WEST DIVISION	W	L	T	PCT
Los Angeles Raiders	8	1	0	.889
San Diego Chargers	6	3	0	.667
Seattle Seahawks	4	5	0	.444
Kansas City Chiefs	3	6	0	.333
Denver Broncos	2	7	0	.222

NFC

EAST DIVISION	W	L	T	PCT
Washington Redskins	8	1	0	.889
Dallas Cowboys	6	3	0	.667
St. Louis Cardinals	5	4	0	.556
New York Giants	4	5	0	.444
Philadelphia Eagles	3	6	0	.333

CENTRAL DIVISION	W	L	T	PCT
Green Bay Packers	5	3	1	.611
Minnesota Vikings	5	4	0	.556
Tampa Bay Buccaneers	5	4	0	.556
Detroit Lions	4	5	0	.444
Chicago Bears	3	6	0	.333

WEST DIVISION	W	L	T	PCT
Atlanta Falcons	5	4	0	.556
New Orleans Saints	4	5	0	.444
San Francisco 49ers	3	6	0	.333
Los Angeles Rams	2	7	0	.222

1983 NFL FINAL STANDINGS

AFC

EAST DIVISION	W	L	T	PCT
Miami Dolphins	12	4	0	.750
New England Patriots	8	8	0	.500
Buffalo Bills	8	8	0	.500
Baltimore Colts	7	9	0	.438
New York Jets	7	9	0	.438

CENTRAL DIVISION	W	L	T	PCT
Pittsburgh Steelers	10	6	0	.625
Cleveland Browns	9	7	0	.563
Cincinnati Bengals	7	9	0	.438
Houston Oilers	2	14	0	.125

WEST DIVISION	W	L	T	PCT
Los Angeles Raiders	12	4	0	.750
Seattle Seahawks	9	7	0	.563
Denver Broncos	9	7	0	.563
San Diego Chargers	6	10	0	.375
Kansas City Chiefs	6	10	0	.375

NFC

EAST DIVISION	W	L	T	PCT
Washington Redskins	14	2	0	.875
Dallas Cowboys	12	4	0	.750
St. Louis Cardinals	8	7	1	.531
Philadelphia Eagles	5	11	0	.313
New York Giants	3	12	1	.219

CENTRAL DIVISION	W	L	T	PCT
Detroit Lions	9	7	0	.563
Green Bay Packers	8	8	0	.500
Chicago Bears	8	8	0	.500
Minnesota Vikings	8	8	0	.500
Tampa Bay Buccaneers	2	14	0	.125

WEST DIVISION	W	L	T	PCT
San Francisco 49ers	10	6	0	.625
Los Angeles Rams	9	7	0	.563
New Orleans Saints	8	8	0	.500
Atlanta Falcons	7	9	0	.438

1984 NFL FINAL STANDINGS

AFC

EAST DIVISION

	W	L	T	PCT
Miami Dolphins	14	2	0	.875
New England Patriots	9	7	0	.563
New York Jets	7	9	0	.438
Indianapolis Colts	4	12	0	.250
Buffalo Bills	2	14	0	.125

CENTRAL DIVISION

	W	L	T	PCT
Pittsburgh Steelers	9	7	0	.563
Cincinnati Bengals	8	8	0	.500
Cleveland Browns	5	11	0	.313
Houston Oilers	3	13	0	.188

WEST DIVISION

	W	L	T	PCT
Denver Broncos	13	3	0	.813
Seattle Seahawks	12	4	0	.750
Los Angeles Raiders	11	5	0	.688
Kansas City Chiefs	8	8	0	.500
San Diego Chargers	7	9	0	.438

NFC

EAST DIVISION

	W	L	T	PCT
Washington Redskins	11	5	0	.688
New York Giants	9	7	0	.563
St. Louis Cardinals	9	7	0	.563
Dallas Cowboys	9	7	0	.563
Philadelphia Eagles	6	9	1	.406

CENTRAL DIVISION

	W	L	T	PCT
Chicago Bears	10	6	0	.625
Green Bay Packers	8	8	0	.500
Tampa Bay Buccaneers	6	10	0	.375
Detroit Lions	4	11	1	.281
Minnesota Vikings	3	13	0	.188

WEST DIVISION

	W	L	T	PCT
San Francisco 49ers	15	1	0	.938
Los Angeles Rams	10	6	0	.625
New Orleans Saints	7	9	0	.438
Atlanta Falcons	4	12	0	.250

1985 NFL FINAL STANDINGS

AFC

EAST DIVISION

	W	L	T	PCT
Miami Dolphins	12	4	0	.750
New York Jets	11	5	0	.688
New England Patriots	11	5	0	.688
Indianapolis Colts	5	11	0	.313
Buffalo Bills	2	14	0	.125

CENTRAL DIVISION

	W	L	T	PCT
Cleveland Browns	8	8	0	.500
Cincinnati Bengals	7	9	0	.438
Pittsburgh Steelers	7	9	0	.438
Houston Oilers	5	11	0	.313

WEST DIVISION

	W	L	T	PCT
Los Angeles Raiders	12	4	0	.750
Denver Broncos	11	5	0	.688
Seattle Seahawks	8	8	0	.500
San Diego Chargers	8	8	0	.500
Kansas City Chiefs	6	10	0	.375

NFC

EAST DIVISION

	W	L	T	PCT
Dallas Cowboys	10	6	0	.625
New York Giants	10	6	0	.625
Washington Redskins	10	6	0	.625
Philadelphia Eagles	7	9	0	.438
St. Louis Cardinals	5	11	0	.313

CENTRAL DIVISION

	W	L	T	PCT
Chicago Bears	15	1	0	.938
Green Bay Packers	8	8	0	.500
Minnesota Vikings	7	9	0	.438
Detroit Lions	7	9	0	.438
Tampa Bay Buccaneers	2	14	0	.125

WEST DIVISION

	W	L	T	PCT
Los Angeles Rams	11	5	0	.688
San Francisco 49ers	10	6	0	.625
New Orleans Saints	5	11	0	.313
Atlanta Falcons	4	12	0	.250

STANDINGS

1986 NFL FINAL STANDINGS

AFC

EAST DIVISION

	W	L	T	PCT
New England Patriots	11	5	0	.688
New York Jets	10	6	0	.625
Miami Dolphins	8	8	0	.500
Buffalo Bills	4	12	0	.250
Indianapolis Colts	3	13	0	.188

CENTRAL DIVISION

	W	L	T	PCT
Cleveland Browns	12	4	0	.750
Cincinnati Bengals	10	6	0	.625
Pittsburgh Steelers	6	10	0	.375
Houston Oilers	5	11	0	.313

WEST DIVISION

	W	L	T	PCT
Denver Broncos	11	5	0	.688
Kansas City Chiefs	10	6	0	.625
Seattle Seahawks	10	6	0	.625
Los Angeles Raiders	8	8	0	.500
San Diego Chargers	4	12	0	.250

NFC

EAST DIVISION

	W	L	T	PCT
New York Giants	14	2	0	.875
Washington Redskins	12	4	0	.750
Dallas Cowboys	7	9	0	.438
Philadelphia Eagles	5	10	1	.344
St. Louis Cardinals	4	11	1	.281

CENTRAL DIVISION

	W	L	T	PCT
Chicago Bears	14	2	0	.875
Minnesota Vikings	9	7	0	.563
Detroit Lions	5	11	0	.313
Green Bay Packers	4	12	0	.250
Tampa Bay Buccaneers	2	14	0	.125

WEST DIVISION

	W	L	T	PCT
San Francisco 49ers	10	5	1	.656
Los Angeles Rams	10	6	0	.625
Atlanta Falcons	7	8	1	.469
New Orleans Saints	7	9	0	.438

1987 NFL FINAL STANDINGS

AFC

EAST DIVISION

	W	L	T	PCT
Indianapolis Colts	9	6	0	.600
New England Patriots	8	7	0	.533
Miami Dolphins	8	7	0	.533
Buffalo Bills	7	8	0	.467
New York Jets	6	9	0	.400

CENTRAL DIVISION

	W	L	T	PCT
Cleveland Browns	10	5	0	.667
Houston Oilers	9	6	0	.600
Pittsburgh Steelers	8	7	0	.533
Cincinnati Bengals	4	11	0	.267

WEST DIVISION

	W	L	T	PCT
Denver Broncos	10	4	1	.700
Seattle Seahawks	9	6	0	.600
San Diego Chargers	8	7	0	.533
Los Angeles Raiders	5	10	0	.333
Kansas City Chiefs	4	11	0	.267

NFC

EAST DIVISION

	W	L	T	PCT
Washington Redskins	11	4	0	.733
Dallas Cowboys	7	8	0	.467
St. Louis Cardinals	7	8	0	.467
Philadelphia Eagles	7	8	0	.467
New York Giants	6	9	0	.400

CENTRAL DIVISION

	W	L	T	PCT
Chicago Bears	11	4	0	.733
Minnesota Vikings	8	7	0	.533
Green Bay Packers	5	9	1	.367
Tampa Bay Buccaneers	4	11	0	.267
Detroit Lions	4	11	0	.267

WEST DIVISION

	W	L	T	PCT
San Francisco 49ers	13	2	0	.867
New Orleans Saints	12	3	0	.800
Los Angeles Rams	6	9	0	.400
Atlanta Falcons	3	12	0	.200

STANDINGS

1988 NFL FINAL STANDINGS

AFC

EAST DIVISION	W	L	T	PCT
Buffalo Bills	12	4	0	.750
Indianapolis Colts	9	7	0	.563
New England Patriots	9	7	0	.563
New York Jets	8	7	1	.531
Miami Dolphins	6	10	0	.375

CENTRAL DIVISION	W	L	T	PCT
Cincinnati Bengals	12	4	0	.750
Cleveland Browns	10	6	0	.625
Houston Oilers	10	6	0	.625
Pittsburgh Steelers	5	11	0	.313

WEST DIVISION	W	L	T	PCT
Seattle Seahawks	9	7	0	.563
Denver Broncos	8	8	0	.500
Los Angeles Raiders	7	9	0	.438
San Diego Chargers	6	10	0	.375
Kansas City Chiefs	4	11	1	.281

NFC

EAST DIVISION	W	L	T	PCT
Philadelphia Eagles	10	6	0	.625
New York Giants	10	6	0	.625
Washington Redskins	7	9	0	.438
Phoenix Cardinals	7	9	0	.438
Dallas Cowboys	3	13	0	.188

CENTRAL DIVISION	W	L	T	PCT
Chicago Bears	12	4	0	.750
Minnesota Vikings	11	5	0	.688
Tampa Bay Buccaneers	5	11	0	.313
Detroit Lions	4	12	0	.250
Green Bay Packers	4	12	0	.250

WEST DIVISION	W	L	T	PCT
San Francisco 49ers	10	6	0	.625
Los Angeles Rams	10	6	0	.625
New Orleans Saints	10	6	0	.625
Atlanta Falcons	5	11	0	.313

1989 NFL FINAL STANDINGS

AFC

EAST DIVISION	W	L	T	PCT
Buffalo Bills	9	7	0	.563
Indianapolis Colts	8	8	0	.500
Miami Dolphins	8	8	0	.500
New England Patriots	5	11	0	.313
New York Jets	4	12	0	.250

CENTRAL DIVISION	W	L	T	PCT
Cleveland Browns	9	6	1	.594
Houston Oilers	9	7	0	.563
Pittsburgh Steelers	9	7	0	.563
Cincinnati Bengals	8	8	0	.500

WEST DIVISION	W	L	T	PCT
Denver Broncos	11	5	0	.688
Kansas City Chiefs	8	7	1	.531
Los Angeles Raiders	8	8	0	.500
Seattle Seahawks	7	9	0	.438
San Diego Chargers	6	10	0	.375

NFC

EAST DIVISION	W	L	T	PCT
New York Giants	12	4	0	.750
Philadelphia Eagles	11	5	0	.688
Washington Redskins	10	6	0	.625
Phoenix Cardinals	5	11	0	.313
Dallas Cowboys	1	15	0	.063

CENTRAL DIVISION	W	L	T	PCT
Minnesota Vikings	10	6	0	.625
Green Bay Packers	10	6	0	.625
Detroit Lions	7	9	0	.438
Chicago Bears	6	10	0	.375
Tampa Bay Buccaneers	5	11	0	.313

WEST DIVISION	W	L	T	PCT
San Francisco 49ers	14	2	0	.875
Los Angeles Rams	11	5	0	.688
New Orleans Saints	9	7	0	.563
Atlanta Falcons	3	13	0	.188

STANDINGS

1990 NFL FINAL STANDINGS

AFC

EAST DIVISION	W	L	T	PCT
Buffalo Bills	13	3	0	.813
Miami Dolphins	12	4	0	.750
Indianapolis Colts	7	9	0	.438
New York Jets	6	10	0	.375
New England Patriots	1	15	0	.063

CENTRAL DIVISION	W	L	T	PCT
Cincinnati Bengals	9	7	0	.563
Houston Oilers	9	7	0	.563
Pittsburgh Steelers	9	7	0	.563
Cleveland Browns	3	13	0	.188

WEST DIVISION	W	L	T	PCT
Los Angeles Raiders	12	4	0	.750
Kansas City Chiefs	11	5	0	.688
Seattle Seahawks	9	7	0	.563
San Diego Chargers	6	10	0	.375
Denver Broncos	5	11	0	.313

NFC

EAST DIVISION	W	L	T	PCT
New York Giants	13	3	0	.813
Philadelphia Eagles	10	6	0	.625
Washington Redskins	10	6	0	.625
Dallas Cowboys	7	9	0	.438
Phoenix Cardinals	5	11	0	.313

CENTRAL DIVISION	W	L	T	PCT
Chicago Bears	11	5	0	.688
Tampa Bay Buccaneers	6	10	0	.375
Detroit Lions	6	10	0	.375
Green Bay Packers	6	10	0	.375
Minnesota Vikings	6	10	0	.375

WEST DIVISION	W	L	T	PCT
San Francisco 49ers	14	2	0	.875
New Orleans Saints	8	8	0	.500
Los Angeles Rams	5	11	0	.313
Atlanta Falcons	5	11	0	.313

1991 NFL FINAL STANDINGS

AFC

EAST DIVISION	W	L	T	PCT
Buffalo Bills	13	3	0	.813
New York Jets	8	8	0	.500
Miami Dolphins	8	8	0	.500
New England Patriots	6	10	0	.375
Indianapolis Colts	1	15	0	.063

CENTRAL DIVISION	W	L	T	PCT
Houston Oilers	11	5	0	.688
Pittsburgh Steelers	7	9	0	.438
Cleveland Browns	6	10	0	.375
Cincinnati Bengals	3	13	0	.188

WEST DIVISION	W	L	T	PCT
Denver Broncos	12	4	0	.750
Kansas City Chiefs	10	6	0	.625
Los Angeles Raiders	9	7	0	.563
Seattle Seahawks	7	9	0	.438
San Diego Chargers	4	12	0	.250

NFC

EAST DIVISION	W	L	T	PCT
Washington Redskins	14	2	0	.875
Dallas Cowboys	11	5	0	.688
Philadelphia Eagles	10	6	0	.625
New York Giants	8	8	0	.500
Phoenix Cardinals	4	12	0	.250

CENTRAL DIVISION	W	L	T	PCT
Detroit Lions	12	4	0	.750
Chicago Bears	11	5	0	.688
Minnesota Vikings	8	8	0	.500
Green Bay Packers	4	12	0	.250
Tampa Bay Buccaneers	3	13	0	.188

WEST DIVISION	W	L	T	PCT
New Orleans Saints	11	5	0	.688
Atlanta Falcons	10	6	0	.625
San Francisco 49ers	10	6	0	.625
Los Angeles Rams	3	13	0	.188

STANDINGS

1992 NFL FINAL STANDINGS

AFC

EAST DIVISION	W	L	T	PCT
Miami Dolphins	11	5	0	.688
Buffalo Bills	11	5	0	.688
Indianapolis Colts	9	7	0	.563
New York Jets	4	12	0	.250
New England Patriots	2	14	0	.125

CENTRAL DIVISION	W	L	T	PCT
Pittsburgh Steelers	11	5	0	.688
Houston Oilers	10	6	0	.625
Cleveland Browns	7	9	0	.438
Cincinnati Bengals	5	11	0	.313

WEST DIVISION	W	L	T	PCT
San Diego Chargers	11	5	0	.688
Kansas City Chiefs	10	6	0	.625
Denver Broncos	8	8	0	.500
Los Angeles Raiders	7	9	0	.438
Seattle Seahawks	2	14	0	.125

NFC

EAST DIVISION	W	L	T	PCT
Dallas Cowboys	13	3	0	.813
Philadelphia Eagles	11	5	0	.688
Washington Redskins	9	7	0	.563
New York Giants	6	10	0	.375
Phoenix Cardinals	4	12	0	.250

CENTRAL DIVISION	W	L	T	PCT
Minnesota Vikings	11	5	0	.688
Green Bay Packers	9	7	0	.563
Tampa Bay Buccaneers	5	11	0	.313
Chicago Bears	5	11	0	.313
Detroit Lions	5	11	0	.313

WEST DIVISION	W	L	T	PCT
San Francisco 49ers	14	2	0	.875
New Orleans Saints	12	4	0	.750
Atlanta Falcons	6	10	0	.375
Los Angeles Rams	6	10	0	.375

1993 NFL FINAL STANDINGS

AFC

EAST DIVISION	W	L	T	PCT
Buffalo Bills	12	4	0	.750
Miami Dolphins	9	7	0	.563
New York Jets	8	8	0	.500
New England Patriots	5	11	0	.313
Indianapolis Colts	4	12	0	.250

CENTRAL DIVISION	W	L	T	PCT
Houston Oilers	12	4	0	.750
Pittsburgh Steelers	9	7	0	.563
Cleveland Browns	7	9	0	.438
Cincinnati Bengals	3	13	0	.188

WEST DIVISION	W	L	T	PCT
Kansas City Chiefs	11	5	0	.688
Los Angeles Raiders	10	6	0	.625
Denver Broncos	9	7	0	.563
San Diego Chargers	8	8	0	.500
Seattle Seahawks	6	10	0	.375

NFC

EAST DIVISION	W	L	T	PCT
Dallas Cowboys	12	4	0	.750
New York Giants	11	5	0	.688
Philadelphia Eagles	8	8	0	.500
Phoenix Cardinals	7	9	0	.438
Washington Redskins	4	12	0	.250

CENTRAL DIVISION	W	L	T	PCT
Detroit Lions	10	6	0	.625
Minnesota Vikings	9	7	0	.563
Green Bay Packers	9	7	0	.563
Chicago Bears	7	9	0	.438
Tampa Bay Buccaneers	5	11	0	.313

WEST DIVISION	W	L	T	PCT
San Francisco 49ers	10	6	0	.625
New Orleans Saints	8	8	0	.500
Atlanta Falcons	6	10	0	.375
Los Angeles Rams	5	11	0	.313

STANDINGS

1994 NFL FINAL STANDINGS

AFC

EAST DIVISION

	W	L	T	PCT
Miami Dolphins	10	6	0	.625
New England Patriots	10	6	0	.625
Indianapolis Colts	8	8	0	.500
Buffalo Bills	7	9	0	.438
New York Jets	6	10	0	.375

CENTRAL DIVISION

	W	L	T	PCT
Pittsburgh Steelers	12	4	0	.750
Cleveland Browns	11	5	0	.688
Cincinnati Bengals	3	13	0	.188
Houston Oilers	2	14	0	.125

WEST DIVISION

	W	L	T	PCT
San Diego Chargers	11	5	0	.688
Kansas City Chiefs	9	7	0	.563
Los Angeles Raiders	9	7	0	.563
Denver Broncos	7	9	0	.438
Seattle Seahawks	6	10	0	.375

NFC

EAST DIVISION

	W	L	T	PCT
Dallas Cowboys	12	4	0	.750
New York Giants	9	7	0	.563
Arizona Cardinals	8	8	0	.500
Philadelphia Eagles	7	9	0	.438
Washington Redskins	3	13	0	.188

CENTRAL DIVISION

	W	L	T	PCT
Minnesota Vikings	10	6	0	.625
Green Bay Packers	9	7	0	.563
Detroit Lions	9	7	0	.563
Chicago Bears	9	7	0	.563
Tampa Bay Buccaneers	6	10	0	.375

WEST DIVISION

	W	L	T	PCT
San Francisco 49ers	13	3	0	.813
New Orleans Saints	7	9	0	.438
Atlanta Falcons	7	9	0	.438
Los Angeles Rams	4	12	0	.250

1995 NFL FINAL STANDINGS

AFC

EAST DIVISION

	W	L	T	PCT
Buffalo Bills	10	6	0	.625
Indianapolis Colts	9	7	0	.563
Miami Dolphins	9	7	0	.563
New England Patriots	6	10	0	.375
New York Jets	3	13	0	.188

CENTRAL DIVISION

	W	L	T	PCT
Pittsburgh Steelers	11	5	0	.688
Cincinnati Bengals	7	9	0	.438
Houston Oilers	7	9	0	.438
Cleveland Browns	5	11	0	.313
Jacksonville Jaguars	4	12	0	.250

WEST DIVISION

	W	L	T	PCT
Kansas City Chiefs	13	3	0	.813
San Diego Chargers	9	7	0	.563
Seattle Seahawks	8	8	0	.500
Denver Broncos	8	8	0	.500
Oakland Raiders	8	8	0	.500

NFC

EAST DIVISION

	W	L	T	PCT
Dallas Cowboys	12	4	0	.750
Philadelphia Eagles	10	6	0	.625
Washington Redskins	6	10	0	.375
New York Giants	5	11	0	.313
Arizona Cardinals	4	12	0	.250

CENTRAL DIVISION

	W	L	T	PCT
Green Bay Packers	11	5	0	.688
Detroit Lions	10	6	0	.625
Chicago Bears	9	7	0	.563
Minnesota Vikings	8	8	0	.500
Tampa Bay Buccaneers	7	9	0	.438

WEST DIVISION

	W	L	T	PCT
San Francisco 49ers	11	5	0	.688
Atlanta Falcons	9	7	0	.563
St. Louis Rams	7	9	0	.438
Carolina Panthers	7	9	0	.438
New Orleans Saints	7	9	0	.438

STANDINGS

1996 NFL FINAL STANDINGS

AFC

EAST DIVISION	W	L	T	PCT
New England Patriots	11	5	0	.688
Buffalo Bills	10	6	0	.625
Indianapolis Colts	9	7	0	.563
Miami Dolphins	8	8	0	.500
New York Jets	1	15	0	.063

CENTRAL DIVISION	W	L	T	PCT
Pittsburgh Steelers	10	6	0	.625
Jacksonville Jaguars	9	7	0	.563
Cincinnati Bengals	8	8	0	.500
Houston Oilers	8	8	0	.500
Baltimore Ravens	4	12	0	.250

WEST DIVISION	W	L	T	PCT
Denver Broncos	13	3	0	.813
Kansas City Chiefs	9	7	0	.563
San Diego Chargers	8	8	0	.500
Oakland Raiders	7	9	0	.438
Seattle Seahawks	7	9	0	.438

NFC

EAST DIVISION	W	L	T	PCT
Dallas Cowboys	10	6	0	.625
Philadelphia Eagles	10	6	0	.625
Washington Redskins	9	7	0	.563
Arizona Cardinals	7	9	0	.438
New York Giants	6	10	0	.375

CENTRAL DIVISION	W	L	T	PCT
Green Bay Packers	13	3	0	.813
Minnesota Vikings	9	7	0	.563
Chicago Bears	7	9	0	.438
Tampa Bay Buccaneers	6	10	0	.375
Detroit Lions	5	11	0	.313

WEST DIVISION	W	L	T	PCT
Carolina Panthers	12	4	0	.750
San Francisco 49ers	12	4	0	.750
St. Louis Rams	6	10	0	.375
Atlanta Falcons	3	13	0	.188
New Orleans Saints	3	13	0	.188

1997 NFL FINAL STANDINGS

AFC

EAST DIVISION	W	L	T	PCT
New England Patriots	10	6	0	.625
Miami Dolphins	9	7	0	.563
New York Jets	9	7	0	.563
Buffalo Bills	6	10	0	.375
Indianapolis Colts	3	13	0	.188

CENTRAL DIVISION	W	L	T	PCT
Pittsburgh Steelers	11	5	0	.688
Jacksonville Jaguars	11	5	0	.688
Tennessee Oilers	8	8	0	.500
Cincinnati Bengals	7	9	0	.438
Baltimore Ravens	6	9	1	.406

WEST DIVISION	W	L	T	PCT
Kansas City Chiefs	13	3	0	.813
Denver Broncos	12	4	0	.750
Seattle Seahawks	8	8	0	.500
Oakland Raiders	4	12	0	.250
San Diego Chargers	4	12	0	.250

NFC

EAST DIVISION	W	L	T	PCT
New York Giants	10	5	1	.656
Washington Redskins	8	7	1	.531
Philadelphia Eagles	6	9	1	.406
Dallas Cowboys	6	10	0	.375
Arizona Cardinals	4	12	0	.250

CENTRAL DIVISION	W	L	T	PCT
Green Bay Packers	13	3	0	.813
Tampa Bay Buccaneers	10	6	0	.625
Detroit Lions	9	7	0	.563
Minnesota Vikings	9	7	0	.563
Chicago Bears	4	12	0	.250

WEST DIVISION	W	L	T	PCT
San Francisco 49ers	13	3	0	.813
Carolina Panthers	7	9	0	.438
Atlanta Falcons	7	9	0	.438
New Orleans Saints	6	10	0	.375
St. Louis Rams	5	11	0	.313

STANDINGS

1998 NFL FINAL STANDINGS
AFC

EAST DIVISION	W	L	T	PCT
New York Jets	12	4	0	.750
Miami Dolphins	10	6	0	.625
Buffalo Bills	10	6	0	.625
New England Patriots	9	7	0	.563
Indianapolis Colts	3	13	0	.188

CENTRAL DIVISION	W	L	T	PCT
Jacksonville Jaguars	11	5	0	.688
Tennessee Oilers	8	8	0	.500
Pittsburgh Steelers	7	9	0	.438
Baltimore Ravens	6	10	0	.375
Cincinnati Bengals	3	13	0	.188

WEST DIVISION	W	L	T	PCT
Denver Broncos	14	2	0	.875
Oakland Raiders	8	8	0	.500
Seattle Seahawks	8	8	0	.500
Kansas City Chiefs	7	9	0	.438
San Diego Chargers	5	11	0	.313

NFC

EAST DIVISION	W	L	T	PCT
Dallas Cowboys	10	6	0	.625
Arizona Cardinals	9	7	0	.563
New York Giants	8	8	0	.500
Washington Redskins	6	10	0	.375
Philadelphia Eagles	3	13	0	.188

CENTRAL DIVISION	W	L	T	PCT
Minnesota Vikings	15	1	0	.938
Green Bay Packers	11	5	0	.688
Tampa Bay Buccaneers	8	8	0	.500
Detroit Lions	5	11	0	.313
Chicago Bears	4	12	0	.250

WEST DIVISION	W	L	T	PCT
Atlanta Falcons	14	2	0	.875
San Francisco 49ers	12	4	0	.750
New Orleans Saints	6	10	0	.375
Carolina Panthers	4	12	0	.250
St. Louis Rams	4	12	0	.250

1999 NFL FINAL STANDINGS
AFC

EAST DIVISION	W	L	T	PCT
Indianapolis Colts	13	3	0	.813
Buffalo Bills	11	5	0	.688
Miami Dolphins	9	7	0	.563
New York Jets	8	8	0	.500
New England Patriots	8	8	0	.500

CENTRAL DIVISION	W	L	T	PCT
Jacksonville Jaguars	14	2	0	.875
Tennessee Titans	13	3	0	.813
Baltimore Ravens	8	8	0	.500
Pittsburgh Steelers	6	10	0	.375
Cincinnati Bengals	4	12	0	.250
Cleveland Browns	2	14	0	.125

WEST DIVISION	W	L	T	PCT
Seattle Seahawks	9	7	0	.563
Kansas City Chiefs	9	7	0	.563
San Diego Chargers	8	8	0	.500
Oakland Raiders	8	8	0	.500
Denver Broncos	6	10	0	.375

NFC

EAST DIVISION	W	L	T	PCT
Washington Redskins	10	6	0	.625
Dallas Cowboys	8	8	0	.500
New York Giants	7	9	0	.438
Arizona Cardinals	6	10	0	.375
Philadelphia Eagles	5	11	0	.313

CENTRAL DIVISION	W	L	T	PCT
Tampa Bay Buccaneers	11	5	0	.688
Minnesota Vikings	10	6	0	.625
Detroit Lions	8	8	0	.500
Green Bay Packers	8	8	0	.500
Chicago Bears	6	10	0	.375

WEST DIVISION	W	L	T	PCT
St. Louis Rams	13	3	0	.813
Carolina Panthers	8	8	0	.500
Atlanta Falcons	5	11	0	.313
San Francisco 49ers	4	12	0	.250
New Orleans Saints	3	13	0	.188

STANDINGS

2000 NFL FINAL STANDINGS

AFC

EAST DIVISION

EAST DIVISION	W	L	T	PCT
Miami Dolphins	11	5	0	.688
Indianapolis Colts	10	6	0	.625
New York Jets	9	7	0	.563
Buffalo Bills	8	8	0	.500
New England Patriots	5	11	0	.313

CENTRAL DIVISION	W	L	T	PCT
Tennessee Titans	13	3	0	.813
Baltimore Ravens	12	4	0	.750
Pittsburgh Steelers	9	7	0	.563
Jacksonville Jaguars	7	9	0	.438
Cincinnati Bengals	4	12	0	.250
Cleveland Browns	3	13	0	.188

WEST DIVISION	W	L	T	PCT
Oakland Raiders	12	4	0	.750
Denver Broncos	11	5	0	.688
Kansas City Chiefs	7	9	0	.438
Seattle Seahawks	6	10	0	.375
San Diego Chargers	1	15	0	.063

NFC

EAST DIVISION	W	L	T	PCT
New York Giants	12	4	0	.750
Philadelphia Eagles	11	5	0	.688
Washington Redskins	8	8	0	.500
Dallas Cowboys	5	11	0	.313
Arizona Cardinals	3	13	0	.188

CENTRAL DIVISION	W	L	T	PCT
Minnesota Vikings	11	5	0	.688
Tampa Bay Buccaneers	10	6	0	.625
Green Bay Packers	9	7	0	.563
Detroit Lions	9	7	0	.563
Chicago Bears	5	11	0	.313

WEST DIVISION	W	L	T	PCT
New Orleans Saints	10	6	0	.625
St. Louis Rams	10	6	0	.625
Carolina Panthers	7	9	0	.438
San Francisco 49ers	6	10	0	.375
Atlanta Falcons	4	12	0	.250

2001 NFL FINAL STANDINGS

AFC

EAST DIVISION	W	L	T	PCT
New England Patriots	11	5	0	.688
Miami Dolphins	11	5	0	.688
New York Jets	10	6	0	.625
Indianapolis Colts	6	10	0	.375
Buffalo Bills	3	13	0	.188

CENTRAL DIVISION	W	L	T	PCT
Pittsburgh Steelers	13	3	0	.813
Baltimore Ravens	10	6	0	.625
Cleveland Browns	7	9	0	.438
Tennessee Titans	7	9	0	.438
Jacksonville Jaguars	6	10	0	.375
Cincinnati Bengals	6	10	0	.375

WEST DIVISION	W	L	T	PCT
Oakland Raiders	10	6	0	.625
Seattle Seahawks	9	7	0	.563
Denver Broncos	8	8	0	.500
Kansas City Chiefs	6	10	0	.375
San Diego Chargers	5	11	0	.313

NFC

EAST DIVISION	W	L	T	PCT
Philadelphia Eagles	11	5	0	.688
Washington Redskins	8	8	0	.500
New York Giants	7	9	0	.438
Arizona Cardinals	7	9	0	.438
Dallas Cowboys	5	11	0	.313

CENTRAL DIVISION	W	L	T	PCT
Chicago Bears	13	3	0	.813
Green Bay Packers	12	4	0	.750
Tampa Bay Buccaneers	9	7	0	.563
Minnesota Vikings	5	11	0	.313
Detroit Lions	2	14	0	.125

WEST DIVISION	W	L	T	PCT
St. Louis Rams	14	2	0	.875
San Francisco 49ers	12	4	0	.750
New Orleans Saints	7	9	0	.438
Atlanta Falcons	7	9	0	.438
Carolina Panthers	1	15	0	.063

STANDINGS

2002 NFL FINAL STANDINGS

AFC

EAST DIVISION

	W	L	T	PCT
New York Jets	9	7	0	.563
Miami Dolphins	9	7	0	.563
New England Patriots	9	7	0	.563
Buffalo Bills	8	8	0	.500

WEST DIVISION

	W	L	T	PCT
Oakland Raiders	11	5	0	.688
Denver Broncos	9	7	0	.563
San Diego Chargers	8	8	0	.500
Kansas City Chiefs	8	8	0	.500

NORTH DIVISION

	W	L	T	PCT
Pittsburgh Steelers	10	5	1	.656
Cleveland Browns	9	7	0	.563
Baltimore Ravens	7	9	0	.438
Cincinnati Bengals	2	14	0	.125

SOUTH DIVISION

	W	L	T	PCT
Tennessee Titans	11	5	0	.688
Indianapolis Colts	10	6	0	.625
Jacksonville Jaguars	6	10	0	.375
Houston Texans	4	12	0	.250

NFC

EAST DIVISION

	W	L	T	PCT
Philadelphia Eagles	12	4	0	.750
New York Giants	10	6	0	.625
Washington Redskins	7	9	0	.438
Dallas Cowboys	5	11	0	.313

WEST DIVISION

	W	L	T	PCT
San Francisco 49ers	10	6	0	.625
St. Louis Rams	7	9	0	.438
Seattle Seahawks	7	9	0	.438
Arizona Cardinals	5	11	0	.313

NORTH DIVISION

	W	L	T	PCT
Green Bay Packers	12	4	0	.750
Minnesota Vikings	6	10	0	.375
Chicago Bears	4	12	0	.250
Detroit Lions	3	13	0	.188

SOUTH DIVISION

	W	L	T	PCT
Tampa Bay Buccaneers	12	4	0	.750
Atlanta Falcons	9	6	1	.594
New Orleans Saints	9	7	0	.563
Carolina Panthers	7	9	0	.438

2003 NFL FINAL STANDINGS

AFC

EAST DIVISION

	W	L	T	PCT
New England Patriots	14	2	0	.875
Miami Dolphins	10	6	0	.625
Buffalo Bills	6	10	0	.375
New York Jets	6	10	0	.375

WEST DIVISION

	W	L	T	PCT
Kansas City Chiefs	13	3	0	.813
Denver Broncos	10	6	0	.625
Oakland Raiders	4	12	0	.250
San Diego Chargers	4	12	0	.250

NORTH DIVISION

	W	L	T	PCT
Baltimore Ravens	10	6	0	.625
Cincinnati Bengals	8	8	0	.500
Pittsburgh Steelers	6	10	0	.375
Cleveland Browns	5	11	0	.313

SOUTH DIVISION

	W	L	T	PCT
Indianapolis Colts	12	4	0	.750
Tennessee Titans	12	4	0	.750
Jacksonville Jaguars	5	11	0	.313
Houston Texans	5	11	0	.313

NFC

EAST DIVISION

	W	L	T	PCT
Philadelphia Eagles	12	4	0	.750
Dallas Cowboys	10	6	0	.625
Washington Redskins	5	11	0	.313
New York Giants	4	12	0	.250

WEST DIVISION

	W	L	T	PCT
St. Louis Rams	12	4	0	.750
Seattle Seahawks	10	6	0	.625
San Francisco 49ers	7	9	0	.438
Arizona Cardinals	4	12	0	.250

NORTH DIVISION

	W	L	T	PCT
Green Bay Packers	10	6	0	.625
Minnesota Vikings	9	7	0	.563
Chicago Bears	7	9	0	.438
Detroit Lions	5	11	0	.313

SOUTH DIVISION

	W	L	T	PCT
Carolina Panthers	11	5	0	.688
New Orleans Saints	8	8	0	.500
Tampa Bay Buccaneers	7	9	0	.438
Atlanta Falcons	5	11	0	.313

POST SEASON RESULTS

NFL/NFC CHAMPIONSHIPS

YEAR	WINNER (DIV OR CONF)	LOSER (DIV OR CONF)
1933	Chicago Bears (West)	New York Giants (East)
1934	New York Giants (East)	Chicago Bears (West)
1935	Detroit Lions (West)	New York Giants (East)
1936	Green Bay Packers (West)	Boston Redskins (East)
1937	Washington Redskins (East)	Chicago Bears (West)
1938	New York Giants (East)	Green Bay Packers (West)
1939	Green Bay Packers (West)	New York Giants (East)
1940	Chicago Bears (West)	Washington Redskins (East)
1941	Chicago Bears (West)	New York Giants (East)
1942	Washington Redskins (East)	Chicago Bears (West)
1943	Chicago Bears (West)	Washington Redskins (East)
1944	Green Bay Packers (West)	New York Giants (East)
1945	Cleveland Rams (West)	Washington Redskins (East)
1946	Chicago Bears (West)	New York Giants (East)
1947	Chicago Cardinals (West)	Philadelphia Eagles (East)
1948	Philadelphia Eagles (East)	Chicago Cardinals (West)
1949	Philadelphia Eagles (East)	Los Angeles Rams (West)
1950	Cleveland Browns (AFC)	Los Angeles Rams (NFC)
1951	Los Angeles Rams (NFC)	Cleveland Browns (AFC)
1952	Detroit Lions (NFC)	Cleveland Browns (AFC)
1953	Detroit Lions (Western)	Cleveland Browns (Eastern)
1954	Cleveland Browns (Eastern)	Detroit Lions (Western)
1955	Cleveland Browns (Eastern)	Los Angeles Rams (Western)
1956	New York Giants (Eastern)	Chicago Bears (Western)
1957	Detroit Lions (Western)	Cleveland Browns (Eastern)
1958	Baltimore Colts (Western)	New York Giants (Eastern)
1959	Baltimore Colts (Western)	New York Giants (Eastern)
1960	Philadelphia Eagles (Eastern)	Green Bay Packers (Western)
1961	Green Bay Packers (Western)	New York Giants (Eastern)
1962	Green Bay Packers (Western)	New York Giants (Eastern)
1963	Chicago Bears (Western)	New York Giants (Eastern)
1964	Cleveland Browns (Eastern)	Baltimore Colts (Western)
1965	Green Bay Packers (Western)	Cleveland Browns (Eastern)
1966	Green Bay Packers (Western)	Dallas Cowboys (Eastern)
1967	Green Bay Packers (Central)	Dallas Cowboys (Capital)
1968	Baltimore Colts (Coastal)	Cleveland Browns (Century)
1969	Minnesota Vikings (Central)	Cleveland Browns (Century)
1970	Dallas Cowboys (East)	San Francisco 49ers (West)
1971	Dallas Cowboys (East)	San Francisco 49ers (West)
1972	Washington Redskins (East)	Dallas Cowboys (East)
1973	Minnesota Vikings (Central)	Dallas Cowboys (East)
1974	Minnesota Vikings (Central)	Los Angeles Rams (West)
1975	Dallas Cowboys (East)	Los Angeles Rams (West)
1976	Minnesota Vikings (Central)	Los Angeles Rams (West)
1977	Dallas Cowboys (East)	Minnesota Vikings (Central)
1978	Dallas Cowboys (East)	Los Angeles Rams (West)

POST SEASON RESULTS

1979	Los Angeles Rams (West)	Tampa Bay Buccaneers (Central)
1980	Philadelphia Eagles (East)	Dallas Cowboys (East)
1981	San Francisco 49ers (West)	Dallas Cowboys (East)
1982	Washington Redskins (East)	Dallas Cowboys (East)
1983	Washington Redskins (East)	San Francisco 49ers (West)
1984	San Francisco 49ers (West)	Chicago Bears (Central)
1985	Chicago Bears (Central)	Los Angeles Rams (West)
1986	New York Giants (East)	Washington Redskins (East)
1987	Washington Redskins (East)	Minnesota Vikings (Central)
1988	San Francisco 49ers (West)	Chicago Bears (Central)
1989	San Francisco 49ers (West)	Los Angeles Rams (West)
1990	New York Giants (East)	San Francisco 49ers (West)
1991	Washington Redskins (East)	Detroit Lions (Central)
1992	Dallas Cowboys (East)	San Francisco 49ers (West)
1993	Dallas Cowboys (East)	San Francisco 49ers (West)
1994	San Francisco 49ers (West)	Dallas Cowboys (East)
1995	Dallas Cowboys (East)	Green Bay Packers (Central)
1996	Green Bay Packers (Central)	Carolina Panthers (West)
1997	Green Bay Packers (Central)	San Francisco 49ers (West)
1998	Atlanta Falcons (West)	Minnesota Vikings (Central)
1999	St. Louis Rams (West)	Tampa Bay Buccaneers (Central)
2000	New York Giants (East)	Minnesota Vikings (Central)
2001	St. Louis Rams (West)	Philadelphia Eagles (East)
2002	Tampa Bay Buccaneers (South)	Philadelphia Eagles (East)
2003	Carolina Panthers (South)	Philadelphia Eagles (East)

POST SEASON RESULTS

AFL/AFC CHAMPIONSHIPS

YEAR	WINNER (DIV OR CONF)	LOSER (DIV OR CONF)
1960	Houston Oilers (East)	Los Angeles Chargers (West)
1961	Houston Oilers (East)	San Diego Chargers (West)
1962	Dallas Texans (West)	Houston Oilers (East)
1963	San Diego Chargers (West)	Boston Patriots (East)
1964	Buffalo Bills (East)	San Diego Chargers (West)
1965	Buffalo Bills (East)	San Diego Chargers (West)
1966	Kansas City Chiefs (West)	Buffalo Bills (East)
1967	Oakland Raiders (West)	Houston Oilers (East)
1968	New York Jets (East)	Oakland Raiders (West)
1969	Kansas City Chiefs (West)	Oakland Raiders (West)
1970	Baltimore Colts (East)	Oakland Raiders (West)
1971	Miami Dolphins (East)	Baltimore Colts (East)
1972	Miami Dolphins (East)	Pittsburgh Steelers (Central)
1973	Miami Dolphins (East)	Oakland Raiders (West)
1974	Pittsburgh Steelers (Central)	Oakland Raiders (West)
1975	Pittsburgh Steelers (Central)	Oakland Raiders (West)
1976	Oakland Raiders (West)	Pittsburgh Steelers (Central)
1977	Denver Broncos (West)	Oakland Raiders (West)
1978	Pittsburgh Steelers (Central)	Houston Oilers (Central)
1979	Pittsburgh Steelers (Central)	Houston Oilers (Central)
1980	Oakland Raiders (West)	San Diego Chargers (West)
1981	Cincinnati Bengals (Central)	San Diego Chargers (West)
1982	Miami Dolphins (East)	New York Jets (East)
1983	Los Angeles Raiders (West)	Seattle Seahawks (West)
1984	Miami Dolphins (East)	Pittsburgh Steelers (Central)
1985	New England Patriots (East)	Miami Dolphins (East)
1986	Denver Broncos (West)	Cleveland Browns (Central)
1987	Denver Broncos (West)	Cleveland Browns (Central)
1988	Cincinnati Bengals (Central)	Buffalo Bills (East)
1989	Denver Broncos (West)	Cleveland Browns (Central)
1990	Buffalo Bills (East)	Los Angeles Raiders (West)
1991	Buffalo Bills (East)	Denver Broncos (West)
1992	Buffalo Bills (East)	Miami Dolphins (East)
1993	Buffalo Bills (East)	Kansas City Chiefs (West)
1994	San Diego Chargers (West)	Pittsburgh Steelers (Central)
1995	Pittsburgh Steelers (Central)	Indianapolis Colts (East)
1996	New England Patriots (East)	Jacksonville Jaguars (Central)
1997	Denver Broncos (West)	Pittsburgh Steelers (Central)
1998	Denver Broncos (West)	New York Jets (East)
1999	Tennessee Titans (Central)	Jacksonville Jaguars (Central)
2000	Baltimore Ravens (Central)	Oakland Raiders (West)
2001	New England Patriots (East)	Pittsburgh Steelers (Central)
2002	Oakland Raiders (West)	Tennessee Titans (South)
2003	New England Patriots (East)	Indianapolis Colts (South)

POST SEASON RESULTS

SUPER BOWL

YEAR	WINNER (DIV OR CONF)	LOSER (DIV OR CONF)
1966	Green Bay Packers (NFL)	Kansas City Chiefs (AFL)
1967	Green Bay Packers (NFL)	Oakland Raiders (AFL)
1968	New York Jets (AFL)	Baltimore Colts (NFL)
1969	Kansas City Chiefs (AFL)	Minnesota Vikings (NFL)
1970	Baltimore Colts (AFC)	Dallas Cowboys (NFC)
1971	Dallas Cowboys (NFC)	Miami Dolphins (AFC)
1972	Miami Dolphins (AFC)	Washington Redskins (NFC)
1973	Miami Dolphins (AFC)	Minnesota Vikings (NFC)
1974	Pittsburgh Steelers (AFC)	Minnesota Vikings (NFC)
1975	Pittsburgh Steelers (AFC)	Dallas Cowboys (NFC)
1976	Oakland Raiders (AFC)	Minnesota Vikings (NFC)
1977	Dallas Cowboys (NFC)	Denver Broncos (AFC)
1978	Pittsburgh Steelers (AFC)	Dallas Cowboys (NFC)
1979	Pittsburgh Steelers (AFC)	Los Angeles Rams (NFC)
1980	Oakland Raiders (AFC)	Philadelphia Eagles (NFC)
1981	San Francisco 49ers (NFC)	Cincinnati Bengals (AFC)
1982	Washington Redskins (NFC)	Miami Dolphins (AFC)
1983	Los Angeles Raiders (AFC)	Washington Redskins (NFC)
1984	San Francisco 49ers (NFC)	Miami Dolphins (AFC)
1985	Chicago Bears (NFC)	New England Patriots (AFC)
1986	New York Giants (NFC)	Denver Broncos (AFC)
1987	Washington Redskins (NFC)	Denver Broncos (AFC)
1988	San Francisco 49ers (NFC)	Cincinnati Bengals (AFC)
1989	San Francisco 49ers (NFC)	Denver Broncos (AFC)
1990	New York Giants (NFC)	Buffalo Bills (AFC)
1991	Washington Redskins (NFC)	Buffalo Bills (AFC)
1992	Dallas Cowboys (NFC)	Buffalo Bills (AFC)
1993	Dallas Cowboys (NFC)	Buffalo Bills (AFC)
1994	San Francisco 49ers (NFC)	San Diego Chargers (AFC)
1995	Dallas Cowboys (NFC)	Pittsburgh Steelers (AFC)
1996	Green Bay Packers (NFC)	New England Patriots (AFC)
1997	Denver Broncos (AFC)	Green Bay Packers (NFC)
1998	Denver Broncos (AFC)	Atlanta Falcons (NFC)
1999	St. Louis Rams (NFC)	Tennessee Titans (AFC)
2000	Baltimore Ravens (AFC)	New York Giants (NFC)
2001	New England Patriots (AFC)	St. Louis Rams (NFC)
2002	Tampa Bay Buccaneers (NFC)	Oakland Raiders (AFC)
2003	New England Patriots (AFC)	Carolina Panthers (NFC)

PRO BOWL RESULTS

YEAR	WINNER	LOSER	SCORE
1970	NFC	AFC	27- 6
1971	AFC	NFC	26-13
1972	AFC	NFC	33-28
1973	AFC	NFC	15-13
1974	NFC	AFC	17-10
1975	NFC	AFC	23-20
1976	AFC	NFC	24-14
1977	NFC	AFC	14-13
1978	NFC	AFC	13- 7
1979	NFC	AFC	37-27
1980	NFC	AFC	21- 7
1981	AFC	NFC	16-13
1982	NFC	AFC	20-19
1983	NFC	AFC	45- 3
1984	AFC	NFC	22-14
1985	NFC	AFC	28-24
1986	AFC	NFC	10- 6
1987	AFC	NFC	15- 6
1988	NFC	AFC	34- 3
1989	NFC	AFC	27-21
1990	AFC	NFC	23-21
1991	NFC	AFC	21-15
1992	AFC	NFC	23-20 (OT)
1993	NFC	AFC	17- 3
1994	AFC	NFC	41-13
1995	NFC	AFC	20-13
1996	AFC	NFC	26-23 (OT)
1997	AFC	NFC	29-24
1998	AFC	NFC	23-10
1999	NFC	AFC	51-31
2000	AFC	NFC	38-17
2001	AFC	NFC	38-30
2002	AFC	NFC	45-20
2003	AFC	NFC	55-52

NFL MVP AWARD

YEAR	PLAYER
1960	Norm Van Brocklin
1960	Joe Schmidt
1961	Paul Hornung
1962	Jim Taylor
1963	Y.A. Tittle
1964	Johnny Unitas
1965	Jim Brown
1966	Bart Starr
1967	Johnny Unitas
1968	Earl Morrall
1969	Roman Gabriel
1970	John Brodie
1971	Alan Page
1972	Larry Brown
1973	O.J. Simpson
1974	Ken Stabler
1975	Fran Tarkenton
1976	Bert Jones
1977	Walter Payton
1978	Terry Bradshaw
1979	Earl Campbell
1980	Brian Sipe
1981	Ken Anderson
1982	Mark Moseley
1983	Joe Theismann
1984	Dan Marino
1985	Marcus Allen
1986	Lawrence Taylor
1987	John Elway
1988	Boomer Esiason
1989	Joe Montana
1990	Joe Montana
1991	Thurman Thomas
1992	Steve Young
1993	Emmitt Smith
1994	Steve Young
1995	Brett Favre
1996	Brett Favre
1997	Barry Sanders
1997	Brett Favre
1998	Terrell Davis
1999	Kurt Warner
2000	Marshall Faulk
2001	Kurt Warner
2002	Rich Gannon
2003	Steve McNair
2003	Peyton Manning

OFFENSIVE MVP AWARD

YEAR	PLAYER
1972	Larry Brown
1973	O.J. Simpson
1974	Ken Stabler
1975	Fran Tarkenton
1976	Bert Jones
1977	Walter Payton
1978	Earl Campbell
1979	Earl Campbell
1980	Earl Campbell
1981	Ken Anderson
1982	Dan Fouts
1983	Joe Theismann
1984	Dan Marino
1985	Marcus Allen
1986	Eric Dickerson
1987	Jerry Rice
1988	Roger Craig
1989	Joe Montana
1990	Warren Moon
1991	Thurman Thomas
1992	Steve Young
1993	Jerry Rice
1994	Barry Sanders
1995	Brett Favre
1996	Terrell Davis
1997	Barry Sanders
1998	Terrell Davis
1999	Marshall Faulk
2000	Marshall Faulk
2001	Marshall Faulk
2002	Priest Holmes
2003	Jamal Lewis

DEFENSIVE MVP AWARD

YEAR	PLAYER
1971	Alan Page
1972	Joe Greene
1973	Dick Anderson
1974	Joe Greene
1975	Mel Blount
1976	Jack Lambert
1977	Harvey Martin
1978	Randy Gradishar
1979	Lee Roy Selmon
1980	Lester Hayes
1981	Lawrence Taylor
1982	Lawrence Taylor
1983	Doug Betters
1984	Kenny Easley
1985	Mike Singletary
1986	Lawrence Taylor
1987	Reggie White
1988	Mike Singletary
1989	Keith Millard
1990	Bruce Smith
1991	Pat Swilling
1992	Cortez Kennedy
1993	Rod Woodson
1994	Deion Sanders
1995	Bryce Paup
1996	Bruce Smith
1997	Dana Stubblefield
1998	Reggie White
1999	Warren Sapp
2000	Ray Lewis
2001	Michael Strahan
2002	Derrick Brooks
2003	Ray Lewis

OFFENSIVE ROOKIE OF THE YEAR

YEAR	PLAYER
1967	Mel Farr
1968	Earl McCullouch
1969	Calvin Hill
1970	Dennis Shaw
1971	John Brockington
1972	Franco Harris
1973	Chuck Foreman
1974	Don Woods
1975	Mike Thomas
1976	Sammy White
1977	Tony Dorsett
1978	Earl Campbell
1979	Ottis Anderson
1980	Billy Sims
1981	George Rogers
1982	Marcus Allen
1983	Eric Dickerson
1984	Louis Lipps
1985	Eddie Brown
1986	Rueben Mayes
1987	Troy Stradford
1988	John Stephens
1989	Barry Sanders
1990	Emmitt Smith
1991	Leonard Russell
1992	Carl Pickens
1993	Jerome Bettis
1994	Marshall Faulk
1995	Curtis Martin
1996	Eddie George
1997	Warrick Dunn
1998	Randy Moss
1999	Edgerrin James
2000	Mike Anderson
2001	Anthony Thomas
2002	Clinton Portis
2003	Anquan Boldin

DEFENSIVE ROOKIE OF THE YEAR

YEAR	PLAYER
1967	Lem Barney
1968	Claude Humphrey
1969	Joe Greene
1970	Bruce Taylor
1971	Isiah Robertson
1972	Willie Buchanon
1973	Wally Chambers
1974	Jack Lambert
1975	Robert Brazile
1976	Mike Haynes
1977	A.J. Duhe
1978	Al Baker
1979	Jim Haslett
1980	Al Richardson
1980	Buddy Curry
1981	Lawrence Taylor
1982	Chip Banks
1983	Vernon Maxwell
1984	Bill Maas
1985	Duane Bickett
1986	Leslie O'Neal
1987	Shane Conlan
1988	Erik McMillan
1989	Derrick Thomas
1990	Mark Carrier
1991	Mike Croel
1992	Dale Carter
1993	Dana Stubblefield
1994	Tim Bowens
1995	Hugh Douglas
1996	Simeon Rice
1997	Peter Boulware
1998	Charles Woodson
1999	Jevon Kearse
2000	Brian Urlacher
2001	Kendrell Bell
2002	Julius Peppers
2003	Terrell Suggs

COACH OF THE YEAR

YEAR	COACH
1970	Paul Brown
1971	George Allen
1972	Don Shula
1973	Chuck Knox
1974	Don Coryell
1975	Ted Marchibroda
1976	Forrest Gregg
1977	Red Miller
1978	Jack Patera
1979	Jack Pardee
1980	Chuck Knox
1981	Bill Walsh
1982	Joe Gibbs
1983	Joe Gibbs
1984	Chuck Knox
1985	Mike Ditka
1986	Bill Parcells
1987	Jim Mora
1988	Mike Ditka
1989	Lindy Infante
1990	Jimmy Johnson
1991	Wayne Fontes
1992	Bill Cowher
1993	Dan Reeves
1994	Bill Parcells
1995	Ray Rhodes
1996	Dom Capers
1997	Jim Fassel
1998	Dan Reeves
1999	Dick Vermeil
2000	Jim Haslett
2001	Dick Jauron
2002	Andy Reid
2003	Bill Belichick

SUPERBOWL MVP

YEAR	TEAM	PLAYER
1966	Green Bay Packers	Bart Starr
1967	Green Bay Packers	Bart Starr
1968	New York Jets	Joe Namath
1969	Kansas City Chiefs	Len Dawson
1970	Dallas Cowboys	Chuck Howley
1971	Dallas Cowboys	Roger Staubach
1972	Miami Dolphins	Jake Scott
1973	Miami Dolphins	Larry Csonka
1974	Pittsburgh Steelers	Franco Harris
1975	Pittsburgh Steelers	Lynn Swann
1976	Oakland Raiders	Fred Biletnikoff
1977	Dallas Cowboys	Randy White
1977	Dallas Cowboys	Harvey Martin
1978	Pittsburgh Steelers	Terry Bradshaw
1979	Pittsburgh Steelers	Terry Bradshaw
1980	Oakland Raiders	Jim Plunkett
1981	San Francisco 49ers	Joe Montana
1982	Washington Redskins	John Riggins
1983	Los Angeles Raiders	Marcus Allen
1984	San Francisco 49ers	Joe Montana
1985	Chicago Bears	Richard Dent
1986	New York Giants	Phil Simms
1987	Washington Redskins	Doug Williams
1988	San Francisco 49ers	Jerry Rice
1989	San Francisco 49ers	Joe Montana
1990	New York Giants	Ottis Anderson
1991	Washington Redskins	Mark Rypien
1992	Dallas Cowboys	Troy Aikman
1993	Dallas Cowboys	Emmitt Smith
1994	San Francisco 49ers	Steve Young
1995	Dallas Cowboys	Larry Brown
1996	Green Bay Packers	Desmond Howard
1997	Denver Broncos	Terrell Davis
1998	Denver Broncos	John Elway
1999	St Louis Rams	Kurt Warner
2000	Baltimore Ravens	Ray Lewis
2001	New England Patriots	Tom Brady
2002	Tampa Bay Buccaneers	Dexter Jackson
2003	New England Patriots	Tom Brady

AUDIBLE: An audible is a play called by the quarterback at the line of scrimmage which changes the play that was previously called in the huddle; a change of plans in game play, just before the ball goes into play. Also called an automatic.

BLITZ: An all-out run by linebackers and defensive backs, charging through the offensive line in an effort to sack the quarterback before he can hand off the ball, or pass it. Also called red dogging.

BOOTLEG: The quarterback fakes a hand-off to backs going one way while goes the other way to run or pass.

CLIPPING: Blocking an opponent from behind, typically at leg level. Clipping is a foul, with a 15-yard penalty.

CLOTHESLINE: A foul. To clothesline is to strike another player across the face with one's extended arm.

CUT: To suddenly change direction to lose a pursuing player. Also, to drop a prospective player from the team roster.

DRAW PLAY: A fake pass which ends with one of the backs carrying the ball after the defensive linemen are "drawn" in on the pass rush.

ENCROACH: Contacting an opposing player before the snap. Encroaching is illegal, with a five-yard penalty.

FLOOD: An attempt to swamp the opposition or an area of the field with sheer numbers of players.

FREEZE: Holding onto the ball for along time without scoring or attempting to score, to freeze the ball.

HAIL MARY: The quarterback throwing the ball up in the air without really targeting any particular receiver, hoping someone on his side catches it. Typically done when the quarterback's about to get sacked!

HASH MARKS: These marks divide the field into thirds. Whenever the ball becomes dead on or outside one of these marks, it is placed on its respective hash mark.

ILLEGAL MOTION: Movement by an offensive player before the snap. Illegal motion is, obviously, illegal, and gets a five-yard penalty.

LATERAL: As a forward pass, but not thrown in the direction of the opponents' goalpost. Rather, the ball is thrown in any direction other than towards the opponents' goal.

MULTIPLE OFFENSE: Offense strategy using a number of formations.

NICKEL DEFENSE: A defensive formation involving five defensive backs, hence the name.

OPTION PLAY: An offensive play wherein the player with the ball has the option of running or passing.

PIGSKIN: Old term for a football.

PLAY ACTION: A passing play set up to draw the Defensive Linebackers towards the Line Of Scrimmage with a Run Fake.

POCKET: The area the quarterback sets up his pass from. Guarded against the opposition to hopefully form a safe "pocket".

PULLING: Leaving one's position to move elsewhere to block.

PUMP FAKE: When the Quarterback draws hi s arm back and fakes a forward pass to draw the Free Safety to an area or cause a Defensive Back to pause in his coverage of a Wide Receiver.

QUARTERBACK SNEAK: An play wherein the quarterback receives the ball after the snap and immediately runs forward through the opposition, with his own team blocking for him.

QUICK COUNT: When the quarterback calls the signals at the line of scrimmage very rapidly so as to throw off the other team.

REVERSE: An offensive play In a reverse, the player with the ball runs in one direction, then hands off the ball to another player going the opposite direction, reversing the ball's direction of travel.

ROUGHING: A personal foul with a 15 yard penalty. Called when a player illegally contacts another player, as in roughing the punter, when a player tackles the punter without touching the ball, or roughing the passer, where a defensive player attempts to tackle the quarterback after the ball has been thrown.

SACK: Tackling the quarterback before he can throw a pass.

SAFETY: When a team forces the opposition to down the ball in their own end zone, they receive two points, called a safety. Also, the player position called safety is a defensive backfield position, the deepest in the backfield. There are two safeties, see Strong Safety and Free Safety.

SCREEN PASS: A pass from behind the line of scrimmage, after a deep drop by the Quarterback. It's a play that allows the rushers to charge through as the offensive linemen fake block them, only to set up a wall for a receiver, or runningback to catch the pass and run behind.

SLANT: Running, with the ball, at an angle.

SLOT: A gap in the offensive line between a receiver and a tackle.

ZONE DEFENSE: A defense strategy where each player has an area, or "zone", of the field to defend. See also man-to-man defense.

ABOUT STATS INC.

In 1981, STATS, Inc. virtually created the high tech sports information industry by developing sophisticated data gathering networks to deliver the most in-depth, innovative sports information services in the world. Now with more than 20 years of experience in sophisticated sports data collection, processing and distribution—STATS, Inc. is the world's leading sports information and statistical analysis company.

Throughout its history, STATS has applied sports information and technology with an innovative flair that has changed the way sports are viewed, reported, and most importantly, enjoyed. STATS provides exclusive information and data from its proprietary databases to fans, professional teams, print and broadcast media, software developers and interactive service providers around the globe while serving as one of the industry's leading fantasy sports game management firms.

You can find STATS, Inc. on the world wide web at *www.stats.com*.

Or write to:

STATS, Inc.

8130 Lehigh Ave.
Morton Grove,
IL 60053

ABOUT THE AUTHOR

John Mehno

John Mehno is a freelance writer based in Pittsburgh. He has written for The Associated Press and United Press International. His byline has appeared in the *Washington Post*, *New York Daily News*, *Chicago Sun-Times*, *Dallas Morning News* and many other newspapers. He has been a correspondent for *The Sporting News* since 1989 and is the author of *The Chronicle of Baseball*.